395

DAVID FELLMAN
Vilas Professor of Political Science, University of Wisconsin
ADVISORY EDITOR TO DODD, MEAD & COMPANY

ABOUT THE AUTHORS

Thomas H. Eliot is Chancellor of Washington University. A graduate of Harvard, he taught there and at the Massachusetts Institute of Technology before becoming Professor of Political Science at Washington University in 1952. He is the author of GOVERNING AMERICA: THE POLITICS OF A FREE PEOPLE, and has contributed articles to the *American Political Science Review* and other publications. Before entering academic life he was a practicing attorney in Buffalo and Boston and served with several government agencies, being General Counsel of the Social Security Board from 1935 until 1938. He was a member of the Seventy-Seventh Congress as a Representative from Massachusetts. He was Visiting Research Professor of Politics at Princeton University in 1958-59.

William N. Chambers is Professor of Political Science at Washington University. He has also taught at Harvard, where he received his B.Sc. degree, and at Columbia University. He has been a visiting scholar at the Center for Advanced Study in the Behavioral Sciences, and has received a Senior Research Award in Governmental Affairs from the Social Science Research Council and a Research Award in Constitutional Democracy from the Rockefeller Foundation. His publications include PO-LITICAL PARTIES IN A NEW NATION: THE AMERICAN EXPERIENCE; OLD BULLION BENTON: SENATOR FROM THE NEW WEST; and THE DEMOCRATS, 1789-1964, as well as other volumes in collaboration. He has contributed to professional journals and is now working on an analytical-historical study of the Democratic party.

Robert H. Salisbury is Associate Professor of Political Science at Washington University. He received his Ph.D. degree from the University of Illinois. He is coauthor of STATE POLITICS AND THE PUBLIC SCHOOLS and a contributing author to FUNCTIONS AND POLICIES OF AMERICAN GOVERNMENT; ETHICS AND STANDARDS IN AMERICAN BUSINESS; COMPARATIVE STATE POLITICS; and THE LIBRARY AND THE CITY. He has contributed articles to the *American Political Science Review*, the *Journal of Politics*, *Public Opinion Quarterly*, and other professional journals. He has been a consultant to various governmental agencies, dealing particularly with urban affairs, and has recently conducted a study of community power structure in an eastern city.

Kenneth Prewitt is Assistant Professor of Political Science at Washington University. He received his M.A. degree from Washington University and his Ph.D. from Stanford, where he has also served as Associate Director of the Stanford Institute of Political Studies Project in Comparative Studies of Legislative Behavior and Small Decision-Making Groups, which has produced reports on "Latent Partisanship in Nonpartisan Elections," "Career Patterns of Local Elected Officials," and "Political Socialization and Political Roles." He has contributed to the NEW ENCYCLOPEDIA OF THE SOCIAL SCIENCES and to the *Journal of Politics*, and to a study in IDEOLOGY AND DISCONTENT, "America's Radical Right: Politics and Ideology," of which he is coauthor.

AMERICAN GOVERNMENT

Problems and Readings
in Political Analysis

SECOND EDITION

THOMAS H. ELIOT
WILLIAM N. CHAMBERS
ROBERT H. SALISBURY
KENNETH PREWITT

DODD, MEAD & COMPANY
NEW YORK · TORONTO · 1966

The First Edition appeared under the following title:
AMERICAN GOVERNMENT: READINGS AND PROBLEMS
FOR ANALYSIS

Third Printing

Printed in the United States of America

ACKNOWLEDGMENTS

Grateful acknowledgment is made to the following for permission to use
copyrighted materials:

AMERICAN POLITICAL SCIENCE REVIEW: John Dickinson, "Democratic Realities and Democratic Dogma," 24 (1930). George Goodwin, Jr., "The
Seniority System in Congress," LIII (1959). Richard E. Neustadt, "Approaches to Staffing the Presidency: Notes on FDR and JFK," LVII
(1963).

AMERICAN ACADEMY OF POLITICAL AND SOCIAL SCIENCE: Henry A. Turner,
"How Pressure Groups Operate," from the Annals of the American Academy of Political and Social Science, 319 (1958).

THE BROOKINGS INSTITUTION: "The Formulation and Administration of
United States Foreign Policy," a study prepared for the U.S. Senate
Committee on Foreign Relations, 86th Congress, 2nd Session. Paul T.
David, Ralph M. Goodwin, and Richard C. Bain, The Politics of National
Party Conventions, revised condensed edition, 1964.

EUGENE BURDICK and THIS WEEK MAGAZINE: Adaptation of "Voting Profile" from This Week Magazine, May 16, 1956, copyright 1956 by The
United Newspapers Magazine Corporation.

COLUMBIA UNIVERSITY PRESS: Paul F. Lazarsfeld, Bernard R. Berelson, and
Hazel Gaudet, The People's Choice, 1944. William Howard Taft, Our
Chief Magistrate and His Power, 1916.

PREFACE

The Uses of Problem Analysis

I

The purpose of this book remains basically what it was in its
first edition. It is to bring the student as actively as possible into
the learning process in the introductory course in American politics. By placing problems before him and calling on him to
work out viable solutions, we hope to lead the student to an
understanding of the relationship between general statements
on the one hand and facts on the other, and to an understanding
of how both theory and data are involved in political analysis.

The present edition differs from the original edition of 1959 in
several important respects. We have had the advice of many
colleagues who have used the book in colleges and universities
across the country, and we have tried to profit by it. We have
eliminated several problems contained in the original edition
which proved less successful than others as teaching tools. We
have also substantially revised and enlarged those that remain,
and have included several entirely or almost entirely new problems. We have substantially enlarged the number and length of
reading materials reproduced within the problems, and have
tried in every case to select those readings that we thought were
most stimulating and enlightening for the subject at hand. In
most cases we have added new introductory materials to the
problems, in an effort to place each problem in the context of
the general framework of American politics and of modern
political analysis. In most cases also the problem instructions

have been significantly changed or enlarged from the original edition. Finally, we have tried to establish as much continuity or progression as possible from problem to problem so that the problems may stand as a more meaningful whole, although it is still true that they can be used piecemeal or in an order different from the one in which they are presented here. In short, while we have sought to make the problems more rigorous we have also tried to keep the book flexible so that it may fit the needs of different instructors and students.

The problems in this book remain as the product of several years of exchange between teachers and students. To an even greater extent than was true with the first edition, they are the winnowing of innumerable problems which we have tested in classes and discussion sections in American politics at Washington University. They were designed from the outset to help in achieving two goals in the introductory course—the goal of stimulating students who are simply "taking the course for credit," and the goal of challenging those who are already concerned with the subject. Among the latter group there are usually students who believe that a high school course has given them an adequate understanding of the American political system. These may particularly benefit from the problems, for despite excellent schooling they are likely to find that they still have much to learn in the realm of serious political analysis.

II

The introductory course may have several objectives. For one thing, it may be a preparation for citizenship or political participation. To play a part in public affairs young men and women must have some knowledge of how those affairs are organized and run, some acquaintance with the dynamic operation of government and politics.

To others the harvest which the introductory course can produce may appear more modest. It may be limited to assuming that in a democracy there is an obligation at least to vote, and vote intelligently. Despite the strictures of prophets of a power elite or the apparent success of new public relations techniques in politics, we are still committed to the democratic ideal of a knowledgeable electorate. Thus though teachers or students may lack eagerness for the political battle, both may have at least the objective of creating or becoming intelligent voters. To achieve this goal there must be information or data. And to serve well, such data must be not only recorded and memorized, but analyzed.

Indeed, the *use* of data in many fields is central to a third major objective of introductory political science—the objective of a liberal education. It is assumed that the freshman comes to the campus to "grow in wisdom." Wisdom is not merely the assimilation of assorted facts, profitable as this may prove in television contests. The greater, vital part is the gradual growth of an ability to make reflective decisions. This is wisdom, or if you will, judgment. The teacher of political science must strive to develop such judgment in his students, even in those who have little interest in the subject matter of the course.

There is a fourth aim that should be of major significance in the introductory course in American politics. Colleges and universities are the seedbeds of scholarship, and among college freshmen there will be a significant few who are potential scholars, the political scientists of the future. These few may be deflected from the scholarly path if their first taste of political science is flat and unappetizing—if, indeed, they are forced to endure only factual exposition or stale indoctrination. The nature of a large and youthful class precludes, to be sure, the advanced application of scientific techniques to the study of politics. But for those who wish to see, it is possible to open some vistas and make familiar some of the fundamentals of the scientific approach. Such vistas are offered in the problems in this book.

The question, then, is how to organize a course which can aim at such objectives, and what materials to use. Commonly the materials are a fat textbook, a shorter compilation of selected readings, and perhaps a few paperback volumes on particular topics. These may serve more or less well, but not well enough, for they leave one great gap for the student, and create one major difficulty for the teacher.

The gap is the absence of active student participation, of direct experience in the application of general principles to concrete cases. A student, for instance, may be letter-perfect in reciting a definition of "federalism," but can he be sure that he knows what the term means until he has tried to apply that definition? In Problem 9 in this book he is asked to do just that, and also, in the revised version of the problem, to carry the definition into an analysis of some of the dynamics of conflict in a federal system. He is likely to emerge with a realization that the words of the definition have a practical meaning and an analytical use, and with a sense of accomplishment at this discovery. He has connected the abstract with the tangible, the concept with the data. So with problems dealing with such other concepts as politics, constitution, democracy, majority rule, consensus, civil liberties, decision making, or judicial review.

The difficulty for the teacher is felt especially in the smaller classes or sections where the subject for discussion is either a portion of the text or one of the selected readings. It is hard to focus such a discussion, and unless it is focused it is likely to be a waste of time. Different questions, only vaguely related, are raised by different students; unimportant aspects of the reading are chewed over at length; the hour may well pass in desultory and profitless conversation. An instructor can avoid this difficulty by simply lecturing, but this sacrifices the values of student participation. Or he can surmount it by careful preparation and rigorous insistence that the discussion be centered on the points he wishes to have discussed. But he can overcome the difficulty much more effectively if the assigned reading is specifically pointed to a particular question or set of questions as it is in the problems in this book. Students can then think out possible answers to such questions in advance of class. On the basis of such focused and common preparation and reflection, discussion can proceed at once freely and relevantly, and with excitement.

Thus the purpose of this book is to aid the teacher and especially to fill the gap for the student. The book can be used in various ways. Conceivably all the problems could be assigned for discussion, one or more a week. Experience in many classes, however, leads to the suggestion that each instructor select among the problems, in accordance with his interests and the needs of his students. Several of the problems are good for two hours of useful discussion, rather than one; some seem especially fit for oral discussion with students preparing outlines in advance; others lend themselves better to full written essays. In a one-semester course a typical program might include one or two problems from each part, eleven or twelve for discussion, and three or four for written essays or outlines, long or short; but the instructor can pick and choose as he sees fit. The arrangement of the book follows the general pattern of most textbooks, but there is nothing hard and fast about it. For instance, Problem 2, dealing with concepts of politics and democracy, can be used appropriately at the conclusion of a course as well as at its beginning. And one or more of the problems in the sections on the executive and judicial branches might serve equally well in the section on the Constitution and the separation of powers.

Eager to drive quickly into the conventional part of the course, some teachers may prefer to defer the problems in Part I. Others, anxious to introduce their students to the difficult business of dealing with concepts, could spend four sessions on those problems alone. Problem 1, for example, requires students to wrestle with a subject that few of them have ever thought about before, the difference between descriptive statements and value judgments. While some instructors may lack time or inclination for this exercise others may find it particularly important as a preliminary to the study of politics, because political analysis is so often encumbered and distorted by a mass of preconceived value judgments or prejudices. Furthermore, the role of value judgments in political analysis is integral to some of the later problems.

Still other rearrangements are possible. Thus, for example,

Problem 3 might be used toward the end of the course as a means of focusing attention on the range of functions a democratic political system must get performed; conversely, Problem 20 might be considered in Part V as it deals with the roles of interest groups and political parties in the formation of legislative policy. The point for the instructor is to use the problems in the order and manner he finds most effective for himself and his students.

III

Two questions may arise that should be dealt with here. The first is: *what are the correct answers to the problems?* These are not geometrical exercises, and for most of them there is no single "correct answer." Thus, for example, there is no pat solution for the student in Problem 25, just as there are no pat answers for the President and his staff in actual decision-making situations. Or again, no one who has worked in political parties will assume that there is any sure answer to the questions posed in Problem 14 on party organization. Yet each of the problems can elicit a thorough, thoughtful response, which shows a comprehension of the issues and an ability to relate facts and theory and arrive at defensible formulations.

The second question may be expressed as a criticism: *why are the factual situations so often set forth in fictional rather than actual "case histories"?* The answer is that most real cases, properly recounted, inevitably involve so many elements that they are ill adapted for use in an introductory course. As a teaching mechanism fiction serves a very useful purpose, for it can enable one to eliminate those elements in a situation which unduly complicate a problem or are irrelevant to the central point. Thus the fixing of a focus is made easier. As a matter of fact a good deal of the fictional material in this book is based on real events. The case history of the Campanella bill in Problem 2, for instance, parallels recent history in a large American city, and the fictional cases in a number of other problems are based on actual events.

This response to the two questions can be given with some assurance because of the reaction to the problems in many classes. The students found the fictitious situations recognizable, realistic, and understandable. The frequent use of role-playing imparted a satisfying sense of involvement in the political or governmental process. The emphasis on analysis and processes allowed the class to escape the futility of uninformed and fruitless argument about whether this policy is better than that.

Another question may be raised—the use of a problems book in courses with large numbers of students, where discussion sections are not scheduled. Here the book may be used simply as a book of readings. More extensively, many of the problems may be dealt with in brief, positive outlines, which students may prepare and submit for grading and comment; and some of the problems can be assigned for fuller essays, possibly in place of an hour quiz. Finally, in large lecture sections oral statements and discussion by a few selected students may be useful, with different students assigned as discussants in different hours to maximize the number who will finally participate.

The task imposed by the American politics course is not easily accomplished. This book has been prepared in constant awareness of the manifold nature of that task. Though it is intended to brighten the hours of the student and lighten the load of the teacher, it is not aimed at softening the job of learning. It is aimed rather at making learning a happier and more satisfying occupation. It is devised in the conviction that intellectual effort and analytical thinking are highly worthwhile.

Throughout the work of revision for this new edition we have kept these larger aims constantly in mind, while at the same time we have sought to bring the problems up-to-date in terms of conceptual or theoretical as well as factual content, and to reshape them to carry the student as deeply as possible into the procedures of political analysis.

IV

We are, of course, greatly indebted to many people who have assisted us in the preparation of this book. Our first debt is to the hundreds of students at Washington University who, since 1953, have worked with the problems or the predecessors of the problems. At the beginning these students were exposed to inevitable ambiguities and imperfections in the problems as they were originally drafted. Their responses—vocal, critical, and in the main enthusiastic—helped us to perfect the problems.

Their instructors, too, including our colleagues in the Department of Political Science, have earned our thanks for their perceptive comments and suggestions, as have many graduate students who have worked with us in one capacity or another. Our appreciation to numerous authors and publishers for permission to reprint selections from their works is hereby warmly expressed. To our own publishers and to their advisory editor in political science, Professor David Fellman of the University of Wisconsin, we are in debt for a happy combination of cooperation and stringent criticism.

The clerical and stenographic work entailed in this project included the production of small mountains of mimeographed material over several years, in addition to the preparation of the final manuscripts for both the original and the revised editions; and we thank all of those who have labored with us on these matters so cheerfully.

THOMAS H. ELIOT
WILLIAM N. CHAMBERS
ROBERT H. SALISBURY
KENNETH PREWITT

Washington University
Saint Louis, Missouri
February 1965

CONTENTS

PART VI. THE LEGISLATIVE POWER

PART VII. THE EXECUTIVE POWER

PART VIII. THE JUDICIAL POWER

PART I

Some Fundamental Questions

PROBLEM 1

Facts and Values in Political Analysis

ANYONE embarking on a study of a "science" deserves to have some idea of what he is letting himself in for. Persons who call themselves political scientists investigate and attempt to explain a wide range of political events, structures, institutions, behavior, values, and ideologies. For example, an election is an event, economic classes are structures, the United States Senate is an institution, voting is an aspect of political behavior, partisan preferences are values, and democracy is a political ideology. The student of politics tries to explain the origin of such phenomena and their function in the political system.

Needless to say, not only political scientists are interested in the world of politics. There are observers who report, commentators who discuss, lobbyists who pressure, ideologues who exhort, and, of course, politicians who practice, to name just a few of the persons who closely follow the political drama. As you are aware from your own experiences, political happenings are grist for almost any conversational mill. It is obvious to the most casual observer that persons have quite different reasons for being interested in politics and select different aspects of politics for that interest. What distinguishes the interest of the political scientist? In brief, a political scientist is one who systematically collects facts (data) in order to develop explanations (theories) which account for why things are as they are in the political world, how they came to be that way, and what they may mean for future generations. This is neither an easy nor an insignificant undertaking, and it is made particularly difficult by some pitfalls which may lead us as students of politics into self-deception, however innocently, as we set out on our task. It may help you in your own endeavors as a neophyte political scientist to become acquainted with some of these dangers.

1. The student should begin by considering what he knows, what he does not know, and how much of what he thinks he knows may actually consist of *misconceptions*. Many people think they "know," for example, that to be democratic a political system must include a written constitution; separation of powers among legislative, executive, and judicial branches; and a federal division of powers between national and state governments—in short, it must conform to the general pattern of our American democracy. Yet, this is not true. The student of comparative politics knows that these things do not necessarily go together, and can cite as evidence the cases of Great Britain, Sweden, and Italy on the one hand, or the Soviet Union and Yugoslavia on the other. The first three are all democracies, yet Britain has no written constitution; and none of them includes separation of powers as we understand it, or federalism in their governmental structure. The last two both encompass federal systems, formally at least, but neither of them is a democracy. Again, many journalists and news commentators think they "know" that most Democrats who move from central-city areas to the suburbs become Republican in their new environments, but the most reliable survey data indicates that this is not usually the case. It is well to become fully aware of the possibility that one's preconceived notions may be quite incorrect, and learn to test them against *evidence*. In this example, "testing against evidence" means to look for cases which could disprove your assumption.

A peculiar kind of misconception or misunderstanding is simplification, or what has been called "the heresy of simplicism." To the uninitiated, for example, the problem of corruption in government or politics may seem very simple indeed—it's all due to bad men in office, and if we just vote the bad men out, corruption will disappear. The informed observer knows that this question is immensely complex, however. He is aware that great pressures operate on government officials and that the source of corruption is frequently someone outside government rather than the man in government; and he is conscious of the degree to which activities that may be thought acceptable in business, such as lavish entertainment, are considered unacceptable when a government official is concerned. Many students bring such oversimplified notions to their study of government and politics, whether they involve corruption, the way pressure groups work, the role of patronage in political parties, or judicial review. Such allegations as "government is corrupt" may have to be retracted as the student becomes more aware of the facts and learns how easily blanket accusations may cover up ignorance of the rules of the game.

2. The political scientist must also be alert to the distinction between what are called *descriptive statements* and *value judgments*. We must interpret "descriptive statement" broadly here. It may be a statement of a particular fact, such as "in 1964, the major-party candidates for president of the United States were Lyndon B. Johnson and Barry Goldwater." It may be a more general statement, such as "in times of national crisis, there is widespread and bipartisan support for the president." Or it may be a forecast, such as "if a serious depression occurs, then the party in power will suffer at the next election." A descriptive statement may be true or false. In political science we speak of testing descriptive statements on the basis of available evidence, or available facts in the case. Technically this is the process of "verification" or "confirmation." A statement may, in terms of the evidence, be confirmed (found to be probably true), be disconfirmed (found to be probably false), or be found indeterminate (neither confirmed nor disconfirmed on the available evidence). The subject of test-

ing statements is a large one and need not be fully covered at this stage. You should, however, keep firmly in mind that a descriptive statement asserts something about political phenomena which can be supported or rejected by testing it against the relevant evidence.

The student of politics has at his disposal a wide range of techniques which help him avoid self-deception when ascertaining the accuracy of a given statement. For example, if you wanted to explain why we have a two-party system in the United States, you might rely on historical and documentary evidence. If you wished to determine the voting behavior of particular groups in a society, you could undertake a systematic survey. For assessing the impact of a newspaper on a political event, you might undertake a content analysis of the paper, an examination of its news coverage and editorial comment, and compare the paper's position with the outcome. To explain why countries have unstable political systems may lead you to census and UNESCO records of the distribution of economic resources among the citizens of those countries. Whatever the question, it is assumed that evidence exists and techniques can be found which permit you to determine the correctness of the statements purporting to answer the question.

What we have called "value judgments," on the other hand, are not efforts simply at description or explanation. Rather they are expressions of one's feelings about a matter, expressions of preference, of liking or disliking, expressions of what one thinks is "good" or "bad," or "right" or "wrong," or "desirable" or "undesirable," of what "should" or "should not" be. However strongly one may defend such value judgments, they cannot as such be tested by observation, by reference to facts, evidence, data. Often value judgments are expressed in a way to make them look at first glance like descriptive statements. To say, "the administration of Lyndon B. Johnson has taken the wrong road by carrying on the New Frontier ideas of John F. Kennedy," is to make a value judgment. Its "rightness" or "wrongness" cannot be demonstrated simply by reference to facts, however strongly one may believe or disbelieve in the sentiment expressed.

All of us subscribe to certain value judgments. Our personal backgrounds—family, economic, social class, community or neighborhood, religious, ethnic or racial, and educational—our particular experiences and situation in life, and our general personality tendencies predispose all of us toward particular attitudes, value judgments, opinions about politics. Usually such attitudes are unexamined in that we have not consciously inquired into them or analyzed the grounds on which they rest. Sometimes such value judgments become so "hardened," so overlaid with emotion, that they take the form of prejudice. Some people are prejudiced against Negroes, Catholics, or Jews, or all or nearly all Democrats or Republicans, and they find it impossible to believe that a person falling into such a category can ever be anything other than "bad." Again, some people may be deeply prejudiced against government welfare programs as noxious "socialism," or against American involvement in world politics as "globaloney." To the extent that an individual holds on, emotionally, to value judgments and consequently refuses to weigh the facts and arguments pro-and-con, his whole view of politics may be distorted.

Thus our value judgments or prejudices may significantly affect our efforts to understand politics. First, they may influence our selection of facts for study, leading us to overlook data that may be unpalatable to our preference. For example, Democrats, bent on "proving" that the Republican party was hostile to civil rights in the election of 1964, might ignore the fact of Republican Congressional support for every major civil rights bill from 1957 through 1964. Second, our value predispositions may lead us to confuse what-we-wish-were-the-case with what-is-the-case. For example, Republicans may want their party to win the next presidential election so badly that they come to believe that the Republicans will win. Third, our value judgments may influence the way in which we interpret data. For example, one observer may state the facts about the legislative process in Congress and conclude that they present a picture of "inefficiency" and "chaos," while another may state the same facts and declare that they represent a "practical" adaptation to social and political "realities." The student should become aware of these factual statement-value judgment pitfalls and the problem of prejudice. He should try to achieve some self-consciousness concerning his own value predispositions and how they may affect him in his role as an observer of politics. In ordinary writing and conversation, factual statements and value judgments tend to mix together. In scientific inquiry a primary step is to get the facts straight and to learn to separate descriptive statements from value judgments.

All this does not, however, mean that a student of politics is precluded from having any opinions or value judgments about politics. He inevitably will, and the point is only that he should become conscious of this and strive to keep the distinction clear between what he prefers, on the one hand, and what is the case (or what is likely to be the case in the future), on the other. A number of problems in this book require the student to take a value position, but in such problems the emphasis is on considering the grounds on which the value judgment rests.

3. Words are tricky and a statement may be vague or ambiguous, capable of being understood in two or more meanings, instead of clear and precise. Where such ambiguity occurs it is often very difficult to distinguish whether a statement was meant as a descriptive statement or as a value judgment. If it was meant as a descriptive statement there may be difficulty in testing it to see if it is true or false because its meaning is unclear. For example, the statement, "political parties play a tremendous role in American elections, national, state, and local," is both vague and ambiguous. Does the word "tremendous" indicate a fact, or express a value judgment? If the former, what does "tremendous" mean in operation, that is, what particular facts would we look for to determine whether parties do or do not play a "tremendous" role? Students should be careful to spot and question ambiguities in what they read or hear, and to avoid ambiguities in their own discussion or writing.

Ambiguity may be reduced by the process of *definition*, and by trying to use a term throughout a piece of discourse in the way in which it has been originally defined. Consider the key term "power," which may be used with some care as the ability of a person or group to secure the cooperation or compliance of others, or may be employed as an emotional scare term, often in such phrases as "power politics," without any definition explicit or implicit. Similarly, the word "influence" may be used in the technical sense in which political scientists generally employ it or as a kind of epithet as in "influence peddling." It is important to be aware of the meanings we attach to key terms in any discourse, and to hold to the assigned meanings throughout.

4. Finally, the student should be aware of how little his own limited personal experience can tell him about the over-all pattern of American government and politics. We all, in a sense, live in the "caves" of our limited experiences, in our own limited environments, and we cannot at firsthand see the world whole. Thus what a person may find in his own "cave," from his own limited observation, may not be the case generally. For instance, it may be true that all the college graduates you happen to know are Republicans; but this does not mean that there is a general truth that all college graduates are Republicans. Firsthand observation is essential to understanding, but we should not take uncritically the findings of our own limited experience and impressions. To do so may be to commit what is called the fallacy of generalizing from the single case.

These four cautions should be kept in mind throughout one's study of political science. The more a student learns about the substance of political science, the more he should understand about the difficulties involved in the position of an observer.

An example of care in the vocabulary of politics may be found in a modern recapitulation of James Madison's central argument concerning checks on power in the American political structure. First read the original argument in the selections from *The Federalist*, reproduced in Problem 6, "Checks and Balances and the Blessings of Liberty," below. Then review carefully the following summary and compare it with the original.

Summary of the Madisonian Argument [1]

I. The basic definitions:

DEFINITION 1: An "external check" for any individual consists of the application of rewards and penalties, or the expectation that they will be applied, by some source other than the given individual himself.

DEFINITION 2: "Tyranny" is every severe deprivation of a natural right.

DEFINITION 3: A republic is a government which (a) derives all of its powers directly or indirectly from the great body of the people, and (b) is administered by persons holding their office during pleasure, for a limited period, or during good behavior.

DEFINITION 4: A faction is "a number of citizens, whether amounting to a majority or a minority of the whole, who are united and actuated by some common impulse of passion, or of interest, adverse to the rights of other citizens, or to the permanent and aggregate interests of the community."

II. The basic axiom: The goal that ought to be attained, at least in the United States, is a non-tyrannical republic.

III. The argument:

Hypothesis 1: If unrestrained by external checks, any given individual or group of individuals will tyrannize over others.

Hypothesis 2: The accumulation of all powers, legislative, executive, and judiciary, in the same hands implies the elimination of external checks.

Hypothesis 3: If unrestrained by external checks, a minority of individuals will tyrannize over a majority of individuals.

Hypothesis 4: If unrestrained by external checks, a majority of individuals will tyrannize over a minority of individuals.

Hypothesis 5: At least two conditions are necessary for the existence of a non-tyrannical republic:

[1] Robert A. Dahl, *A Preface to Democratic Theory* (Chicago: University of Chicago Press, 1956), 32–33.

    First Condition: The accumulation of all powers, legislative, executive, and judiciary, in the same hands, whether of one, a few, or many, and whether hereditary, self appointed, or elective, must be avoided.

    Second Condition: Factions must be so controlled that they do not succeed in acting adversely to the rights of other citizens or to the permanent and aggregate interests of the community.

    Hypothesis 6: Frequent popular elections will not provide an external check sufficient to prevent tyranny.

    Hypothesis 7: If factions are to be controlled and tyranny is to be avoided, this must be attained by controlling the effects of faction.

    Hypothesis 8: If a faction consists of less than a majority, it can be controlled by the operation of "the republican principle."

    Hypothesis 9: The development of majority factions can be limited if the electorate is numerous, extended, and diverse in interests.

    Hypothesis 10: To the extent that the electorate is numerous, extended, and diverse in interests, a majority faction is less likely to exist, and if it does exist, it is less likely to act as a unity.

It may be noted in the summary that the problem of ambiguity is dealt with as far as possible by explicit *definitions,* as set forth in Part I; that the basic *value judgment* is explicitly stated as such in an axiom which hinges on the value-oriented words "goal" and "ought," in Part II; and that the argument then follows in a series of *descriptive statements,* Part III, all of which are generalizations about politics and some of which are predictions. As hypotheses, all of these statements are subject to investigation or test as to their truth or falsity.

Consider carefully the points made in the above discussion and then undertake the following projects:

A. Write out three *descriptive statements* about American government or politics that you believe to be true. These descriptive vote in higher proportions in American national elections than those who have attended college.

6. In a democracy, the will of a majority should take precedence over the wishes of a minority.

7. Despite talk of international cooperation and mutual security, American aid to foreign nations has really become, in fact, just a giveaway program.

8. National political parties in the United States tend to place greater emphasis on the function of conducting and winning elections than they do on the function of shaping and carrying through party policies in government.

9. The form of government the United States now has is best described as a republic, not as a democracy.

D. In class discussion try to determine how many of the statements you subscribed to in Questions A and C above may really be misconceptions of what is actually the case (facts), and how many statements you took to be descriptive statements turn out on analysis to be partially or wholly value judgments.

E. Try to think through the factors in your own background or position as an observer that may have led you to such misconceptions or to such confusions of descriptive statements with value judgments.

PROBLEM 2

Democracy, Interests, and Government Decisions

ALL social systems of any size, whether traditionalist or modern, whether oligarchic, monarchical, or dictatorial, exhibit something we call politics. Yet only a few societies have developed political systems that may be thought of as democratic, and of these the United States is probably the one that has subscribed to democratic politics longest. Yet we are often confused as to what we mean by "democracy," and we sometimes feel that our democratic ideals are violated in the day-to-day practice of politics. Thus we may think, on the one hand, of democracy as something that should give expression to the "general welfare" or the "public interest," and on the other, of the presumably selfish machinations of "pressure groups" or "politicians." Often, indeed, we think of democracy as good and politics as bad. Profession and practice seem to be in conflict, and this adds to the confusion.

In part this uncertainty stems from the nature of the democratic tradition as we have unconsciously internalized it. For John Locke or Thomas Jefferson and other prophets of the seventeenth- and eighteenth-century Enlightenment a democratic polity was one in which free, rational individuals or their representatives deliberated on public issues and arrived at policies which were best for the whole community, or at least at policies which the majority of the community thought were best. The judgment of the majority was expected by and large to be the prime expression of the general will or "public interest," and this judgment of the majority was to be discovered through elections and carried out by government. Yet other political thinkers like Montesquieu and James Madison argued that it was in the nature of politics that particular classes or groups in the society would make special claims on government; and spokesmen in this tradition have maintained that the balancing, adjustment, and compromising of such claims is the regular business of democratic politics. Such claims are not always easy to compromise, however, particularly when a situation develops in which there seems to be no feasible middle ground. Those who in a given situation oppose the claims of special groups, moreover, may argue that needs of the whole community or the "public interest" must in a showdown take precedence over the interests of any segment of the community.

Before you go any further write down briefly, but as clearly and comprehensively as you can, what you think the term "democracy" means. Retain what you have written for future reference.

Keeping in mind your definition of "democracy," read and analyze the following case study of politics in operation. This case history, though it is derived from the actual facts of a recent political conflict in an American city, involves general concepts, questions, and principles which could relate as well to politics in a state, or to politics in the United States as a whole. It is an attempt to present some of the problems of democratic politics in microcosm.

The Campanella Bill—A Political Case History

The city of Zenith, in the state of Winnemac, is an American city of about 350,000 population. Like many other cities in the Midwest in recent years it has suffered a relative loss of economic position as a result of the concentration of new defense, electronic, and space industries on the East and West coasts. The population of the central city actually declined between the census of 1950 and the census of 1960, with the movement of many people and industries to the suburbs. The people of Zenith are predominantly white and Protestant, though Roman Catholics comprise about 35 percent of the population and a substantial number of Negroes live in the city's central wards.

In the northeastern corner of Zenith a district known as the "Hill" is occupied by a closely knit group of Italo-Americans. They still speak Italian frequently and adhere to many "old world" or Italian customs. This ethnic minority, about seven percent of the total population of Zenith, usually supports in a relatively united way the dominant Italo-American leader of the moment, who is often referred to as the "King of the Hill." Thus the Italo-Americans tend to act as a cohesive, though not formally organized, interest group in Zenith politics. For the past twenty years Giuseppe "Buster" Campanella, Alderman for the Eighteenth Ward, a Democrat, has been the recognized spokesman of the Italo-Americans, and has attained a position of considerable influence in the city as a whole. He attended Zenith City College and law school, and is widely respected as an intelligent, capable political leader.

In Zenith there is substantial competition between the Republican and Democratic parties, but in recent years the Democrats have been dominant.

At the 1963 election for mayor the Democratic candidate was Rufus Barker, a professor of civil engineering at Jefferson University in Zenith. In a strenuous campaign Professor Barker was supported by many business, labor, and professional groups, by both Protestants and Catholics, by several Negro leaders, and by Zenith's crusading morning newspaper, the *Sentinel-Telegraph*. This, coupled with his great personal appeal as a candidate and his program to "make Zenith a better city to live in," gave him victory by an overwhelming majority. The keynote of his campaign was: "Progress or Decay? Zenith must Decide!"

In office Mayor Barker moved promptly to put his program for "Progress" into effect. Among many other things he worked with the Zenith Chamber of Commerce and a conference of Midwestern senators and governors to bring new, modern industry to Zenith. At the same time he launched a city-wide survey of local zoning patterns by the City Planning Commission and a Citizens' statements must be such that they can be subjected to empirical analysis. What evidence would confirm that your statements are true, and what evidence might refute them?

B. Write out three *statements of value* about American government or politics to which you personally subscribe. On what grounds would you defend these value judgments?

C. Think over carefully the following nine statements, and for each of the nine indicate:

> (a) whether you would classify it as an effort to make a descriptive statement (whether true or false), or a value judgment;
>
> (b) if it is a descriptive statement, what evidence would be needed to determine the truth or falsity of the statement;
>
> (c) if it is a value judgment, what makes it so. Do you agree or disagree with it? Why?
>
> (d) at what points do you find ambiguities in the statements, and how would you go about clearing them up?

1. The men who framed the Constitution of the United States in 1787 were primarily concerned with broadening political democracy for American citizens.

2. The Constitution of the United States does not now need amending in any important way, because it contains an amending clause and has been amended when circumstances required it in the past.

3. Although lawyers compose only a small part of the total population, there are more lawyers among the members of Congress than there are persons from any other occupation.

4. The national government has no business requiring hotels, restaurants, and theaters to admit Negroes along with whites in communities where a majority of the people are opposed to such integration.

5. Despite the civic activities of many college-educated men and women, people without college educations generally

Committee for Land Use, to which he appointed representatives of important groups throughout the community. The result of this survey was a comprehensive zoning proposal aimed at planned use of the city's land areas for industrial, commercial, residential, recreational, and other purposes, to promote economic "Progress" and new industrial development and at the same time provide neighborhood environments that would help "make Zenith a better city to live in." The Mayor recommended to the Board of Aldermen a comprehensive zoning ordinance based on the survey proposal.

The members of the Board of Aldermen, where the Democrats had a fourteen-to-eight majority, are elected one from each of twenty-two wards. Mayor Barker's comprehensive zoning proposal was immediately denounced by some aldermen who thought that people in the wards they represented would be injured by the new zoning plan. With the support of community leaders and the local newspapers the Mayor was able to insist on acceptance of his plan, and the Board of Aldermen voted thirteen-to-nine to adopt it. Six Republicans and three Democrats voted against it. In the following months, however, when individual aldermen submitted bills of specific interest to their particular wards—proposals, for example, to enact "spot zoning" ordinances to open certain lots in areas previously classified as residential, so retail stores could be built—the Board of Aldermen often carried such bills over Mayor Barker's objections and even overrode his vetoes. Usually such measures were carried by the long-established practice of "aldermanic courtesy." Under this practice members of the Board would regularly "go along" with nearly any request by a particular alderman for an ordinance of special interest to people in his ward. The Mayor vehemently condemned the practice of aldermanic courtesy and charged that it was "a device to serve narrow interests in the wards at the expense of general, community-wide purposes and the public interest." On the other hand several aldermen stoutly defended aldermanic courtesy as "grass-roots democracy in action." They argued that the people of their neighborhoods, and the aldermen as their representatives, knew what was best for their neighborhoods, and that they had a right to expect their elected ward representatives to be responsive to their needs.

Toward the end of his first four-year term in 1967 Mayor Barker announced that he would be a candidate for re-election. In a campaign similar to that which first put him in office, he specifically condemned the practice of aldermanic courtesy and suggested that aldermen ought to be elected from the city at large instead of from particular wards. Numerous opponents of city-wide election of aldermen, however, charged that this would make it possible for "a few downtown big business leaders and the Squash Club big shots to control the city government," at the expense of "the plain people in the poorer neighborhoods," whose interests could be given fair consideration only by aldermen who were in close contact with their constituents on a neighborhood basis. In fact, the Mayor's ties with large business groups had become increasingly close during his first term. In addition, many party leaders now felt that Mayor Barker was becoming too impressed with himself and his position in Zenith—"He thinks he's the cheese, the big-I-am, and he gets bossier every day," one prominent Democrat declared privately. Nonetheless the Mayor won re-election easily, though by a slightly decreased vote.

Shortly after the beginning of Mayor Barker's second term the aldermen and the Mayor faced an important decision on a zoning issue. It involved a twenty-acre tract of vacant land in the Mill-bank Valley, adjacent to the Italo-American occupied Hill and within the boundaries of Campanella's Eighteenth Ward. The land, owned by the Penn-Matthewson Lumber Company, whose chief lumber yard was adjacent to the tract, had originally been zoned as a residential area. The report of the City Planning Commission and the Citizens' Committee for Land Use, and Mayor Barker's comprehensive zoning ordinance passed in 1964 by the Board of Aldermen, had reclassified it as an area for industry only. The main line of the Winnemac-Atlantic railroad ran about half a mile from the tract, and the railroad had expressed its willingness to build a spur to serve any industry that might be built there. As the Alderman from the Eighteenth Ward the "King of the Hill" now offered a bill to return the area to residential use only and open it to the construction of multiple-family dwellings. He had introduced his bill, Campanella said, in response to the requests of several people in his ward, some of whom had approached him informally to point out what they called "the need for more living room near their families" for the expanding Italo-American population. Many families were doubling up in the existing homes in the overcrowded Hill district. The local leader of the demand to have the area returned to residential classification was a Catholic priest, the Rev. Patrick McCarthy, who was a respected and influential figure among Catholics and non-Catholics throughout Zenith and popular among his present parishioners in the Hill district. Under Father McCarthy's quiet but effective leadership a petition to limit the tract to residential use was signed by 634 citizens in the Eighteenth Ward and delivered to Alderman Campanella. In addition a syndicate of real estate men and contractors supported Campanella's motion; these men, some of whom lived on the Hill and others elsewhere in Zenith, hoped to build two-family frame dwellings and one large apartment house in the area. Finally the Campanella bill was supported by the United Clothing Workers' Union, AFL-CIO, one of the labor groups most active politically in Zenith, which happened to include among its membership many Italo-Americans who lived in the Hill district. The residential zoning proposal was opposed by the City Planning Commission, the Citizens' Committee for Land Use, the Zenith Chamber of Commerce, some of Zenith's labor unions, and other civic groups who maintained that the area was an ideal site for the location of new industries. It was also opposed by two business firms who had a direct interest in the area. One of these was the Penn-Matthewson Lumber Company, who maintained that the land they owned had a value of $400,000 as an industrial area but would be valued at only $150,000 if it were classified as residential. Another was Thyssen Ionics, Incorporated, which had already drawn up plans to build on the tract a new plant employing about 1,500 men. Many Negro leaders also opposed the Campanella bill in the hope that new industry in the area might provide jobs for unemployed Negro workers.

The Mayor promptly took sides in this conflict. He opposed Campanella's bill as another attack by special, local groups on his efforts for "Progress" against "Decay," for which the people of Zenith had voted twice by electing him mayor. He also argued that Zenith badly needed industrial sites and industrial development, and that the Millbank Valley area was better suited to industrial than to residential use. In this stand Mayor Barker was vigorously supported by the *Sentinel-Telegraph,* which printed the results of a carefully conducted public opinion survey indicating that 36 percent of Zenith's citizens supported the Mayor's stand while only 11 percent opposed it. Of the rest, 39 percent did not know about the issue at all and another 14 percent expressed no opinion.

Meanwhile Campanella had been busy in the Board of Aldermen where the initial decision would be made. He spoke privately to James Michael Rooney, who as majority floor leader in the Board of Aldermen had virtual control over deciding when bills would be brought before the Board for action. During long years of service on the Board together Campanella and Rooney had become close personal friends and Campanella now told Rooney, "Jim, this bill means a lot to me." When the Board took up the bill, the "King of the Hill" reminded his fellow aldermen that he had represented the Eighteenth Ward for twenty years, declared that his rezoning bill was "of vital concern to the people of my neighborhood," and asked that it be passed. In reply Alderman Benton Reeves, of the "silk stocking" Twentieth Ward, a Democratic intellectual who was sometimes called the "Bow-Tie Liberal," denounced the bill as "the selfish, bastard progeny of the illicit, undemocratic practice of aldermanic courtesy," as "the spawn of a dark liaison between 'Buster' Campanella and his political friends and playmates on the Board." He also said that he was "tired of seeing the public interest, the general welfare, constantly being obstructed by the outcries of little, local, selfish pressure groups with narrow-minded politicians as their fugle-men." When Reeves had finished, Campanella angrily retorted that he didn't know what Reeves meant by "fuglemen," but that he was sure that the opposition to his bill was "another example of the power of big-business groups and the Squash Club big shots in Zenith." These men, and the Mayor as their spokesman in this case, he complained, were "putting the interests of profit ahead of the interests of people—in this case the interests of industrial expansion ahead of the welfare of the men and women I represent in my ward, who ought to have homes." He reiterated that he had been "the chosen representative of my people on the Hill for twenty years," and that he and his "people" knew what was "best for their welfare—and *that* is democracy." The Board then passed the Campanella bill without further discussion, thir-teen to eight; five of the eight Republicans and three of the fourteen Democrats voted against it, with one Democratic mem-ber absent. Many factors affected this decision. They included (1) loyalty to the practice of aldermanic courtesy; (2) friendship toward Campanella or antagonism toward Mayor Barker; (3) a feeling among some aldermen that similar situations might arise in their own wards when they would be expected to "get results" for local groups; (4) deference to the substantial Catholic support for the bill resulting from Father McCarthy's influence; and (5) the influence in several wards of the militant United Clothing Workers' Union, which supported the bill in the interest of their members in the Hill area.

The Zenith city charter gave the Mayor power to veto bills by returning them to the Board of Aldermen without his signature. In such cases bills did not become law unless the Board repassed them by a simple majority. The Campanella bill was promptly vetoed by Mayor Barker. In a stinging veto message he insisted that industrial zoning of the Millbank tract was "in the public interest," and called upon "all truly democratic, all genuinely Zenith-minded aldermen" to sustain his veto. This would require a majority of the whole Board, or twelve votes. In an interview with a *Sentinel-Telegraph* reporter Campanella said, "I have always felt that my first duty was to the Eighteenth Ward and the people there," and declared hotly that Mayor Barker's veto was a "fresh example of his big-I-am, big-business attitude." The *Sentinel-Telegraph's* survey showed that the Hill dwellers supported the "King" overwhelmingly.

With only one day available before the Board of Aldermen considered Mayor Barker's veto Alderman Reeves set to work to try to get it sustained, so that the ultimate decision would leave the Millbank Valley tract open to industry. He talked to as many members of the Board as he could, insisting that a "clear majority of the people of Zenith" had shown that they supported the Mayor's program of planned land use for "Progress." As evidence he cited the election and re-election of Mayor Barker on a clear program and the fact that the *Sentinel-Telegraph* poll showed widespread popular support specifically for the Mayor's stand against the Campanella bill. He proclaimed that "loyalty to the ideas of democratic government and community welfare" required that the aldermen vote to sustain the veto. Getting wind of this, Alderman Campanella also talked with members of the Board, asking them in the name of aldermanic courtesy to him as a spokesman for his ward to override the veto.

Now, study, analyze, reflect on, and compare carefully the following four statements:

I. A Model of Democratic Government [1]

Most writers on democracy, whatever else they may insist must be present in order for a government to be called a "democracy," are . . . committed to the view that it must exhibit the following minimum characteristics: (1) Those who hold office in it must stand ready, *in some sense,* to do whatever the people want them to do,

[1] Austin Ranney and Willmoore Kendall, *Democracy and the American Party System* (New York: Harcourt, Brace and Co., 1956), 23, 54–55. Emphasis added in some instances.

and to refrain from doing anything the people oppose; (2) each member of the "community" for which it acts should have, *in some sense*, as good a chance as his fellows to participate in the community's decision-making—not better and not worse; and (3) it must operate in terms of an understanding that when the enfranchised members of the community disagree as to what ought to be done, the last word lies, *in some sense*, with the larger number and never the smaller—i.e., the *majority* of the electorate and not the minority should carry the day. . . .

Let us . . . present in summary form a list of the leading characteristics of [a] model of democracy . . .

1. *Popular sovereignty.* The whole power of government resides in the whole people—that is, in all the members of the community, and not in any special ruling class or in any single individual.

2. *Political equality.* Each member of the community has the same formal right as all the other members to participate in the community's total decision-making process.

3. *Popular consultation.*

   (a) The community's laws are made by a representative assembly.

   (b) The electoral arrangements for selecting members of the representative assembly are such that the assembly will be as subordinate to the people as the latter wish it to be.

   (c) Failing (b), the members of the assembly make decisions as the *whole people* would make them if the latter were present and voting.

   (d) The assembly supervises, holds accountable, and has full control over all other public officials.

   (e) There are arrangements for communicating to the people full factual knowledge and understanding of all public problems they wish to do something about.

   (f) The citizens participate in the development of proposals for public policy as well as give or withhold consent to such proposals.

4. *Majority rule.*

   (a) No decision as to public policy or procedure is deemed valid if *opposed by more than half of the members of the community.*

(b) A majority of the representative assembly has the same power over the assembly's decisions as a majority of the town meeting has over the latter's decisions.

(c) Majorities forebear from tyranny and minorities from irredentism and civil war because of a sense of *obligation* to do so on the part of *all* the members of the community (and of their elected representatives) based on the feeling of each that he needs to keep all the others loyal to the community if he is to realize his own values.

(d) Decisions are made after a process of creative discussion in which all the members of the community are trying to find out what is *best for the community*.

II. An Alternative Model for Democracy [2]

A system of democratic theology has grown up; and the temptation to take it seriously and apply it literally can be held responsible for many [misunderstandings]. . . . The keystone of this doctrine is the assumption that there exists in every political society a "will of the people" which declares itself at elections and operates through the instrumentality of elected officials; and it is thought to be the object of democracy to see that this "popular will" gets itself translated into governmental [decisions], and that governmental action is determined by nothing else. . . . One of the principal grounds of [criticism of] democratic institutions is that they do not achieve this aim—that instead of ensuring that governmental action shall be guided solely by *the popular will*, they permit it to take its direction from *the will of small groups or special interests.* . . .

[But] the larger number of members of any political society have no opinion, and hence no will, on nearly all the matters on which government acts. The only opinion, the only will which exists is the opinion, the will, of special groups . . . The [actual] task of government, and hence of democracy as a form of government, is not to express an imaginary popular will, but to *effect adjustments among the various special wills and purposes* which at any given time are pressing for realization. . . .

[2] John Dickinson, "Democratic Realities and Democratic Dogma," *American Political Science Review*, 24 (1930), 288, 291–93. Emphasis added.

This is the task of governmental decisions ranging in importance from where to locate a new street or sewage-disposal plant to whether or not to go to war. Government, from this point of view, is primarily an arbitrator, and since practically every arbitration must result in giving to one side more of what it thinks it ought to have than the other side is willing to admit, every governmental [decision] can be viewed as favoring in some degree some particular and partial "will," or special interest. It is therefore meaningless to criticize government, whether democratic or not, merely because it allows special interests to attain some measure of what they think themselves entitled to. . . .

Where a society in its normal condition embraces a wide variety of competing interests of approximately equal strength, which are pressing restlessly and aggressively against one another . . . a type of government is required through which *the conflict of interests can result in compromises,* and in compromises, furthermore, whose necessity is brought directly home to the warring [interest groups] themselves. . . .

This may be something quite different from *pure* democracy, or government by mass-meeting, which is almost as archaic a governmental type as pure monarchy.

III. Groups in the Political Process [3]

The late William James is said to have observed that democracy is a system in which the government does something and waits to see who "hollers." Then it does something else in order to relieve the "hollering" as best it can and waits to see who "hollers" at the adjustment. No one who has ever been a public official will dismiss this as merely a humorous remark. . . .

For example, a municipal council is confronted with what appears to be a public demand that the prevailing diagonal system of parking automobiles on business streets be changed to parallel parking. Characteristically the council decides to proceed cautiously by enacting an ordinance that leaves parking as it has been on one side of the street but changes to parallel parking on the other side. No

[3] Wilfred E. Binkley and Malcolm C. Moos, *A Grammar of American Politics* (New York: Alfred A. Knopf, 1952), 3, 7–11, 14.

sooner does the ordinance go into effect than protests arise from the merchants who have parallel parking on their side of the street because the number of automobiles able to park near their businesses has been reduced. At the next meeting of the municipal council the ordinance is repealed, diagonal parking is restored, and the tumult subsides. . . .

The basic concept needed for an understanding of the dynamics of government is the multi-group nature of modern society or the modern state . . . The framers of the American Constitution understood the multi-group structure of society, and Madison gave classic expression to their conception in the tenth article of the *Federalist.* The late Charles A. Beard gave a modern version of Madison's interpretation in the following apt paraphrase: "A landed interest, a transport interest, a railway interest, a shipping interest, an engineering interest, a manufacturing interest, with many lesser interests, grow up of necessity in all great societies and divide them into different classes actuated by different sentiments and views. The regulation of these various and interfering interests . . . constitutes the principal task of modern statesmen . . . in the necessary and ordinary operation of the government."

Democratic government is presumed to be controlled only by public opinion. In a democratic system public policy slowly and hesitatingly emerges from innumerable planned conferences and unplanned conversations. Pressure groups, the press, radio and television commentators, and all other agencies of communication utilized by a free people contribute to the formulation of public opinion. In a multi-group society public opinion tends to become a resultant of the competing influences of the various groups. With respect to a specific issue one might conceive of progressive forces pushing forward, conservatives thrusting to the right, and radicals to the left, and reactionary forces shoving back. The resultant movement of public opinion depends upon the relative strength of the several forces. Sometimes one, sometimes another, is strongest. Professor H. L. Childs conceives the process to be analogous to the play of mechanical forces: "Were it possible to plot pressure groups objectively as parallelograms of forces and compute the resultant, significant predictions might be made . . . as to significant trends in public policy."

Democracy often provides the opportunity for competing groups to coordinate their aims in programs they can all support. This is done through institutional means for discovering common ground, as through legislatures, the chief organ for giving formal or legal expression to ultimate agreement. The policies thus declared "tend to become a series of compromises along lines of least resistance." . . .

It was long customary to assume that concepts of the public interest were determined logically by the reasoning of "right thinking" persons. [Yet] in our multi-group society, functioning as a democracy, there seems to be no way for the public interest to be determined and established other than through the free competition of interest groups. The necessary composing or compromising of their differences is the practical test of what constitutes the public interest. . . .

The high function of the legislator is to translate social ideas, influences, and pressures into public policies if he is to be, in the truest sense, a representative. . . . Theoretically, legislation represents the will of the majority, but actually, as Judge Learned Hand observes: "Most legislation is not of that kind; it represents the insistence of a compact and formidable minority. Nor are we to complain of that, for while we may be right to say that the problem of democracy lies in minorities, we are not to suppose that the bulk of government can go on on any other terms." . . .

[In] the case of all great controversial issues before legislative bodies, the outcome . . . also depends upon whichever side can exert the greater pressure for or against the legislation required to consummate the plan.

[Yet] the American social structure [also] contains powerful forces that tend to counteract each other and thereby prevent the mastery of the government by any single force. For example, neither management nor labor is able to influence the government as it might wish, and in the relative though shifting balance between the two social forces, safety seems to lie. The public when thoroughly aroused will permit neither to attain a dangerous advantage but will use the ballot to restore what it deems to be a salutary balance.

In the American governmental system the executive, who is head of the administrative system as well as a leader in legislation, can provide the focal point for rallying public opinion against selfish private interests. More than once a dynamic executive has frustrated the designs of powerful interests exerting pressure upon the legislature.

At his best, the executive, as the synthesizer of the public interest, can symbolize the unity of the state and become an instrument for translating it into established policies of the public good. . . .

IV. Politics as People

As Calvin Coolidge once remarked, "Politics is people: it is personal, it is individual, and nothing more." By this statement he meant to stress that politics consisted of individuals working with, or opposing, other individuals, and that elements of friendship or personal antagonism were basic to politics. He also suggested that at bottom all politics could be understood in terms of individual action, and that basically politics was "nothing more" than this. This is a view quite commonly held among working politicians, who see politics as kind of individualistic, "who's who," or "who is doing what with or to whom," game.

Now, consider carefully for class discussion or for a written exercise the following lines of analysis.

Two warnings: Remember that you are called upon to relate *all four* of the general statements I–IV to the Campanella bill case, and remember that there is no "set answer."

1. Suppose, *first*, that the Board *overrides* the Mayor's veto and thus Campanella's bill becomes law:
   (a) To what extent is the full case history of the Campanella bill, thus completed, in accord with or not in accord with the two different conceptions of democracy contained in Statement I, and alternatively in Statement II?
   (b) What does the history of the Campanella bill, thus completed, suggest concerning the practicality of each of the two statements of democracy, considered in terms of the points made in Statements III and IV as well as the case history itself?

2. Suppose, *second,* that the Board *sustains* the Mayor's veto and the Campanella bill thus does not become law. If this happened what changes, if any, would you make in your assessment

of how the completed history of the Campanella bill would "fit" or fail to "fit" the conceptions and analyses contained in Statements I, II, III, and IV.

3. If *you* were the alderman who was absent on the first vote on the Campanella rezoning bill, how would *you* vote—to sustain the Mayor's veto, or to override it and thus make Campanella's bill law? What factors would you have to take into account in making your decision? Justify your decision in terms of (a) your own general *conception of democracy*, as you originally stated it and as you may want to revise it as a result of your study of this problem; and (b) the particular factors described here as these would relate to the necessities of practical political action and that you would have to face as an alderman, in the Board and in your ward.

4. Think through carefully what you have learned from the case history of the Campanella bill, and from your reading of Statements I–IV as you have related them to this case history. How would you *now* define *your own* conception of "democracy," at least as it might operate in the American context?

Bear in mind that it might be possible to draw on both of the models on democracy contained in Statements I and II as well as on the analyses of Statements III and IV in preparing a more nearly adequate conception or definition of "democracy."

PROBLEM 3

Democratic Functions and Political Parties

DEMOCRACY has been called the most difficult form of government ever devised, and certainly democratic political systems must find ways to perform a bewildering variety of political functions. Group interests must be expressed or articulated in political terms, and different interests must be brought together or adjusted so that the political system will not be torn apart. Ordinary citizens must in some degree be educated about the workings of the system, as they must also in some measure be kept informed about its problems, procedures, and policies. Leaders must be recruited and trained in quantity; and there must be some reasonably orderly way in which voters can select leaders and then choose to retain them in office or replace them. Majorities must somehow be formed in the electorate or at least in legislative assemblies; and some means must be found to secure popular support for the officials and policies of government while at the same time criticism is permitted. Finally, governmental decisions must be made and carried out and governmental policies must be set. It might be said that democracy is like the bumblebee, which shouldn't be able to fly but does.

In the United States a number of institutions have contributed to the functioning of our democratic polity. These have ranged from the school system to various means for assimilating immigrants into the American political culture, from organized interest groups to the free communications network of press, television, and radio. From the outset, however, many of the most crucial democratic functions in the United States have been performed in large measure by our political parties. As the first new nation of modern times and the first democratic republic of its magnitude in history, the United States was also the first to generate modern, representative parties. The Federalist and first Republican parties appeared in the American political arena at a time when the politics of Great Britain, where the right to vote was still severely limited, was still a scramble of loose persuasions labeled "Whig" and "Tory," and underneath of shifting factions, personal "connexions" built around dominant aristocrats or great magnates, and *ad hoc* parliamentary combinations. Yet the original thirteen American states had begun their independent political careers without parties. They had also generated their own version of the loose, shifting politics of factions, personal cliques, and caucuses in which the performance of democratic functions was erratic. It was not until six or seven years after the ratification of the Constitution that the United States was able to arrive at a going party system. Since that time different parties have come and gone, but for more than a century now the Democrats and Republicans have survived as stable formations performing crucial political tasks.

In terms of the functions required in a democratic political system, the development of American political parties raises a number of important questions. Why did parties arise in the first place? What functions have parties actually undertaken in American politics, and if parties did not exist how would these functions be performed? What connections can be traced between the origins of parties and their functions in a democracy?

Now read the following statements, one dealing with early party development and the other with party functions today.

I. Party Origins [1]

Political parties in America did not spring from growing resistance to colonial rule from 1763 to 1776, in a manner that is familiar in

[1] William Nisbet Chambers, "Party System and Nation-Building in America," Conference on Political Parties and Political Development, Social Sci-

many new nations in Asia and Africa today. In the Revolutionary struggle sharp divisions did develop between "Patriots" and "Loyalists." The Patriots established committees of correspondence in the thirteen colonies or states, formed the Continental Congress as a coordinating agency for the Revolutionary effort and as a quasi-government thereafter, and undertook other means of agitation, cooperation, and action. Yet the Patriots did not become a party in the full sense and did not persist as a distinct political formation past the period of the struggle for independence. Cleavage between so-called "Federalists" and "anti-Federalists" also appeared in the controversy over the ratification of the new Constitution in 1788–1789. Yet once again these alignments did not take on party form and the actual contest over ratification was waged among a pluralistic congeries of leaders and groups. . . . In the internal politics of the several states, moreover, the contest for power was waged by a variety of factional formations rather than by parties. Only relatively advanced Pennsylvania developed something like a party system.

Thus the first American parties, or national parties, emerged out of new conflicts only in the decade of the 1790s. Broadly speaking what marked Federalists off from Republicans were cleavages between mercantile, investing, and manufacturing interests and certain segments of agriculture on the one side, and most planting and agrarian interests on the other. Differences also arose out of disagreements over the degree to which power should be consolidated in the new national government; over proposed policies to promote economic growth and capitalist development through government action; and over the extent to which foreign policy should be oriented toward traditionalist-monarchist England or revolutionary-republican France. Finally, conflict grew out of contentions between leading personalities like the Federalists Alexander Hamilton or John Adams on the one hand and the Republicans James Madison or Thomas Jefferson on the other, contentions that were sometimes as petty as they were colorful; and out of cleavages among a variety of other group, sectional, religious, local, and personal interests and

ence Research Council, Rome, Italy, January 1964, 2–9, 11–13. Scheduled for publication in Myron Weiner and Joseph LaPalombara, eds., *Political Parties and Political Development* (Princeton: Princeton University Press, 1965).

persuasions. The whole story does not require retelling in its historical detail. The Federalists and Republicans also developed out of a set of basic conditions, and these are more to the point here.

As a general theory or hypothesis, the most basic conditions associated with the development of political parties in the modern sense may be summarized under four major headings—

1. The emergence or prospect of a significant national or common political arena, within which influence or power may be sought with reference to the decision-making centers and the offices of a common political system.

2. The development of differentiation or complexity within the political system in terms of divergences in group structures and conflicts of interest and opinion, and in terms of governmental structures and functions.

3. The emergence of social structures and of ideologies . . . which permit or encourage some form of popular or mass politics and a substantial electorate.

4. The consequent need to develop political structures to establish relationships between leaders and popular followings, if leaders are to win and hold power and governmental functions are to be performed.

This statement of conditions can readily be related to the American instance. . . . The recital of American conditions will be given in summary form, as a set of middle-range generalizations about American political development.

1. A national political arena was opened with the ratification of the new Constitution and the establishment of the national government in 1789.

Even in the colonial years a considerable degree of inter-colonial communication and what might be called "continental consciousness," or proto-national identity, had begun to emerge on the American scene. This development at once helped to sustain and received new impetus from the Revolutionary War effort and the Continental Congress of 1775–1789. The limited powers of this Congress, however, together with the fact that it could not exercise direct power over citizens but was only a quasi-government which depended on the states, and the fact that the Congress consisted of delegates appointed by state legislatures rather than of representatives chosen by the voters, all kept it from providing a truly national political arena. The new general government with its single, indirectly-elected executive and its representative, two-house Congress did become the center of a rapidly developing national arena. It was in and around this government that groups, leaders, and parties struggled and the great issues of the day were fought out.

2. The indigenous pluralism within the American nation produced a high degree of differentiation among groups, social strata, and states or sections, and a complex interplay of interests, loyalties, sentiments, and opinions; and most of these forces quickly found expression in politics.

The cross-currents which the pluralism of early American life threw up were complex indeed. There were small-freehold farmers and great planters owning thousands of slaves; merchants, shippers and shipbuilders, importers and exporters, investors, and struggling manufacturers; artisans or "mechanics"; varied ethnic stocks and different religious faiths; would-be "aristocrats" and nascent "democrats," and sanguine "Gallomen" [partisans of France] and sober "Anglomen" [friends of England]; states competing with one another; and a host of sub-groupings, such as near-subsistence farmers or farmers who looked to the market. A congeries of interests extended across the new nation which had to be given expression and adjusted if the political system was to sustain itself and perform its functions; and parties developed in considerable part as a response to such felt needs. Certain interstate comparisons are also revealing in connection with this condition for party formation. Indices are difficult to assign, but Pennsylvania exhibited a particularly high degree of differentiation in the interplay of interests; and this phenomenon helps to explain the fact that Pennsylvania alone developed a state party system in the 1780s and also moved rapidly toward shaping local units of the national parties in the 1790s. A significant degree of complexity might also be attributed to New York, for example, where the pace of national party development was second only to that of Pennsylvania; but in New York old patterns of domination by great families and clique politics, characteristics which were much less in evidence in Pennsylvania, impeded party development. It may be suggested in general as a hypothesis that the higher the degree of differentiation of group and other relationships is in a political system, the greater the probability for the development of political parties is, though this probability may be reduced by the presence of other impeding conditions.

Substantial differentiation also characterized the national government. It was not only formally separated into executive, legislative and judicial branches with different prescribed powers, but the two houses of Congress had different electoral foundations and constituencies and somewhat different functions. The Constitution also provided an intricate set of checks or reciprocal relationships among the various organs of government which in effect constituted a further differentiation of functions. Again, parties arose in part in response to the problems leaders faced in trying to operate this complex governmental machinery effectively.

3. Social structures and basic perspectives in the American experience provided a strong impetus for popular involvement in politics, demands for representation and mechanisms of consent, and the emergence of a substantial electorate.

In comparison with European societies of the time American society was remarkably open, atomistic, affluent, and fluid. It was not bound to feudal traditions, graded structures of estates or classes, or old-corporate configurations. Most men owned a piece of farm land or other property as a foundation for individual independence; a vast continent and its wealth of resources offered unprecedented opportunities; distances between rich and poor were not so great as they were in Old World societies; social distinctions and deference patterns were not so sharp or rigid and there was no genuine aristocracy or hierarchy of fixed orders; and social mobility was a frequent fact as well as a hope. Distinctions there were, particularly between great planters and lesser farmers and Negro slaves in the South; and where social gradations were particularly sharp and persistent patterns of deference held on longer than they did elsewhere. Yet distinctions were generally on the wane, partly as a result of economic opportunity and partly because of the democratization that had accompanied the national Revolution and swept many states in the 1780s. This development was furthered by the impact of the social outlook, *ethos,* or mood which . . . placed heavy stress on such important if sometimes conflicting values as free individualism, op-

portunity, individual achievement, equalitarianism, and liberal democracy. It is not surprising that movement toward democratic
participation, representation, and consent was rapid, and it is also
not surprising that these forces brought the emergence of an extensive electorate in state after state. In terms of inter-state
comparisons, all of these forces and particularly the stress on
equalitarianism and a mass base for politics were especially pronounced in Pennsylvania, where party action developed most rapidly. On the other hand equalitarianism and the extension of
suffrage took hold more slowly in the Southern states, where full-
scale party structures and action came comparatively late, although
even there the impact of remaining tax or property qualifications
on suffrage has been exaggerated by older historians. It may be suggested as a further general hypothesis that the greater the degree
to which equalitarian political ideologies and extended suffrage
obtain, the greater the probability is that political parties will develop, in the absence of other impeding factors. The balance of
recent research findings for the American case is that after the
Revolution the great majority of white adult males in an era of
widely held agricultural property could vote. Not all of them did
but the democratic impulse and keen party competition brought
voting participation in the period 1799–1802 and after to the substantial proportion of 39 percent or more of white adult males in
important elections, a level that was not to be exceeded until new
party rivalry appeared in the Jacksonian era. Moreover, access to
other avenues to the political arena was comparatively open. Freedom of political belief, expression, and action was also generally
accepted, despite important uncertainties and exceptions in the
early years.

    4. Given the three preceding conditions, a sense of felt need
    gradually arose for efficient means to represent and combine in-
    terests, amass power, conduct elections, and manage government.

Innumerable obstacles stood in the way of party development
and no one set out to construct parties with a blueprint in mind.
Men thought in terms of devices to meet immediate needs, or bick-
ered about immediate interests; many important political figures
including George Washington spoke out against the idea of parties;
the process of party-building was one of groping expediencies as

well as brilliant innovations; and it was some time before leaders came to think consciously in party-building terms. Yet in the space of a few years after the ratification of the Constitution in 1789 stable structures were evolved, and the Federalist and Republican formations emerged as parties. . . .

In the American case the emergence of parties marked a significant elaboration of structures and a movement toward relative political efficiency. Before the advent of parties politics was a pluralistic, kaleidoscopic flux of personal cliques like those that gathered around the great magnate families in New York, caucuses of the sort that came and went in many New England towns, select and often half-invisible juntos in the capitals or courthouse villages in the Southern states, or other more or less popular but usually evanescent factions. All of these political formations in their pluralistic variety may be brought under the general heading of faction politics. With few exceptions such old-style "connexions" or multiple factions were characterized by lack of continuity from election to election, by tenuous or shifting relationships between leaders in government on the one hand and the electorate on the other, by comparatively narrow ranges of support from interest groupings, and thus by a confusing degree of raw, un-aggregated pluralism in politics. One result was that it was difficult for the voters to hold any one group of men responsible for the direction of public policy. Another was that policy-making was generally erratic or incoherent, except where it was under the control of a dominant "connexion," clique, or junto.

The advent of the Federalists and Republicans as comprehensive parties, on the other hand, brought a new dualistic ardor into politics. The parties emerged as durable, differentiated, visible, rationalized formations which developed stable operating structures. Continuing relationships were evolved between leaders and cadre at the center of government, and lesser leaders and cadre in the states, counties, and towns; and in turn between this structure and broad popular followings in the electorate. It is appropriate in the American instance to consider the structure of leaders and cadre as "the party," or party proper, and its supporters or adherents in the public as its following. At the beginning American parties accomplished little toward organization strictly construed. . . . Yet both party structures in the 1790s did reach out to amass stable popular followings of considerable range and density which carried them well beyond the fluid and limited support pre-party factions had enjoyed. Finally both parties developed distinctive sets of in-group perspectives with emotional overtones, or ideologies, which helped to bind party structures together and popular followings to the parties. In short the first American parties can be described as developing historical patterns of stable structures linked to broad popular followings, with distinguishing ideologies, and as structures that were able and ready to perform crucial political functions. It is in terms of this general idea of what a party is that the Federalists and Republicans may be thought of as the first modern parties.

II. Party Functions [2]

Unquestionably the most common function among the parties of the world's democracies—and the one that separates them most efficiently from other political organizations—is the mobilization of voters behind candidates for election. The major American parties, far more than most other parties, are dominated by the electing function. They are, indeed, great and overt conspiracies for the capture of public office. Yet within the entire American party system parties differ in the vigor and seriousness with which they pursue the electing function. For the major parties it is virtually the alpha and the omega. The cycle and seasons of their activity depend almost completely on the calendar of elections. . . .

Second only to the electing function is the party's role as a teacher—its function as a propagandist for political attitudes, ideas, and programs. Generally, the American parties have avoided the burden of promoting the vast world view that ideological parties such as the European Socialists assume. Their ambitions are more modest: a diffuse identification with the interests of labor or business or agriculture, for instance, or a platform with indistinct and often ambiguous policy stands. At a given time the American party may even adopt no more than a broad posture as the party of peace or prosperity.

The American parties—as all others—also perform the even more general educational role of political socialization. For its loyalists

[2] Frank J. Sorauf, *Political Parties in the American System* (Boston: Little, Brown and Co., 1964), 2–6, 8–10.

the party arranges the confusion of the political world. It teaches them how to view the political universe and its options. Its symbols offer them a point of reference in judging officeholders or in finding the "right" side in an issue or controversy. At the simplest level the parties help their clienteles to divide the political world into the statesmen and the scoundrels. For the more sophisticated follower the party relates a value or set of values—conservatism, racial equality, or national pride—to the policy or candidate alternatives he faces. Even though the American political parties share this function of organizing and directing political perceptions with the mass media and interest groups, they remain nonetheless a potent focus for organizing knowledge about American politics.

The parties of the democracies, third, assume in varying degrees the function of organizing the policy-making machinery of government. In the United States Congress and in state legislatures the basic unit of organization is the party caucus; from it flows the appointment of powerful presiding officers, committee chairmen, floor leaders, and steering committees. Performance of this function, of course, depends on the party's success as an electoral organization. The American party unable to win more than a handful of legislative seats and only an occasional executive post plays little or no part in organizing legislative and executive branches. Even though small bodies of voters may enable parties in multi-party systems to garner a share of parliamentary and cabinet power, policy-making power within the American political system depends on majorities.

The failure of the American parties to seize and use the policy-making power they so frantically pursue in their electing function has occasioned a fifteen-year debate within American political science. The academic advocates of "party responsibility" castigate the parties for failing to elect men who are loyal to an articulated program and who will enact the program into public policy once elected. . . . Indeed, the major share of the history of the major American parties has been marked by an inversion of the usual party policy-making roles within government. Within the parliamentary systems of the Western democracies the parties have organized legislative majorities and blocs, at the same time as inviolable traditions of professional administrative services have kept them isolated from much of executive and administrative control. In the United States, though, the major parties have traditionally organized legislative chambers without using the party power for party-originated and party-identified policies. But they have, thanks to a long and largely honorable tradition of patronage, often been able to control the selection and operation of administrative services. Even as they yield the bulk of the patronage to merit-system appointees, they continue to control more top-level administrative appointments than do, say, the British political parties.

Finally, the political parties seem to be involved in a series of "non-political" functions. European parties, more frequently than the American, sponsor boy scout troops, social clubs for senior citizens, adult-education classes, and benevolent societies that offer group health and life insurance programs. In its fabled heyday the urban machine in America offered the new arrivals to the cities a range of services that made it, in contemporary terms, a combination of employment agency, legal aid society, social worker, domestic relations counselor, and community social center. And in the new style, urban "club" parties in the American cities and suburbs, the parties cater to the social and intellectual needs of a mobile, educated, ideological, often isolated upper middle class. The style may have changed from "beer all around" at the local tavern to martinis at the cocktail hour, but the parties continue to concern themselves with more than just campaigns and elections.

To refer to these functions as "non-political" is, of course, somewhat misleading. Although they may not seem to promise an immediate political payoff, the party hopes that in the long run they will create loyalties, obligations, and ties that will facilitate the successful performance of the other, more directly political tasks. The political party, in fact, exists solely for political purposes and performs only political functions. The other forms of political organization— the Church, the ethnic group, the informal community elite, the voluntary interest group such as a trade union or medical association —move freely from the non-political to the political function and quickly back again. Not so the political party. Its exclusively political character sets it apart from the other political organizations. . . .

The fact that political parties are exclusively political in function is no assurance that they monopolize the functions of contesting elections, proclaiming political programs and values, and organizing the machinery of government. The American parties, in fact, share the function of selecting and electing candidates with informal community elites in many localities. They also share with interest groups the maintenance of a system of responsibility in the American legislature. And in the function of spelling out political programs and alternatives they operate in uneasy competition with the mass media, educational institutions, and voluntary associations. The class urban machine in the United States came close to monopolizing these functions, but its palmier days are past. That the parties can no longer monopolize them suggests a changing role for them within the American political system. . . .

When we talked earlier of the functions the parties perform, we referred only to their immediate ones: the manifest functions. These are the tasks party leadership sets out consciously to perform and on the performance of which the party's immediate success or failure depends. In performing them the parties also perform remoter, indirect, "latent" functions. It is as if, by performing immediate functions A, B, and C, the party fortuitously performs also the useful functions X, Y, and Z. For example, as the party goes about the immediate tasks of nominating and electing candidates for office, it is at the same time recruiting political leadership. Indeed, as it selects candidates from its own cadre of active workers, it may also be functioning as a training school for political leaders. To put the matter in another way, the party performs certain tasks (the manifest ones) that ensure its own successful functioning, at the same time performing others (the latent ones) that contribute to the functioning of the entire political system.

Only in the party's latent functions is the relationship between it and the political system clear. The chief manifest functions the parties perform—the nomination and election of candidates, the support of issues and ideology, and the organization of government power—can be and are performed by the parties of totalitarian political systems as well as by the democratic parties. But the ways in which the parties choose, and are permitted, to perform them determine the sharply different latent consequences. When one begins to list the latent functions of the American and British parties it soon becomes clear that he is talking of parties operating in and forming an integral part of democratic political systems. And a comparison of those of the British and American parties with those of the parties of the new nations of Asia and Africa soon indicates the different party contributions to differing varieties of democracy. The dominant, single parties of some of the new nations clearly function within a Rousseauist democracy of solidarity and national purpose rather than in the pluralist, competitive democracy of the United States.

The parties of the democracies, both by supporting candidates for office and by representing interests and issues, simplify the choices confronting the voters. By reducing the contestants for public office and the options of public policy to two, three, or even a handful, the party simplifies—doubtless oversimplifies—the political choices into terms the average citizen can grasp. The stability and continuity of the party symbols, heroes, and slogans gives him fixed points of political reference, thus maintaining the simplicity of choices over the years. In the various ways in which the parties nominate and elect they play a crucial role in the recruitment of political leadership. Especially in those vigorous American party organizations in which the office-seeker must work his way tortuously up the party hierarchy, the party is the gateway through which the ambitious must pass and be passed. Finally, by organizing individuals, interests, and groups into broader political aggregates, the parties mediate and compromise the clash of political interests and ideologies.

In all of these ways the tie between the political party and the democratic regime is clear. The parties facilitate the popular participation, the representation of interests, and the presentation of alternatives on which the processes of democracy depend. They augment the representational processes of the democratic system by providing an organizational link between political man and the institutions of government beyond the one provided by the formal election machinery. They organize the loyal opposition and the democratic dialogue of the "ins" and "outs." So closely are our concepts of party tied, not only to democracy, but also to Western democracy, that they have limited relevance to the parties of national independence and development in the newer nations. Most Americans find it difficult to think of the single, dominant parties of these nations as "genuine" political parties. Much less than the parties of the older democracies do they propose alternative candidates and programs, but to a far greater extent, they do carry out the more general functions of political education, socialization, and communication.

In both of these reading selections the idea is implicit that any political system must get essential functions performed if it is to operate efficiently. Just what these functions will be and the structures that may develop to perform them, however, depends on the nature and conditions of the society and the character of the political system that evolves out of it. Thus a feudal, hierarchical society of manorial lords, knights, yeomen, and serfs, for example, will not generate the same kind of political system or find it necessary to perform quite the same functions as a modern, democratic, mass society. The American political system developed in a direction that emphasized its democratic characteristics and produced political parties that came to perform a broad range of political functions in a two-party system. The direction of American political development also gave rise to the conditions which apparently brought about the emergence of political parties in the first place. These conditions—specifically, a national political arena, complex conflicts of interest and opinion and complex governmental machinery, social structures and attitudes which encouraged democratic participation and a large number of voters, and the need to establish stable relationships between leaders and followers— can also be related to the functions American parties have come to undertake. Even so the American political system might conceivably have found other means or structures to get essential political functions performed. It might have depended on faction politics as it has operated in certain one-party American states even in the twentieth century, for example, or on systems of expert bureaucratic administration in government which might be more or less responsive to interest demands or public opinion. Yet the question remains whether these or other devices could perform essential political functions as *efficiently* or as *democratically* as political parties have done. It might also be asked if such devices could get the essential functions performed at all.

Review in your text and your class notes materials concerning contemporary American social structure and ideology and the

contemporary operation and role of American political parties.
Then prepare careful, thoughtful, analytical answers to the
following questions as they relate to the problem of key demo-
cratic political functions and the present role of political parties.

1. Do the four general conditions listed in Statement I as contributing to the rise of political parties still exist in the United States today? In what ways that may be important for the activity of political parties has the specific nature or content of each of these four conditions changed?

2. In your own words, summarize briefly but carefully the major functions performed by political parties in American democracy today, as set forth in Statement II, and in other summaries with which you are familiar. What relationships can you trace between the conditions which apparently gave rise to American political parties on the one hand, and each of the particular functions they have come to perform on the other? To what extent can the four general conditions which brought about the emergence of political parties explain the functions of parties, as these four conditions may continue to exist in modified form today? Do these conditions explain all of the functions parties undertake today? What other institutions can you identify that perform some of the functions parties also undertake? What functions do these institutions perform?

3. Many of the founding fathers were opposed to political parties and there has been much criticism of political parties in our own time.

Given the democratic character of the American political system, however, it has been said that if parties did not exist it would be necessary to invent them in order to keep our democratic system going and get essential functions performed.

How would you evaluate this statement, and on what grounds?

In terms of the performance of essential functions in the American political system, retaining its basic democratic form, what alternatives to parties can you suggest?

PART II

Rules and the Political Culture

PROBLEM 4

American Ideology and the Constitutional Order

STABLE political systems appear to require at least some degree of acceptance of certain political values, structures, and procedures among the people in the society involved. This acceptance may range from bare acquiescence in key political institutions among a comparatively small number of people to broad agreement on the basic purposes of government and on the way in which the political game is to be played. Agreements of the latter sort become emotionally tinged ideologies and assumptions about the proper conduct of political life, which individuals absorb and internalize as they grow up in a particular culture, even though they are not fully aware of it. Acceptance is often more a matter of passive accommodation than of active belief, though it may include the latter as well.

In broad outline the underlying principles of a stable political system may be thought of as encompassing:

1. *Basic values, traditions, ideology.* Some examples in American political development are personal liberty, consent of the

governed, political democracy including majority rule and minority rights, limited government, and equality.

2. *Major formal rules for government and politics.* Some examples in the American political system are periodic election of major officials, procedures of majority rule modified by separation of powers and checks and balances, a regularized system of law, the federal system, and judicial review of national and state government action.

3. *Informal norms concerning politics.* Some examples in American political culture are freedom or tolerance for differences in political opinions, readiness to stop short of pursuing political disagreements to the point where they endanger the system, fair play in politics.

The extent to which all Americans have subscribed to these values, rules, and norms is questionable. Indeed the evidence indicates that their currency among the articulate, influential, civic strata of American society is much greater than it is among the mass of the population, where far less in the way of understanding and support for such fundamental principles is to be found, particularly when the question becomes one of specific applications rather than general statements of belief. Such underlying principles remain those on which the American political system rests, however, whether endorsement of them is unanimous or not.

Many of the basic assumptions of the American political system have their origins in the founding of the nation itself. Usually the Declaration of Independence of 1776 and the Constitution of 1789 together with its later amendments are cited as the documents which provide the foundations for the ideology, basic rules, and informal norms of our political culture. Yet at the outset any new nation must find its way to acceptance of such fundamentals; and initial acceptance may grow out of disagreement and conflict as well as out of whatever traditions or shared understandings a people may have at hand. In the nation-building decades of the late eighteenth century the American experience was no exception to this pattern of development. The Revolution, protracted arguments over the state constitutions and the Articles of Confederation of 1781–1789, and the controversy over the Constitution itself testify to this fact. Nonetheless we still conduct our government and politics within the general tradition and framework our founders bequeathed to us almost two centuries ago. With the partial exception of Great Britain, the United States is the only major nation today which can trace such an ancient lineage for its way of political life.

Read and analyze carefully the following statements, paying particular attention to the differences as well as similarities between them.

I. The Revolutionary Impulse [1]

The American Revolution was . . . primarily a struggle between the Colonies and Great Britain over the question of self-government. . . . But there was also another phase of the Revolution, and that was the struggle within the Colonies themselves between the little commercial and landowning aristocracies that had hitherto governed the Colonies and the "people," the unfranchised "humble folk," who now were coming to demand a measure of political equality.

This struggle runs throughout the period of the controversy with Great Britain from 1765 to 1776; and while it was somewhat diminished during the period of the [Revolutionary] war itself, it broke out again with renewed force after the war was over. In fact, the American Revolution was not only a movement for national independence from Great Britain; it was also a movement for the democratization of American society and politics—a movement which has continued from that day to this and which is the central theme of our history. [In most American colonies conditions] were such as to place a determining influence in the hands of a small coterie of wealthy families—the so-called "best families" of the province. . . . Sharply distinguished from these "gentlefolk," in dress and manners as well as in social and political influence, was

[1] Carl Becker, *Our Great Experiment in Democracy* (New York: Harper and Brothers, 1927), 34–40, 47–48, 50–51, 108–114.

the great mass of the population—artisans and laborers, tenant and small freehold farmers. . . .

The conflict between the interests and ideals of these two classes . . . was already beginning when the controversy between the British government and the Colonies began; and from the first the two issues became more or less identified. . . . The radicals wanted to democratize . . . social and political institutions . . . while the old leaders wanted to maintain their supremacy. . . .

As the Revolution ceased to be a mere contest [for independence] and took on the character of a contest for the rights of man . . . . American patriots came to think of themselves as hazarding their lives and their fortunes for the sake of a new social order, the ideal society founded upon the enduring principles of liberty, equality, and fraternity. There is a striking similarity between the ideals and the language of the American patriots and the radical leaders of the French Revolution. . . .

It is thus clear that the American Revolution was a twofold movement: it was a movement for the separation from Great Britain; it was also a movement for the abolition of class privilege, for the democratization of American politics and society, in some measure for the inauguration of an ideal state. The Declaration of Independence reflects and expresses this twofold character of the Revolution. On the one hand it is a declaration of the reasons which justified the separation from Great Britain; on the other hand it is a charter of democracy. . . .

The first years of independence were taken up with attempts to solve the many problems of peaceful reconstruction under a federal government which was one of the weakest ever devised by the hand of man . . . the movement for strengthening the Articles of Confederation resulted in the Constitutional Convention of 1787 which formulated the present Constitution. . . . It was essentially over the questions giving rise to the formation of a new Constitution, and over the question of the new Constitution itself and of its approval or rejection, that the people gradually divided into two chief political parties. . . . They differed in their respective attitudes toward popular government, its sources of strength and of weakness, and the limitations which should be placed upon it. The [opponents of the new Constitution] were what would today be called a radical party, the Federalists [proponents of the Constitution] a conservative party. Hamilton had little faith in the virtue or the wisdom of "the people," and none at all in their capacity for efficient government. According to him only the people with property had a sufficient interest in good government to be intrusted with political power. . . .

Many Federalists were not so frank as Hamilton in expressing their views, but they all shared his anti-democratic philosophy. The experience of the Revolutionary War and the years immediately following had made many men more conservative than they had once been. . . .

The Federalists therefore voted for the Federal Constitution and were in favor of enlarging the functions of the federal government, not only because a strong federal government would serve the economic interests of the industrial and moneyed classes, but also because it would be less amenable to popular control than state governments had been, and would serve as a needed check upon such radical political tendencies as might find expression in certain parts of the country. . . .

[Meanwhile] Jefferson, the author of the Declaration of Independence, still held to the doctrine that "all men are created equal," and never lost his faith in those ideals of popular government and republican virtue . . . which furnished the driving force of the American and French revolutions. . . .

II. *The Meaning of the Declaration of Independence* [2]

The American Revolution was a successful rebellion against the constituted authority. It was not a crusade undertaken in behalf of a creed formulated in advance, but a summary effect of interests and of mental dispositions, compounded among themselves and facilitated by the circumstances of time and place. Nevertheless, since the revolution assumed the form of a deliberate enterprise, calling for unanimity, prolonged effort, and sacrifice, it was necessary to invoke "reasons." There was need of an approving conscience, an assenting judgment, and a confirmation by the disinterested opinion of mankind. There was need for these because they are elements of strength and bonds of effective union. . . .

On July 2, 1776, the Continental Congress, on the motion of Richard Henry Lee, adopted the following resolution: "That these

[2] Ralph Barton Perry, *Puritanism and Democracy* (New York: Vanguard Press, 1944), 123, 124–25, 130–32, 133.

United Colonies are, and of right ought to be, free and independent States, that they are absolved from all allegiance to the British Crown, and that all political connection between them and the State of Great Britain is, and ought to be, totally dissolved." The resolve and the act were unmistakably and uncompromisingly illegal. The Declaration of Independence, which was adopted two days later, was a philosophical creed designed to justify the action of men who had taken the law into their own hands. It was at one and the same time a justification of rebellion and a statement of those common principles on which was to be founded a new state. It is as though men should say: "This is what government and law are for. Judged by this standard, the existing authority has forfeited its claim to obedience. This is at the same time the ground on which to erect a new authority which shall in the future be obeyed as commending itself to our reason and conscience." History affords few parallel instances of a state thus abruptly created, and consciously dedicated to a body of ideas whose acceptance constitutes its underlying bond of agreement.

This American democratic creed, designed to justify the past and chart the future, began as follows:

When in the Course of human events, it becomes necessary for one people to dissolve the political bands which have connected them with another, and to assume among the powers of the earth the separate and equal station to which the Laws of Nature and of Nature's God entitle them, a decent respect to the opinions of mankind requires that they should declare the causes which impel them to the separation.—We hold these truths to be self-evident, that all men are created equal, that they are endowed by their Creator with certain unalienable Rights, that among these are Life, Liberty and the pursuit of Happiness. That to secure these rights, Governments are instituted among Men, deriving their just powers from the consent of the governed.—That whenever any Form of Government becomes destructive of these ends, it is the Right of the People to alter or to abolish it, and to institute new Government, laying its foundation on such principles and organizing its powers in such form, as to them shall seem most likely to effect their Safety and Happiness.

. . . The Declaration of Independence contains the essential ideas of American democracy, and has remained its creed and standard throughout the years of its subsequent development . . . These principles have been challenged by individual thinkers, and even, as in the epoch of the Civil War, by sections or classes; but they have invariably been invoked in times of crisis or of patriotic fervor as constituting the moral bond of American nationality. The later history of the ideas of the Declaration concerns us only so far as may be necessary to establish their permanence and pervasiveness. They were promptly embodied, if they had not been anticipated, in the constitutions of the several states. . . .

When the Federal Constitution was under discussion in the year 1787–1788 the problem of the colonists had shifted from revolution to reconstruction. It was a time of recoil and suspended activity. Even the conquest of the continent had lost much of its momentum. Men felt the pains and costs of change rather than its impetus. . . . The "political bands which [had] connected them with another" had been dissolved, and it was now imperative for Americans "to form a more perfect union" among themselves.

The sentiment and emphasis which are effective for purposes of revolution are the precise opposites of those required "to institute new Government." Revolution is associated with the defiance of authority and the resort to violence; it is the task of political reconstruction to persuade men once again to obey. Revolution begets the feeling that a man can have what he wants; reconstruction compels him again to submit his particular interest to law and to the general good. The problem of reconstruction is to escape from that state of nature to which, in the act of revolution, society has reverted. In 1783 factionalism and personal jealousies were rife. The defects of human nature and the evils of anarchy were everywhere apparent. It was natural that in such a mood, and in response to the exigencies of such a crisis, there should be a swing toward political conservatism.

The Federal Constitution, then, expressed a fear of the excesses of revolutionary democracy, and of the mind of the masses. These fears inspired John Adams, Alexander Hamilton, and other leaders of the Federalist party; they represented the mood of reconstruction, as had Samuel Adams that of revolution. The motive of these leaders was to set such limits to popular government as should save it from self-destruction. . . . To this end they retarded the popular will and multiplied its intermediaries. They sought to accomplish their purpose not by strengthening the executive, but by a division of powers, and by the six-year term of senators. *The Federalist* defended this last provision as follows:

To a people as little blinded by prejudice or corrupted by flattery as those whom I address, I shall not scruple to add that such an institution may be sometimes necessary as a defence to the people against their own temporary errors and delusions. As the cool and deliberate sense of the community ought, in all governments, and actually will, in all free governments, ultimately prevail over the views of its rulers; so there are particular moments in public affairs when the people, stimulated by some irregular passion, or some illicit advantage, or misled by the artful misrepresentations of interested men, may call for measures which they themselves will afterwards be most ready to lament and condemn. In these critical moments, how salutary will be the interference of some temperate and respectable body of citizens in order to check the misguided career, and to suspend the blow meditated by the people against themselves, until reason, justice, and truth can regain their authority over the public mind.

. . . During its later history American democracy has had, under various names, its constitutional and its revolutionary parties. The constitutional party has emphasized the system of government in its integrity and has insisted on legality of procedure. It has attracted those whose advantage lay in economic stability, and in the status quo. The revolutionary party, on the other hand, has emphasized the popular will as directly expressed in the vote of the majority, and has attracted those whose advantage lay in change. The second of these parties represents the forward impulses of American democracy; the first, its sober thought. The second has been retarded by the first, but never stopped or reversed. The history of American democracy is a gradual realization, too slow for some and too rapid for others, of the implications of the Declaration of Independence.

III. The American Liberal Tradition [3]

Once the American Revolution was thought of as a purely political revolution, involving independence from Great Britain. It

[3] Adapted with permission of the author from Louis Hartz, *The Liberal Tradition in America: An Interpretation of American Political Thought Since the Revolution* (New York: Harcourt, Brace and Co., 1955), *passim;* Chapter III.

could thus be distinguished from the Puritan Revolution in England in the Seventeenth century or the French Revolution of the Eighteenth century where the whole structure of the old social order was attacked.

More recently, however, historians have sought to classify the American Revolution as a "social" or "democratic" revolution also. They have pointed to the attack on the principle of monarchy, to the abolition of such "feudal" practices as quitrents, primogeniture, and entail in the South, and to the disestablishment of the Anglican church and the separation of church and state. Thus the American Revolution is equated, at least in part, with the great European democratic revolutions as an attack on outmoded feudal and aristocratic institutions to clear the way for a new democracy, and the American Revolution and the Declaration of Independence are seen as great "liberal," even "radical" milestones. By contrast the adoption of the Federal Constitution in 1787 is painted as a "conservative reaction," quite out of keeping with the revolutionary democratic ferment of the previous decade.

This social revolution theory, however, and any attempt to equate the American Revolution with the great European revolutions distorts the whole picture. Social changes there were in the America of the 1770s. But they were not on a par with the revolutions which took place in Europe. These really did involve attempts to destroy an old feudal order and to establish a new bourgeois order; and these efforts were followed in turn by genuinely conservative or aristocratic reactions, the return of the Stuart monarchs or the restoration of the Bourbon kings and the old order or *ancien regime* which they symbolized. In America, however, matters were different. Feudalism never found real foothold on this side of the Atlantic; property ownership, particularly in small, freehold farms, was widespread; and there never was a true American aristocracy (at least of any size or importance) in the old European, feudal sense. To use the European term "aristocracy" for American planters or bourgeois merchants who happened to be well-to-do, and paint them as locked in basic conflict with a submerged "people," is grossly misleading. By contrast with Europe, with a centuries-old feudal tradition, American society was always in fact, and even more in belief or ideology, free or liberal, broadly equalitarian, and middle class in outlook. In short it was unusually hospitable to the central ideas of classical liberal thought as it was propounded by such prophets as

John Locke in Europe and taken up by Jefferson in 1776 and expressed in the Declaration of Independence, the first great statement of the liberal tradition in America. The peculiar fact of American life, as the French observer Tocqueville put it in 1835, was that Americans "arrived at a state of democracy without having to endure a democratic revolution; and that they [were] born equal, instead of becoming so." Practices such as primogeniture were abolished with surprising ease and little conflict, simply because they were relics or shadows, rather than integral parts of a going feudalism. Even the Virginia "aristocrats" of 1785 succumbed with scarcely a blow, evoking as Jefferson said more "pity than anger" from the people. Similarly the American "radicalism" of the Revolutionary period and the 1780s was tame as compared to European radicalism, because it had no entrenched feudal aristocracy to fight. Even at the outmost limits of American "radicalism" Daniel Shays and Shays's Rebellion were unable to generate anything like the leveling or socialist vision of the radicals of the Puritan and French revolutions, of a Wynstanley or a Babeuf; and Shays like other American "radicals" represented a fundamentally middle class, property-holding or bourgeois outlook. Where there is no significant feudal order or *ancien regime* to fight back, where property ownership is widespread, and where "radicals" like "conservatives" are fundamentally middle class in their ideas, it simply confuses matters to speak of a social revolution or a revolutionary democratic movement.

It follows that where there is no going old order or aristocracy there can be no full-blooded conservative reaction on the model of the Stuart or Bourbon restorations. It is thus misleading again to paint in bold, black-and-white strokes the framing of the Constitution of 1787 as a thoroughgoing "conservative reaction," though this is just what many of our recent historians have done. If it was a reaction at all, it was a reaction of moderate liberalism, quite middle class in outlook, rather than an "aristocratic reaction" or a basically "conservative reaction."

It was something more fundamental to American society than Washington's modesty or self-abnegation that preserved us from monarchy or dictatorship, something more concrete in the American social order than lucky Providence that rescued us from aristocratic rule at the hands of the Constitution-framers and the Federalist party. It was, as James Madison pointed out, the fact that the country would not stand for autocratic rule that saved us from monarchy or dictatorship. It was, as John Dickinson explained, the fact that there was no genuine American aristocracy and that an aristocracy cannot be manufactured overnight that saved us from aristocrat rule.

It can perhaps be argued that the Declaration of Independence speaks more in the spirit of democracy and equalitarianism as well as liberty than the original Constitution does, and that the Constitution places a more nearly exclusive emphasis on individual liberty. It is true that Eighteenth century Enlightenment conceptions of liberty, as men like Montesquieu or Madison saw it, were not identical with ideas of democracy or equality as they have developed in the American experience over the years. Yet in the post-Revolutionary decade such questions were matters of degree rather than of the clash of different social systems or basically contradictory ideologies; and the Constitution as it was ratified in 1789 established what was then the most democratic government in the world. In short, both the Declaration and the Constitution were in the mainstream of the liberal tradition as it stemmed from Locke and was made manifest on American soil.

Read the Declaration of Independence in its entirety and analyze it carefully to pick out the main ideas concerning the foundations, basic purposes, and basic structure of government. Observe that the same basic ideas may be touched on in different ways at different points in the document as a whole.

Read the Constitution of the United States as it was originally written and ratified in 1787–1789, without the later amendments, and analyze it carefully to pick out the main ideas concerning the foundations, basic purposes, and basic structure of government it contains or which are implied in the rules it establishes.

Note that the Declaration, as a political manifesto, not surprisingly emphasizes values or ideology rather than structure or rules. The Constitution on the other hand, intended to serve as an operating frame of government, consists largely of the statement of structure or rules. Yet a careful analysis of the full text of the Declaration will bring to light a number of judgments concerning the proper rules or norms for the conduct of government (some of them by negative implication in the charges against the King or government of Great Britain); and the provisions of the Constitution will also be found to be related to certain ideological assumptions or values. Thus, though they were written with different functions in mind, the two documents are nonetheless subject to comparative analysis.

Review in your text and in your lecture notes materials relating to the proclamation of the Declaration of Independence and to the formulation and ratification of the Constitution.

Assume that you are an impartial, well-informed observer of American politics in 1789. A European friend who sympathized with the ideas of the "radicals" in the American Revolution and with the ideas expressed in the Declaration writes you that he has heard that the new Constitution does not fully embody these ideas, and indeed represents a "conservative reaction" against what he thinks of as the "democratic" or "radical" aspects of the American Revolution, which he sees as underlying the Declaration of Independence. He asks you if this is the case, and if so, to what extent the Constitution itself is "reactionary," fails to embody the ideas of the Declaration of Independence, and instead gives effect to other ideas, and specifically in what ways. He also asks for an explanation of how this situation came about, as you understand it. You review all you know about the political forces that were involved in and led up to the Revolution and the Declaration on the one hand and the framing of the new Constitution on the other, and you also review both documents carefully. You then answer the questions your European friend has addressed to you.

Bearing in mind the somewhat different interpretations given in the statements above, work out carefully the answer you would give to your European friend with particular attention to:

1. The main ideas concerning the fundamentals of a political system which are to be found in the Declaration of Independence,

as they relate to basic values, major formal rules for government and politics, and informal norms concerning politics.

2. The extent and ways in which the Constitution
    (a) reflects or applies each of these ideas, or fails to reflect or apply them; and
    (b) contains other or contrary ideas.

3. Possible explanations for these similarities and differences between the Declaration and the Constitution, in terms of the different contexts of the nation-building process and political conflict in which they were written as well as the different functions the two documents were intended to serve.

Be as precise and specific as you can throughout.

PROBLEM 5

Politics and the Framing
of the Constitution

FROM the vantage point of more than a century and three-quarters it is easy to envision the shapers of the Constitution of the United States at Philadelphia in 1787 as a collection of political Moseses handing down the tablets of the law. The basic framework of the document is taken so much for granted, it has such long standing as "the supreme Law of the Land" (Article VI), that it is hard to think of it as the handiwork of mortal men who were moved by ordinary human purposes. Conflicts over the *meaning* of the Constitution have appeared in plenty, but these have almost always erupted in the form of arguments over *interpretations* or *applications* of various clauses of the document to specific situations. The question has been the meaning of these clauses as they have been read by Congress, the President, or the Supreme Court. More often than not the provisions of the document itself—in their presumably "true" meaning—have been held up as sacrosanct.

In fact the Constitution as a statement of the basic rules for the conduct of politics was itself a product of politics. As every nation or political system has a history and is shaped by the course and happenstance of its political development, so is every constitution the product of political development and active politics. The great English political leader William E. Gladstone once commented: "As the British Constitution is the most subtle organism which has proceeded from progressive history, so the American Constitution is the most wonderful work ever struck off at a given time by the brain and purpose of man." Busy as he was trying to move England into the mainstream of classical nineteenth-century liberal ways, Gladstone could readily perceive that the largely unwritten British constitution was a series of precedents and accretions extending across eight centuries. What he did not seem to see was that the American Constitution, even though it was written in one long, hot summer, also came out of the course of political American development and was shaped by the realities and conflicts of the politics of the day.

One of the issues in controversy was how democratic the new American republic was to be at its moment of launching. To many men of the time (as well as to others since) democracy implied majority rule, construed as meaning in its strictest sense that political decisions are to be made by *fifty percent plus one* of those who vote, whether as voters in a general election or representatives in a legislative assembly. This view does not deny the importance of minority liberties or rights, particularly the freedom of what may be today's minority to engage in political persuasion in the hope of winning enough converts to become tomorrow's majority. Yet, according to this notion of democracy, "government by the people" is a meaningless phrase if in fact a majority of the people are prevented from having their way in important political decisions; and conversely a system in which a minority can regularly or frequently block action desired by most of the people is not truly democratic. An argument can be made against this position, of course, and in any case most of the framers of the Constitution in 1787 opposed straight majority rule and especially feared the action of "self-interested," "temporary," or "fleeting" majorities. Thus should the poor farmers, the "debtor class," gain majorities in all the organs of government they might promptly enact laws wiping out all debts and ruin the creditors, the minority. Other men of the time thought differently, however, and more in terms of the democratic norms that have been absorbed into the American political system.

During the great debate that followed the drafting of the Constitution and preceded its ratification by state conventions, an article published in the New York *Packet* of December 14, 1787, included the following paragraphs concerning majority rule:

> The fundamental maxim of republican government . . . requires that the sense of the majority [of the people] should prevail. . . .
>
> *To give a minority a negative* upon the majority (which is always the case where more than a majority is requisite to a decision), is, in its tendency, to subject the sense of the greater number to that of the lesser. . . . The necessity of unanimity in public bodies, or of something approaching towards it, has been founded upon a supposition that it would contribute to security. But its real operation *is to embarrass the administration, to destroy the energy of the government, and to substitute the pleasure, caprice, or artifices of an insignificant, turbulent, or corrupt junto, to the regular deliberations and decisions of a . . . majority.* In those emergencies of a nation, in which the goodness or badness, the weakness or strength of its government, is of the greatest importance, there is commonly a necessity for action. The public business must, in some way or other, go forward. If a pertinacious minority can control the opinion of [prevent decisions by] a majority, respecting the best mode of conducting it, the majority, in order that something may be done, must conform to the views of the minority; and thus the sense of the smaller number will overrule that of the greater, and give a tone to the national proceedings. Hence, tedious delays; continual negotiation and intrigue; contemptible compromises of the public good. And yet, in such a system . . . upon some occasions things will not admit of accommodation [compromise]; and then the measures of government must be injuriously suspended, or fatally defeated. It is often, by the impracticability of obtaining the concurrence of the necessary number of votes, kept in a state of inaction. Its situation must always savor of weakness, sometimes border upon anarchy.
>
> It is not difficult to discover, that a principle of this kind [allowing a minority to prevent action] gives greater scope to . . . domestic faction [the action of self-seeking interest groups] than that which permits the sense of the majority to decide; though the contrary of this has been presumed. The mistake has proceeded from not attending with due care to the mischiefs that may be occasioned by obstructing the progress of government at certain critical seasons. When the concurrence of a large number is required by the Con-

stitution to the doing of any national act, we are apt to rest satisfied that all is safe, because nothing improper will be likely *to be done;* but we forget how much good may be prevented, and how much ill may be produced, by the power of hindering the doing what may be necessary, and of keeping affairs in the same unfavorable posture in which they may happen to stand at particular periods . . .

At the time this article appeared the proposed Constitution had been criticized as an undemocratic document which in numerous respects denied majority rule in an effort to protect the interests of a minority of owners of large amounts of property. Thus, for example, the Constitution called for a vote of two-thirds of both houses of Congress and three-fourths of the states as the readiest available way to amend its provisions, and for a two-thirds vote of the Senate to ratify treaties with foreign powers. There are also other, more important, and subtler checks on majority rule in the national Constitution and the total framework of government it provides. Even so it generally requires only a simple majority or plurality to elect public officials in the American system, and only a simple majority of the House and Senate to pass ordinary legislation. As an aspect of the fundamental sanctions of democratic choice, at least, notions of majority rule have become basic ingredients in the American political system.

Various interpretations or analyses of the Constitution as a product of the politics of the 1780's in the United States have been offered, and these interpretations have not always been consistent with one another.

One of the most striking was set forth in 1913 by Charles A. Beard, in an attempt to demonstrate that the economic interests of particular groups were the key factors in shaping the Constitution as it originally appeared: [1]

> The requirements for an economic interpretation of the formation and adoption of the Constitution may be stated in a hypothetical proposition which, although it cannot be verified absolutely from

[1] From Charles A. Beard, *An Economic Interpretation of the Constitution of the United States* (New York: The Macmillan Co., 1913), 16–17, 63–65, 73, 149–51, 324–25.

ascertainable data, will at once illustrate the problem and furnish a guide to research and generalization. . . .

Suppose it could be shown from the classification of the men who supported and opposed the Constitution that there was no line of property division at all; that is, that men owning substantially the same amounts of the same kinds of property were equally divided on the matter of adoption or rejection—it would then become apparent that the Constitution had no ascertainable relation to economic groups or classes, but was the product of some abstract causes remote from the chief business of life—gaining a livelihood.

Suppose, on the other hand, that substantially all of the merchants, money lenders, security holders, manufacturers, shippers, capitalists, and financiers and their professional associates are to be found on one side in support of the Constitution and that substantially all or the major portion of the opposition came from the non-slaveholding farmers and the debtors—would it not be pretty conclusively demonstrated that our fundamental law was not the product of an abstraction known as "the whole people," but of a group of economic interests which must have expected beneficial results from its adoption? Obviously all the facts here desired cannot be discovered, but the data bear out the latter hypothesis, and thus a reasonable presumption in favor of the theory is created. . . .

Large and important groups of economic interests were adversely affected by the system of government under the Articles of Confederation, namely, those of public securities, shipping and manufacturing, money at interest; in short, capital as opposed to land.

The representatives of these important interests attempted through the regular legal channels to secure amendments to the Articles of Confederation which would safeguard their rights in the future, particularly those of the public creditors.

Having failed to realize their great purposes through the regular means, the leaders in the movement set to work to secure by a circuitous route the assemblying of a Convention to "revise" the Articles of Confederation with the hope of obtaining, outside of the existing legal framework, the adoption of a revolutionary programme.

Ostensibly, however, the formal plan of approval by Congress and the state legislatures was to be preserved.

Under the protection afforded by these outward signs of regularity, the leaders in the movement for the new Constitution set to work in their respective legislatures to secure the choice of delegates prepared to take the heroic measures which the circumstances demanded. The zealous and dynamic element, of course, was favored by the inertness, ignorance, and indifference of the masses, and the confidence of the legislatures in their ability to exercise the ultimate control through the ratifying power. No special popular elections were called to complicate the problem of securing the right kind of a Convention and the leaders were confronted with the comparatively simple task of convincing the legislatures of the advisability of sending delegates. Naturally the most strenuous and interested advocates of change came forward as candidates. . . .

A further safeguard against the injection of too much popular feeling into the choice of delegates to the Convention was afforded by the property qualifications generally placed on voters and members of the legislatures by the state constitutions and laws in force in 1787. . . .

Having shown that four groups of property rights were adversely affected by the government under the Articles of Confederation, and that economic motives were behind the movement for a reconstruction of the system, it is now necessary to inquire whether the members of the Convention which drafted the Constitution represented in their own property affiliations any or all of these groups. In other words, did the men who formulated the fundamental law of the land possess the kinds of property which were immediately and directly increased in value or made more secure by the results of their labors at Philadelphia? Did they have money at interest? Did they own public securities? Did they hold western lands for appreciation? Were they interested in shipping and manufactures?

The purpose of such an inquiry is not, of course, to show that the Constitution was made for the personal benefit of the members of the Convention . . . The only point here considered is: Did they represent distinct groups whose economic interests they understood and felt in concrete, definite form through their own personal experience with identical property rights, or were they working merely under the guidance of abstract principles of political science? . . .

[At this point the analysis continues with biographies of members of the constitutional Convention, designed to show the economic concerns and interests they shared.]

A survey of the economic interests of the members of the Convention presents certain conclusions. . . . Most of the members came from towns, on or near the coast, that is, from the regions in which personalty [money invested at interest, in shipping and manufactures or merchandising, in public securities, or in speculation in western lands] was largely concentrated. Not one member represented in his immediate personal economic interests the small farming or mechanic classes. The overwhelming majority of members, at least five-sixths, were immediately, directly, and personally interested in the outcome of their labors at Philadelphia, and were to a greater or less extent economic beneficiaries from the adoption of the Constitution. 1) Public security interests were extensively represented in the Convention. Of the fifty-five members who attended no less than forty appear on the Records of the Treasury Department for sums varying from a few dollars up to more than one hundred thousand dollars. . . . 2) Personalty invested in lands for speculation was represented by at least fourteen members. . . . 3) Personalty in the form of money loaned at interest was represented by at least twenty-four members . . . 4) Personalty in mercantile, manufacturing, and shipping lines was represented by at least eleven members. . . . 5) Personalty in slaves was represented by at least fifteen members. . . .

It cannot be said, therefore, that the members of the Convention were "disinterested." On the contrary, we are forced to accept the profoundly significant conclusion that they knew through their personal experiences in economic affairs the precise results which the new government that they were setting up was designed to attain. As a group of doctrinaires . . . they would have failed miserably; but as practical men they were able to build the new government upon the only foundations which could be stable; fundamental economic interests. . . .

[Thus], the movement for the Constitution of the United States was originated and carried through principally by four groups of personalty interests which had been adversely affected under the Articles of Confederation: money, public securities, manufactures, and trade and shipping.

The first firm steps toward the formation of the Constitution were taken by a small and active group of men immediately interested through their personal possessions in the outcome of their labors.

No popular vote was taken directly or indirectly on the proposition to call the Convention which drafted the Constitution.

A large propertyless mass was, under the prevailing suffrage qualifications, excluded at the outset from participation (through representatives) in the work of framing the Constitution.

The members of the Philadelphia Convention which drafted the Constitution were, with a few exceptions, immediately, directly, and personally interested in, and derived economic advantages from, the establishment of the new system.

The Constitution was essentially an economic document based upon the concept that the fundamental private rights of property are anterior to government and morally beyond the reach of the popular majorities.

The major portion of the members of the Convention are on record as recognizing the claim of property to a special and defensive position in the Constitution.

In the ratification of the Constitution, about three-fourths of the adult males failed to vote on the question, having abstained from the elections at which delegates to the state conventions were chosen, either on account of their indifference or their disfranchisement by property qualifications.

The Constitution was ratified by a vote of probably not more than one-sixth of the adult males. . . .

The leaders who supported the Constitution in the ratifying conventions represented the same economic groups as the members of the Philadelphia Convention; and in a large number of instances they were also directly and personally interested in the outcome of their efforts.

In the ratification, it became manifest that the line of cleavage for and against the Constitution was between substantial personalty interests on the one hand and the small farming and debtor interests on the other.

The Constitution was not created by "the whole people" as the jurists have said; neither was it created by "the states" as Southern nullifiers long contended; but it was the work of a consolidated group whose interests knew no state boundaries and were truly national in their scope.

The interpretation Beard offered in 1913 as a reaction against pietistic rather than political understandings of the Constitution enjoyed a long period of influence, but in recent years it has come under attack on a number of grounds.

One of the sharpest criticisms appeared in a volume by Forrest McDonald, *We the People* (1959), an elaborate and intricate analysis of Beard's central contentions. The salient features of McDonald's extended critique are summarized in the following book review: [2]

WE THE PEOPLE: THE ECONOMIC ORIGINS OF THE CONSTITUTION, by Forrest McDonald. University of Chicago Press, 436 Pages, 1959. Reviewed by Julian S. Rammelkamp

It is altogether possible that this painstaking, exhaustive restudy of the forces which produced the Constitution of the United States will administer the coup de grace to another era of historical interpretation. Just as Charles A. Beard, then a young professor of politics at Columbia University, in 1913 demolished an age of formalistic eulogy of the Founding Fathers when he published "An Economic Interpretation of the Constitution," so the present book appears to provide chapter and verse to a growing list of hostile critics of Beard's own thesis.

Reacting against what, in his own day, was the fashionable view that the Constitution was the near-perfect product of the Anglo-Saxon genius for self-government, Professor Beard injected the jarring idea that the Founding Fathers were motivated less by eternal verities of political science than by down-to-earth economic self-interest. Worse, he held that in reality the Constitution was a reactionary document, the carefully devised handiwork of capitalistic interests—loosely, the entrepreneur classes—who, determined to rescue property from the threat of attack by popular majorities, cleverly managed to formulate and impose the Constitution upon the masses of the American people.

Beard's study was originally presented somewhat tentatively and was frankly based upon only partial research. But he believed that when a really thorough investigation of the sources was made his theory would be confirmed. The years went by and no such investigation was made, but in the meantime the "Economic Interpretation" took on the aspect, not of a suggestion, but of a proved analysis. More and more, although bitter controversy raged, Beard's

[2] *St. Louis Post-Dispatch,* March 1, 1959.

underlying theory of class conflict gained headway until it colored most of the accounts of the adoption of the Constitution.

In recent years, however—and notably since World War II—a new generation of historians has arisen to question the validity of Beard's famous book. Such students as Robert Brown of Michigan State University, Oscar Handlin of Harvard, and Frederick Tolles of Swarthmore College have sharply criticized both Beard's methods and conclusions. Now, as a climax, comes this thoroughly devastating work by McDonald which at last does what Beard said should be done; it is a systematic and comprehensive examination of the sources. But the conclusions are not those that Beard anticipated.

Actually this book is much more than its title indicates. Far from being merely a study of economic forces, it is an amazingly detailed state-by-state compilation of the host of influences—political, social, geographic, historical as well as economic—which shaped the Constitution-making era. And from this welter of material—expertly handled—emerge two general conclusions, one positive and one negative.

Negatively, the Beardian thesis that the Constitution was "put over" on the masses of the American people by the clever management of a cohesive, self-conscious capitalistic minority simply does not stand up. Both in the Philadelphia convention itself and in the subsequent state ratifying conventions the entrepreneur class is shown to have been almost evenly divided, some for and some against the Constitution and its key economic clauses. Moreover, far from being opposed to the Constitution, as Beard suggests, the masses—that is, the preponderant small-farmer element of the population—in a number of states were instrumental in securing its approval.

Positively, and more important, McDonald's study clearly shows that in any case no simple, over-all "explanation" of the Constitution or its adoption is possible. A manifold number of causes—both economic and non-economic—must be considered and, furthermore, no single force or set of forces, economic or otherwise, will do for the thirteen states generally. The situation in each state must be analyzed separately, no two being alike. In short, due to the very nature of the sprawling new nation, which was essentially a congeries of distinct localities, only a pluralistic approach in any way could produce a satisfactory study of the period.

And what of Mr. Beard? It seems, despite McDonald's rejection of the old master's thesis as such, that one can still note a strong Beardian influence. For, like his great predecessor, McDonald, too, approaches the problem as one which may best be explained in terms of the practical needs, interests, prejudices, ambitions of a people in the throes of establishing a nation. The Founding Fathers, as Beard brought out long ago, were not demigods but able men of affairs seeking to solve practical problems of government. And, no doubt, were he alive today, Mr. Beard would not object to the dismissal of his main thesis. As a believer in historical relativism, he would probably agree that his explanation, like the one before it, had seen its day. As he himself said, each generation must inevitably write history anew.

The impact on the Constitution of political factors other than those of particular group interests and economic concerns is suggested by Richard Hofstadter in an analysis of a possible balance of political and other forces among the purposes that led the framers to shape the Constitution as they did: [3]

Democratic ideas are most likely to take root among discontented and oppressed classes, rising middle classes, or perhaps some sections of an old, alienated, and partially disinherited aristocracy, but they do not appeal to a privileged class that is still amplifying its privileges. With a half-dozen exceptions at the most, the men of the Philadelphia [constitutional] Convention were sons of men who had considerable position and wealth, and as a group they had advanced well beyond their fathers. Only one of them, William Few of Georgia, could be said in any sense to represent the yeoman farmer class which constituted the overwhelming majority of the free population. In the late Eighteenth century "the better kind of people" found themselves set off from the mass by a hundred visible, tangible, and audible distinctions of dress, speech, manners, and education. There was a continuous lineage of upper-class contempt, from pre-Revolutionary Tories like Peggy Hutchinson, the Governor's daughter, who wrote one day: "The dirty mob was all about me as I drove into town," to a Federalist like Hamilton, who candidly dis-

[3] Richard Hofstadter, *The American Political Tradition and the Men Who Made It* (New York: Alfred A. Knopf, 1948), 4–9, 13–14, 15.

dained the people. Mass unrest was often received in the spirit of young Gouverneur Morris: "The mob begin to think and reason. Poor reptiles! . . . They bask in the sun, and ere noon they will bite, depend upon it. The gentry begin to fear this." . . . Whether the Fathers [of the Constitution] looked to the cynically illuminated intellectuals of contemporary Europe or to their own Christian heritage of the idea of original sin, they found quick confirmation of the notion that man is an unregenerate rebel who has to be controlled.

And yet there was another side to the picture. The Fathers were intellectual heirs of seventeenth-century English republicanism with its opposition to arbitrary rule and faith in popular sovereignty. If they feared the advance of democracy, they also had misgivings about turning to the extreme right. Having recently experienced a bitter revolutionary struggle with an external power beyond their control, they were in no mood to follow Hobbes to his conclusion that any kind of government must be accepted in order to avert the anarchy and terror of a state of nature. They were uneasily aware that both military dictatorship and a return to monarchy were being seriously discussed in some quarters—the former chiefly among unpaid and discontented army officers, the latter in rich and fashionable Northern circles. John Jay, familiar with sentiment among New York's mercantile aristocracy, wrote to Washington, June 27, 1786, that he feared that "the better kind of people (by which I mean the people who are orderly and industrious, who are content with their situations, and not uneasy in their circumstances) will be led, by the insecurity of property, the loss of confidence in their rulers, and the want of public faith and rectitude, to consider the charms of liberty as imaginary and delusive." Such men, he thought, might be prepared for "almost any change that may promise them quiet and security." Washington, who had already repudiated a suggestion that he become a military dictator, agreed, remarking that "we are apt to run from one extreme to the other."

Unwilling to turn their backs upon republicanism, the Fathers also wished to avoid violating the prejudices of the people. "Notwithstanding the oppression and injustice experienced among us from democracy," said George Mason, "the genius of the people is in favor of it, and the genius of the people must be consulted." Mason admitted "that we had been too democratic," but feared that "we should incautiously run into the opposite extreme." James Madison, who has quite rightfully been called the philosopher of the Constitution, told the delegates: "It seems indispensable that the mass of citizens should not be without a voice in making the laws which they are to obey, and in choosing the magistrates who are to administer them." James Wilson, the outstanding jurist of the age, later appointed to the Supreme Court by Washington, said again and again that the ultimate power of government must of necessity reside in the people. This the Fathers commonly accepted, for if government did not proceed from the people, from what other source could it legitimately come? To adopt any other premise not only would be inconsistent with everything they had said against British rule in the past but would open the gates to an extreme concentration of power in the future. . . .

If the masses were turbulent and unregenerate, and yet if government must be founded upon their suffrage and consent, what could a Constitution-maker do? One thing that the Fathers did not propose to do, because they thought it impossible, was to change the nature of man to conform with a more ideal system. They were inordinately confident that they knew what man always had been and what he always would be. The eighteenth-century mind had great faith in universals. Its method, as Carl Becker has said, was "to go up and down the field of history looking for man in general, the universal man, stripped of the accidents of time and place." Madison declared that the causes of political differences and of the formation of factions were "sown in the nature of man" and could never be eradicated. . . .

Since man was an unchangeable creature of self-interest, it would not do to leave anything to his capacity for restraint. It was too much to expect that vice could be checked by virtue; the Fathers relied instead upon checking vice with vice. Madison once objected during the Convention that Gouverneur Morris was "forever inculcating the utter political depravity of men and the necessity of opposing one vice and interest to another vice and interest." And yet Madison himself in the Federalist Number 51 later set forth an excellent statement of the same thesis. . . .

What the Fathers wanted was known as "balanced government," an idea at least as old as Aristotle and Polybius. This ancient conception had won new sanction in the eighteenth century, which was dominated intellectually by the scientific work of Newton and in which mechanical metaphors sprang as naturally to men's minds as did biological metaphors in the Darwinian atmosphere of the late nineteenth century. Men had found a rational order in the universe and they hoped that it could be transferred to politics, or, as John Adams put it, that governments could be "erected on the simple principles of nature." Madison spoke in the most precise Newtonian language when he said that such a "natural" government must be so constructed "that its several constituent parts may, by their mutual relations, be the means of keeping each other in their proper places." A properly designed state, the Fathers believed, would check interest with interest, class with class, faction with faction, and one branch of government with another in a harmonious system of mutual frustration. . . .

Government, thought the Fathers, is based on property. Men who have no property lack the necessary stake in an orderly society to make stable or reliable citizens. Dread of the propertyless masses of the towns was all but universal. George Washington, Gouverneur Morris, John Dickinson, and James Madison spoke of their anxieties about the urban working class that might arise some time in the future—"men without property and principle," as Dickinson described them—and even the democratic Jefferson shared this prejudice. Madison, stating the problem, came close to anticipating the modern threats to conservative republicanism from both communism and fascism:

In future times, a great majority of the people will not only be without landed but any other sort of property. These will either combine, under the influence of their common situation—in which case the rights of property and the public liberty will not be secure in their hands—or, what is more probable, they will become the tools of opulence and ambition, in which case there will be equal danger on another side.

What encouraged the Fathers about their own era, however, was the broad dispersion of landed property. The small landowning farmers had been troublesome in recent years, but there was a general conviction that under a properly made Constitution a *modus vivendi* could be worked out with them. The possession of moderate plots of property presumably gave them a sufficient stake in society to be safe and responsible citizens under the restraints of balanced government. Influence in government would be proportionate to property: merchants and great landholders would be dominant, but small property-owners would have an independent and far from negligible voice. It was "politic as well as just," said Madison, "that the interests and rights of every class should be duly represented and understood in the public councils," and John Adams declared that there could be "no free government without a democratical branch in the constitution."

The farming element already satisfied the property requirements for suffrage in most of the states, and the Fathers generally had no quarrel with their enfranchisement. . . .

There is common agreement among modern critics that the debate over the Constitution was carried on at an intellectual level that is rare in politics, and that the Constitution itself is one of the world's masterpieces of practical statecraft. On other grounds there has been controversy. At the very beginning contemporary opponents of the Constitution foresaw an apocalyptic destruction of local government and popular institutions, while conservative Europeans of the old regime thought the young American Republic was a dangerous leftist experiment. Modern critical scholarship, which reached a high point in Charles A. Beard's *An Economic Interpretation of the Constitution of the United States,* started a new turn in the debate. The antagonism, long latent, between the philosophy of the Constitution and the philosophy of American democracy again came into the open. Professor Beard's work appeared in 1913 at the peak of the Progressive era, when the muckraking fever was still high; some readers tended to conclude from his findings that the Fathers were selfish reactionaries who do not deserve their high place in American esteem. Still more recently, other writers, inverting this logic, have used Beard's facts to praise the Fathers for their opposition to "democracy" and as an argument for returning again to the idea of a "republic."

In fact, the Fathers' image of themselves as moderate republicans standing between political extremes was quite accurate. They were impelled by class motives more than pietistic writers like to admit, but they were also controlled . . . by a statesmanlike sense of moderation and a scrupulously republican philosophy.

Review in your text and in your lecture notes materials relating to:

A. The political development and conflicts which immediately preceded, and which resulted in, the calling of the constitutional convention of 1787.

B. The delegates to the convention, including the social backgrounds from which they came, the main interests with which they were identified, and the ideas concerning government in which they believed.

C. The deliberations of the convention, the main decisions it made as to the structure and operation of government under the new Constitution, and the probable reasons for those decisions.

Now read in its entirety the Constitution as originally written (without any amendments) and analyze it carefully in relation to the defense of majority rule in the *Packet* article.

For class discussion, or as a written exercise, prepare careful, well-thought-out, complete answers to the following questions:

1. To what extent and in what ways, both in the general structure of government it establishes and in the particular provisions for the operation of government it includes, does the Constitution as framed at Philadelphia embody the views concerning majority rule expressed in the *Packet* argument, as reproduced above? To what extent and in what ways does the Constitution fail to embody these views?

2. What particular provisions of the Constitution can be cited to support the thesis that the original Constitution was an "economic document," serving particular economic interests, as Beard maintains? In view of the countertheses advanced by McDonald and Hofstadter, is it necessary to qualify the contention that these provisions were written into the Constitution as a result of the pressures of the economic interest groups to which Beard attrib-

utes them? If so, what qualifications would you consider necessary?

3. What general features or particular provisions of the original Constitution can be cited to support the thesis advanced by Hofstadter that the Constitution was the product of a "scrupulously republican philosophy," and thus an adherence to the basic principles of popular government as the Revolutionary generation saw them?

4. On the basis of all of the information and analysis that you have at hand, what is *your own* assessment of the various factors in the politics of constitution-making that resulted in the Constitution taking the shape that it did?

OPTIONAL: *Review all of the amendments to the Constitution to date, and materials in your text and lecture notes relating to the changing Constitution through interpretation and usage.*

5. In what ways has the Constitution as it now stands and is interpreted in practice moved from the framers' notion of a "republic" toward "democracy," as democracy may imply increased popular influence in government or the principle of majority rule?

PROBLEM 6

Checks and Balances and the Blessings of Liberty

ABSTRACT ideological statements such as those found in the preamble to the Constitution of the United States are ambiguous and elusive. For example, "establish Justice," "secure the Blessings of Liberty," and "promote the general Welfare" are phrases which must be translated into workable political institutions to become meaningful. The constitutional framers were well aware that protecting liberty, a value on which there was nearly unanimous agreement, required institutional engineering if principle was to be linked with practice. This is a challenge difficult to meet under any conditions and the political problems facing the United States in 1787 compounded the task. The colonial heritage, the Revolutionary War, and the experiences of the Confederation each contributed to the stream of ideas and plans that culminated in the Constitution and the pattern of government it established.

A major feature of the Constitution was a system of separation of powers and checks and balances. It is important to keep in mind that the framers were pessimistic in their assessment of how people behaved in politics. Rightly or wrongly, they felt that political leaders were not to be trusted; regardless of how the office-holder was chosen, whether by inheritance or election or selection, he was subject to the temptress ambition—ambition for power—and he often succumbed. The framers felt that a major way in which to guard against the possibility of tyranny by a wayward official was to circumscribe the powers he exercised by dividing the authority of government into separate legislative, executive, and judicial branches and then double-lock the door by an intricate system of checks and balances among these branches. Power was also to be distributed between two main layers of public officialdom, national and local, and thus the influences attending political office were to be checked both horizontally and vertically, not only by the separation of powers but also by the federal division of authority. Fragmentation of power is a notion which will crop up repeatedly in the study of the American political system; indeed it is built into nearly every aspect of the American political process and governmental structure. Because the fragmentation of power and the idea of checks and balances is so crucial to an understanding of American politics, it is wise for us to inquire into just what purposes the framers had in mind.

Fundamentally the framers feared that the concentration of political or governmental power would result in what they called "tyranny"—the oppression, particularly, of minority groups or individuals. Moreover they feared the possible tyrannical or oppressive exercise of power not only by officials acting *within* government, but also by factions, interest groups, or parties acting *through* government, particularly if such groups constituted a majority of the population. For instance, if a majority of the voters were poor debtors they might gain control of the government and wipe out their debt—which would mean serious injury to the minority, the creditors. The separation-of-powers, checks-and-balances system was established to guard against such "dangers," as the framers saw them.

The framers did not rest content with what James Madison called mere "parchment barriers" against oppressive power. That is, they did not rely solely on the constitutional structure of government, such as the separation between legislative, executive, and judicial powers, and the legal checks among these branches of government, such as the president's veto. The framers also considered the possibility of relating the national government to the whole social and political system so that, in the conflict or inter-play of many varied, widely dispersed interests or factions, the chance of any group or faction achieving preponderant power would be kept to a minimum. Thus, *within the government,* James Madison saw the prevention of tyranny depending not only on "the constitutional rights of the place," or office or branch, but also on "the interest of the man" in office. As he put it, one office-holder's "ambition must be made to counteract [another office-holder's] ambition." In addition, *outside the governmental structure,* Madison saw another bulwark against possible tyranny in the interplay of "opposite and rival interests" in the whole field of politics, which would prevent any group or combination of groups from becoming strong enough to dominate the government. In short, the framers saw possible barriers to tyrannical power not only in the legal structure of government, but also in the action-and-reaction of day-to-day politics. In this insight Madison and others articulated an important distinction for all political analysis —the distinction between what we may call formal and nonformal power relations. Restraints on power provided by the separation of powers and checks and balances of the Constitution we may call *formal.* Restraints on power that depend primarily upon pit-ting persons against persons or groups against groups, upon the conflict of "opposite and rival interests" (either individual ambi-tion countering individual ambition within government or the political action of one party or interest group counteracting the power of another group), we may call *nonformal. This important distinction should be held firmly in mind.* It should become clearer as you proceed with the analysis involved in this problem.

A classic statement of the over-all character of separation of powers and checks and balances is contained in *The Federalist,* Essays 47, 51, and 10. Read thoughtfully, and pause to digest, the following selections from these essays, which were written by James Madison. A brief modern restatement of some parts of his argument is given in Problem 1, "Facts and Values in Political Analysis," above.

From *Federalist 47*

No political truth is certainly of greater intrinsic value, or is stamped with the authority of more enlightened patrons of liberty, than . . . the political maxim, that the legislative, executive, and judiciary departments ought to be separate and distinct. . . . The accumulation of all powers, legislative, executive, and judiciary, in the same hands, whether of one, a few, or many, and whether hereditary, self-appointed, or elective, may justly be pronounced the very definition of tyranny. . . . In order to form correct ideas on this important subject, it will be proper to investigate the sense in which the preservation of liberty requires that the three great departments of power should be separate and distinct.

The oracle who is always consulted and cited on this subject is the celebrated Montesquieu [1689–1755]. . . .

The British Constitution was to Montesquieu what Homer has been to the didactic writers on epic poetry. . . .

On the slightest view of the British Constitution, we must perceive that the legislative, executive, and judiciary departments are by no means totally separate and distinct from each other. The executive magistrate forms an integral part of the legislative authority. He alone has the prerogative of making treaties with foreign sovereigns, which, when made, have, under certain limitations, the force of legislative acts. All the members of the judiciary department are appointed by him, can be removed by him on the address of the two Houses of Parliament, and form, when he pleases to consult them, one of his constitutional councils. . . .

From these facts, by which Montesquieu was guided, it may clearly be inferred that, in saying "There can be no liberty where the legislative and executive powers are united in the same person, or body of magistrates," or, "if the power of judging be not separated from the legislative and executive powers," he did not mean that these departments ought to have no *partial agency* in, or no *control* over, the acts of each other. His meaning, as his own words import, and still more conclusively as illustrated by the example in his eye, can amount to no more than this, that where the *whole* power of one department is exercised by the same hands which possess the *whole* power of another department, the fundamental principles of a free constitution are subverted. . . .

The reasons on which Montesquieu grounds his maxim are a further demonstration of his meaning. "When the legislative and executive powers are united in the same person or body," says he, "there can be no liberty, because apprehensions may arise lest *the same* monarch or senate should *enact* tyrannical laws to *execute* them in a tyrannical manner." Again: "Were the power of judging joined with the legislative, the life and liberty of the subject would be exposed to arbitrary control, for *the judge* would then be *the legislator*. Were it joined to the executive power, *the judge* might behave with all the violence of *an oppressor*." Some of these reasons are more fully explained in other passages; but briefly stated as they are here, they sufficiently establish the meaning which we have put on this celebrated maxim of this celebrated author. . . .

From *Federalist 51*

To what expedient . . . shall we finally resort, for maintaining in practice the necessary partition of power among the several departments, as laid down in the Constitution? The only answer that can be given is, that as [merely paper barriers] are found to be inadequate, the defect must be supplied, by so contriving the interior structure of the government as that its several constituent parts may, by their mutual relations, be the means of keeping each other in their proper places. . . .

In order to lay a due foundation for that separate and distinct exercise of the different powers of government, which to a certain extent is admitted on all hands to be essential to the preservation of liberty, it is evident that each department should have a will of its own; and consequently should be so constituted that the members of each should have as little agency as possible in the appointment of the members of the others. Were this principle rigorously adhered to, it would require that all the appointments for the supreme executive, legislative, and judiciary magistracies should be drawn from the same fountain of authority, the people, through channels having no communication whatever with one another. Perhaps such a plan of constructing the several departments would be less difficult in practice than it may in contemplation appear. Some difficulties, however, and some additional expense would attend the execution of it. Some deviations, therefore, from the principle must be admitted. . . .

It is equally evident, that the members of each department should be as little dependent as possible on those of the others, for the emoluments [pay] annexed to their offices. Were the executive magistrate, or the judges, not independent of the legislature in this particular, their independence in every other would be merely nominal.

But the great security against a gradual concentration of the several powers in the same department, consists in giving to those who administer each department the necessary constitutional means and personal motives to resist encroachments of the others. The provision for defence must in this, as in all other cases, be made commensurate to the danger of attack. Ambition must be made to counteract ambition. The interest of the man must be connected with the constitutional rights of the place. It may be a reflection on human nature, that such devices should be necessary to control the abuses of government. But what is government itself, but the greatest of all reflections on human nature? If men were angels, no government would be necessary. If angels were to govern men, neither external nor internal controls on government would be necessary. In framing a government which is to be administered by men over men, the great difficulty lies in this: you must first enable the government to control the governed; and in the next place oblige it to control itself. A dependence on the people is, no doubt, the primary control on the government; but experience has taught mankind the necessity of auxiliary precautions.

This policy of supplying, by opposite and rival interests, the defect of better motives, might be traced through the whole system of human affairs, private as well as public. We see it particularly displayed in all the subordinate distributions of power, where the constant aim is to divide and arrange the several offices in such a manner as that each may be a check on the other—that the private interest of every individual may be a sentinel over the public rights. These inventions of prudence cannot be less requisite in the distribution of the supreme powers of the State.

But it is not possible to give to each department an equal power of self-defence. In republican government, the legislative authority necessarily predominates. The remedy for this inconveniency is to divide the legislature into different branches; and to render them, by different modes of election and different principles of action, as little connected with each other as the nature of their common functions and their common dependence on the society will admit. It may even be necessary to guard against dangerous encroachments by still further precautions. As the weight of the legislative authority requires that it should be thus divided, the weakness of the executive may require, on the other hand, that it should be fortified. An absolute negative [veto] on the legislature appears, at first view, to be the natural defence with which the executive magistrate [President] should be armed. But perhaps it would be neither altogether safe nor alone sufficient. On ordinary occasions it might not be exerted with the requisite firmness, and on extraordinary occasions it might be perfidiously abused. May not this defect of an absolute negative be supplied by some qualified connection between this weaker department and the weaker branch of the stronger department, by which the latter may be led to support the constitutional rights of the former, without being too much detached from the rights of its own department? . . .

There are, moreover, two considerations particularly applicable to the *federal system* of America, which place that system in a very interesting point of view.

First. In a single republic, all the power surrendered by the people is submitted to the administration of a single government; and the usurpations are guarded against by a division of the government into distinct and separate departments. In the compound republic of America, the power surrendered by the people is first divided between two distinct governments [federal, and state] and then the portion allotted to each subdivided among distinct and separate departments. Hence a double security arises to the rights of the people. The different governments will control each other, at the same time that each will be controlled by itself.

Second. It is of great importance in a republic not only to guard the society against the oppression of its rulers, but to guard one part of the society against the injustice of the other part. Different interests necessarily exist in different classes of citizens. If a majority be united by a common interest, the rights of the minority will be insecure. There are but two methods of providing against this evil: the one by creating a will in the community independent of the majority—that is, of the society itself; the other, by comprehending in the society so many separate descriptions of citizens as will render an unjust combination of a majority of the whole very improbable, if not impracticable. The first method prevails in all governments possessing an hereditary or self-appointed authority [king or dictator]. . . . The second method will be exemplified in the federal republic of the United States. Whilst all authority in it will be derived from and dependent on the society, the society itself will be broken into so many parts, interests and classes of citizens, that the rights of individuals, or of the minority, will be in little danger from interested combinations of the majority. In a free government the security for civil rights must be the same as that for religious rights. It consists in the one case in the multiplicity of interests, and in the other in the multiplicity of sects. The degree of security in both cases will depend on the number of interests and sects; and this may be presumed to depend on the extent of country and number of people comprehended under the same government. This view of the subject must particularly recommend a proper federal system to all the sincere and considerate friends of republican government, since it shows that in exact proportion as the territory of the Union may be formed into more circumscribed Confederacies, or States, oppressive combinations of a majority will be facilitated. . . .

In the extended republic of the United States, and among the great variety of interests, parties, and sects which it embraces, a coalition of a majority of the whole society could seldom take place on any other principles than those of justice and the general good . . . there being thus less danger to a minor from the will of a major party. . . .

From *Federalist 10*

Among the numerous advantages promised by a well-constructed Union, none deserves to be more accurately developed than its tendency to break and control the violence of faction [conflict of groups, and pursuit of total power by any group]. The friend of popular governments never finds himself so much alarmed for their character and fate, as when he contemplates their propensity to this dangerous vice. He will not fail, therefore, to set a due value on any plan which, without violating the principles to which he is attached, provides a proper cure for it. . . . The valuable improvements made by the American [state] constitutions on the popular models, both ancient and modern, cannot certainly be too much admired; but it would be an unwarrantable partiality, to contend that they have as effectually obviated the danger on this side, as was wished and expected. Complaints are everywhere heard from our most considerate and virtuous citizens, equally the friends of public and private faith, and of public and personal liberty, that our governments are too unstable, that the public good is disregarded in the conflicts of rival parties, and that measures are too often decided, not according to the rules of justice and the rights of the minor party, but by the superior force of an interested and overbearing majority. However anxiously we may wish that these complaints had no foundation, the evidence of known facts will not permit us to deny that they are in some degree true. . . .

There are two methods of curing the mischiefs of faction: the one, by removing its causes; the other by controlling its effects. . . .

[But] the latent causes of faction are . . . sown in the nature of man; and we see them everywhere brought into different degrees of activity, according to the different circumstances of civil society. A zeal for different opinions concerning government, and many other points, as well of speculation as of practice; an attachment to different leaders ambitiously contending for pre-eminence and power; or to persons of other descriptions whose fortunes have been interesting to the human passions, have, in turn, divided mankind into parties, inflamed them with mutual animosity, and rendered them much more disposed to vex and oppress each other than to co-operate for their common good. So strong is this propensity of mankind to fall into mutual animosities, that where no substantial occasion presents itself, the most frivolous and fanciful distinctions have been sufficient to kindle their unfriendly passions and excite their most violent conflicts. But the most common and durable source of factions has been the various and unequal distribution of property. Those who hold and those who are without property have ever formed distinct interests in society. Those who are creditors, and those who are debtors, fall under a like discrimination. A landed interest, a manufacturing interest, a mercantile interest, a moneyed interest, with many lesser interests, grow up of necessity in civilized nations, and divide them into different classes, actuated by different sentiments and views. The regulation of these various and interfering interests forms the principal task of modern legislation, and involves the spirit of party and faction in the necessary and ordinary operations of the government.

The inference to which we are brought is, that the *causes* of faction cannot be removed, and that relief is only to be sought in the means of controlling its *effects*.

If a faction consists of less than a majority, relief is supplied by the republican principle, which enables the majority to defeat its sinister views by regular vote. It may clog the administration, it may convulse the society; but it will be unable to execute and mask its violence under the forms of the Constitution. When a majority is included in a faction, the form of popular government, on the other hand, enables it to sacrifice to its ruling passion or interest both the public good and the rights of other citizens. To secure [make safe] the public good and private rights against the danger of such a faction, and at the same time to preserve the spirit and the form of popular government, is then the great object to which our inquiries are directed. . . .

From this view of the subject it may be concluded that a pure democracy, by which I mean a society consisting of a small number of citizens, who assemble and administer the government in person, can admit of no cure for the mischiefs of faction. A common passion or interest will, in almost every case, be felt by a majority of the whole; a communication and concert result from the form of government itself; and there is nothing to check the inducements to sacrifice the weaker party or an obnoxious individual. Hence it is that such democracies have ever been spectacles of turbulence and contention; have ever been found incompatible with personal security or the rights of property; and have in general been as short in their lives as they have been violent in their deaths. . . .

A republic, by which I mean a government in which the scheme of representation takes place, opens a different prospect, and promises the cure for which we are seeking. Let us examine the points in which it varies from pure democracy, and we shall comprehend both the nature of the cure and the efficacy which it must derive from the Union.

The two great points of difference between a democracy and a republic are: first, the delegation of the government, in the latter, to a small number of citizens elected by the rest; secondly, the greater number of citizens, and greater sphere of country, over which the latter may be extended.

The effect of the first difference is, on the one hand, to refine and enlarge the public views, by passing them through the medium of a chosen body of citizens, whose wisdom may best discern the true interest of their country, and whose patriotism and love of justice will be least likely to sacrifice it to temporary or partial considerations. Under such a regulation, it may well happen that the public voice, pronounced by the representatives of the people, will be more consonant to the public good than if pronounced by the people themselves, convened for the purpose. . . .

The other point of difference is, the greater number of citizens and extent of territory which may be brought within the compass of republican than of [a pure] democratic government; and it is this circumstance principally which renders factious combinations less to be dreaded in the former than in the latter. The smaller the society, the fewer probably will be the distinct parties and interests composing it; the fewer the distinct parties and interests, the more frequently will a majority be found of the same party; and the smaller the number of individuals composing a majority, and the smaller the compass within which they are placed, the more easily will they concert and execute their plans of oppression. Extend the sphere and you take in a greater variety of parties and interests; you make it less probable that a majority of the whole will have a common motive to invade the rights of other citizens; or if such a common motive exists, it will be more difficult for all who feel it to discover their own strength, and to act in unison with each other. . . .

Hence, it clearly appears, that the same advantage which a republic has over a democracy, in controlling the effects of faction, is enjoyed by a large over a small republic,—is enjoyed by the Union over the States composing it. Does the advantage consist in the substitution of representatives whose enlightened views and virtuous sentiments render them superior to local prejudices and to schemes of injustice? It will not be denied that the representation of the Union will be most likely to possess these requisite endowments. Does it consist in the greater security afforded by a greater variety of parties [or groups] against the event of any one party [or group] being able to outnumber and oppress the rest? In an equal degree does the increased variety of parties [or groups] comprised within the Union, increase this security? Does it, in fine, consist in the greater obstacles opposed to the concert and accomplishment of the secret wishes of an unjust and interested majority? Here, again, the extent of the Union gives it the most palpable advantage.

The influence of factious leaders may kindle a flame within their particular States, but will be unable to spread a general conflagration through the other States. . . .

Review in your text and in your class notes materials relating to the formation of the Constitution and particularly to the doctrine and practice of separation of powers and checks and balances. Read in your text also materials concerning the character and diversity of modern American society and the interplay or action-and-reaction of interest groups and of parties.

As a written assignment or for class discussion:

1. Read carefully the Constitution of the United States, and LIST and DESCRIBE BRIEFLY four important examples of formal checks and balances or legally prescribed restraints on one branch or organ of government by another. An example is the Senate's power to confirm or withhold consent to certain presidential appointments.

2. Applying to modern conditions the ideas of James Madison concerning what we have called nonformal restraints on power, LIST and DESCRIBE BRIEFLY four important restraints you can identify, on the basis of your present knowledge, operating in American government and politics today. An example is two-party competition, with the "outs" ready to criticize the "ins."

3. As briefly as possible state the rationale which Madison would offer for each of the Constitutional provisions and nonformal restraints you have listed. In some cases the selections you have just read will give you the answer; in others you will have to rely on inferences from Madison's basic argument to reconstruct how he would defend the particular restraint.

PROBLEM 7

Separation of Powers and Delegation of Powers

ONE of the fundamental principles of the United States Constitution is that the power to govern must be divided among three coequal branches, the legislative, the executive, and the judicial. Yet the three branches were not to be isolated in watertight compartments, but were intertwined in their relationships with each other in an elaborate fashion. Nevertheless, the basic separation of power between them was regarded by James Madison, "the Father of the Constitution," as of the first importance in preserving liberty. In this connection Madison quoted Montesquieu approvingly: "When the legislative and executive powers are united in the same person or body, there can be no liberty, because apprehensions may arise lest the same monarch or senate should enact tyrannical laws to execute them in a tyrannical manner."

[*See also the full discussion of the subject by Madison in* The Federalist, *Essay 47 and 51, in Problem 6, "Checks and Balances and the Blessings of Liberty," above.*]

To the Founding Fathers tyranny meant arbitrary action by rulers. Although a tyrant might sometimes be benevolent he could act as he pleased, unrestrained by laws, constitutions, or customs, and such arbitrary authority in the hands of any ruler, the Founding Fathers believed, was always a threat to liberty. Subscribing to this principle, they were explicit and direct in the Constitution:

Article I. Section 1. All legislative Powers herein granted shall be vested in a Congress of the United States. . . .

Article II. Section 1. The executive Power shall be vested in a President of the United States of America. . . .

Article III. Section 1. The judicial Power of the United States, shall be vested in one supreme Court, and in such inferior Courts as the Congress may from time to time ordain and establish. . . .

Yet the matter is not quite so simple as it may seem. What *is* the legislative power as distinct from the executive power? Where *is* the line that separates one from the other? These questions may not have seemed difficult when the problems were those of writing down basic rules of government, but when it actually came to governing, the vagueness of many words such as "legislative" or "executive" became apparent. Furthermore the social and economic conditions within which government operates have changed greatly since 1787 and with these changes the words of the Constitutional separation of powers, already unclear, have become even more clouded in their meaning.

In recent years the tendency has been for Congress to delegate to the president or the executive branch the authority to "fill in the details" of rather broad and sweeping declarations of legislative policy. This tendency has been regarded by some as a sensible adaptation of an eighteenth-century concept of separation of powers to twentieth-century needs. Others, however, have seen this delegation of power to the executive as the very threat to liberty that the Founding Fathers feared. Intermingled in this debate about principle has been a variety of interests which are affected in one way or another by changes in the degree of authority and discretion to be exercised by the various branches of government. Thus some vigorous political conflicts have arisen over the question of the scope of authority each branch possesses, and the extent to which the Congress may authorize the president to make essentially legislative decisions.

The following letter was written by a member of the House of Representatives, Clem Miller of California, to a friend in his home district. As an exceptionally perceptive member of Congress, Representative Miller understood that the line between the executive branch and the legislative branch is often difficult to maintain. This particular letter also includes some observations about the effectiveness of making an organized claim on public officials.[1]

Dear Friend:

In today's world most people are ready to admit that, as much as they dislike the word "lobbying," the function carried on under this name is essential to government. (In fact, the right to lobby is protected by the First Amendment.) In recent months there has been a graphic contrast here in effectiveness of lobbying activity between two segments of agriculture important to the economic health of our district: walnut growers and poultrymen. Both groups are in economic trouble because of abundance.

The walnut growers have a large carry-over from last year which, if placed on top of this year's record production, would break the market. The growers wanted the government to buy walnuts for diversion into the school lunch program, to be financed from existing tariffs on foreign walnut imports.

In the poultry industry, overproduction led by huge combines of bankers and feed companies, with million-hen farms, has broken the egg and meat-bird markets wide open. Independent poultrymen are losing six to eight cents per dozen eggs and four to eight cents per pound of meat, and are going bankrupt in droves.

The walnut industry is well organized. They have been proud that they don't have supports and don't ask the government for "handouts." This is easy to understand. One marketing cooperative controls seventy per cent of the state's production. So, when the industry got in trouble and came to Washington, they came well prepared. Each California congressman received a personal, carefully reasoned, five-page letter. It was followed up by another, shorter letter. Then, a telegram called attention to the letters. Finally, there was a telephone call, asking for comments on the letters. By this time, we were fairly wide awake. Quite properly, the group worked through the congressman in whose district the

[1] Clem Miller, *Member of the House: Letters of a Congressman,* John W. Baker, ed. (New York: Charles Scribner's Sons, 1962), 137–40.

association offices and many growers are located. We received several calls from the congressman's staff, alerting us, keeping us posted, offering help in answering questions.

After this preliminary barrage, the walnut growers' representative was ready to come to town. He set up headquarters at a nearby hotel. He called on congressmen several times, accompanied by a gentleman from the packing and canning section of the industry. He talked to my legislative assistant. Then we were all invited to a luncheon at the hotel, where the plight of the industry was laid before us and it was announced that a meeting was set up with the Secretary of Agriculture. Meticulous care was taken to be sure that all congressmen and senators who represent walnut growers would be there. In a large Department of Agriculture conference room with numerous department officials present, a skillful "presentation" for the industry was made. Immediately afterward, the walnut congressmen jumped up to demand action. One was self-contained but bitter about department inaction. Another pointed out the illogical Administration position in caustic terms. In turn, each congressman added his bit to the complaint. The Administration was bland and quite self-righteous ("We have more confidence in the walnut grower than he has in himself"). The exasperation of the Republican congressmen toward the Republican Secretary of Agriculture mounted. "Would a 'shaded' market price have to become a rout before the government moved?" they wanted to know. Administration officials were apparently unshaken.

However, two weeks later, the Administration did act. The industry was delighted. The work of the lobby had been effective.

Let's contrast this with the way things are developing in the egg industry. Some time ago I received a long letter from a constituent asking what congressional action was expected in poultry. A check revealed that nothing was contemplated in Congress. Of the seven thousand bills in Congress, there was not one on poultry or eggs. No hearings were scheduled. My interest piqued, I discussed the situation with House Agriculture Committee staff members and with the acting chairman of the subcommittee. The prevailing view was that since there was no leadership in the industry, and no agreement on policy, hearings would serve no purpose. I urged that hearings be scheduled to see if policy might materialize. A day or so later, I heard that a group of distressed poultrymen from New Jersey were asking to meet with their government. The Georgia and Alabama broiler people also asked to be heard.

All of a sudden, we learned that there was to be a hearing. Citizens were petitioning their government for a redress of grievances. At the hearing a crowd of two hundred poultrymen swarmed into the Agriculture Committee room which had been designed for about seventy-five people. Poultrymen-witnesses testified that the lowest prices in eighteen years for eggs and chickens were bankrupting an industry. As one witness said, in 1957 we were separating the men from the boys; in 1959 it was the men from the giants. One poultryman gave a stark, moving account of his town's plight. He gestured to his friends, sitting somberly at his side. They had been against federal help until a month or so previously, he said. "We called the people who were down here in 1957 looking for handouts 'radicals.' Now, we are here ourselves."

Throughout two days the same depressing story was recounted as the farmer-witnesses, speaking for themselves and other small producers, took their turn. Technological advances, together with banker-feed company-grower integration, were destroying the independent poultryman. Then the Department of Agriculture spokesman told its story. He confirmed the growers' story but indicated that nothing could be done. It was the inexorable law of supply and demand. Significantly absent were representatives of the larger organized farm groups. At nightfall, the poultrymen had to return to their farms.

What was the next step? It is up to the interested congressmen, they told us. How come, we asked? What are we to do? The leader of the poultrymen said that we had been told the problem. Yes, was the response, but he and his friends should go to see the Secretary of Agriculture. Testimony had indicated that Congress had already given the Secretary all of the authority he needed to act. It would do no good to pass more laws, particularly since they would certainly end with Presidential vetoes.

All of the men were active poultrymen who had to get back to their flocks. They were leaving that night. Who was to carry the ball for them here in Washington during the next critical weeks? Who was going to do the telephoning? Who was going to coordinate policy between New Jersey, California, Alabama, Wisconsin, Georgia, and Kansas? The answer from them was, "No one." We had

been given a problem. It was ours now. The result to date: a resolution of the Agriculture Committee urging the Secretary to "implement such programs of purchase, diversion, and export of poultry
products as will lead toward improvement of the present critical
situation." Results for the poultrymen: nothing.

Very sincerely,
Clem Miller

*Summarize the kinds of functions performed by the Congress-
men on the one hand and the Administration on the other in each
of the two instances described in the letter above.*

Each of the following two paragraphs describes situations similar to those discussed by Representative Miller. In each case Congress has authorized the president to carry out a program. These
hypothetical situations are not intended to be exact accounts of
real events, although the first one is similar to a program which
actually has been undertaken. The primary purpose of these
paragraphs is to illustrate the problem of distinguishing between
the legislative and executive functions.

Each situation differs from the other in one or more of the
factors relevant to the question of whether the delegation of
power by Congress to the president is consistent with the idea of
the separation of powers. The cases are different also in the circumstances that may account for Congress having taken this kind
of action. Think about both aspects of this problem as you read.

A. Congress has enacted a law directing the president to carry
out a program of supports for the prices of agricultural commodities. The law says that support prices are to be based on per-
centages of parity—the relationship at a given time between what
a farmer pays for the things he buys and what he receives for the
things he sells—and support prices may range from 75 percent to
90 percent of parity. The law specifies how parity is to be calcu-
lated. It also specifies that the president (or his subordinate) is to
estimate in advance of each year's planting whether there is
likely to be a surplus of each of several commodities. If he finds

that a surplus is probable he may at his discretion reduce the support price, but not to less than 75 percent of parity. If, in contrast, he finds that a shortage is likely he may raise the support price to not more than 90 percent of parity. The statute specifies in detail the administrative procedures to be used in carrying out this program.

B. After a short paragraph which states that subversive organizations in the service of hostile governments threaten to undermine the nation, Congress authorizes and directs the president to determine whether any organization functioning in the United States is an agency of a hostile foreign government. If the president finds organizations to be serving the interests of hostile foreign governments, he may promulgate whatever regulations and take whatever action he deems necessary to prevent such organizations from accomplishing their purposes. No other provisions are contained in the statute.

Review in your text and lecture notes materials relating to the doctrine of separation of powers and to the problems of delegation of power by Congress to the president.

For a written exercise or class discussion, prepare answers to each of the following questions:

1. In each of the two cases described, what factors do you think may have led Congress to decide that the president should make the decisions rather than Congress?

2. In what respects does the action taken in each case appear to be in keeping with the idea that the legislative and executive powers should be kept separate? In what respects does the action taken in each case conflict with the doctrine of separation of powers?

3. The two statutes you have considered are not mere figments of the imagination. The first is an adaptation of an existing law, and they both put into concrete terms the kinds of actions performed by the two branches of government. Keeping these concrete examples in mind, prepare a brief statement distinguishing

as carefully and as exactly as you can between the "legislative" and the "executive" functions of government. Make sure that your definitions are consistent with the tasks that the president and Congress actually perform.

4. In view of the vastly different conditions which confront governmental operation today, compared with the eighteenth century, how would you evaluate the present importance of separation of powers as a safeguard of individual liberty?

PROBLEM 8

Judicial Review and the Legislative Process

ONE of the knottiest problems confronting students of American politics is to distinguish criticisms of *political processes* from criticisms of *political policies*. The term "process" refers (1) to the procedures and mechanisms which direct and constrain the manner in which political leaders are selected; (2) to the regulations which officeholders must observe when arriving at policy decisions; and (3) to the rules which assure that decisions are implemented and enforced in legitimate, that is, nonarbitrary, ways. Such matters are usually grounded in the basic ideology, values, and norms on which the political system rests. Judicial review is an example of a process by which the constitutionality of legislation or of executive action is judged. The word "policies" on the other hand directs attention to the *content* of the bills, laws, acts, and decisions which affect how the nation's resources are to be distributed or its affairs are to be conducted. Such matters are of course regularly subject to controversy.

Yet controversy over policies may often lead to controversy over processes. Thus, for example, the Supreme Court decision (*Brown* v. *Board of Education of Topeka,* 1954) which held that state laws requiring segregated schools conflicted with the Fourteenth Amendment was arrived at by the workings of the process of judicial review. The content of the decision affected the social structure within many states. In recent years the Supreme Court has been criticized for various other decisions, the content of

93

which displeased one group or another. Some of the critics have
gone on to claim that the Court was "usurping power" and have
sought to restrain its judicial authority; thus, because they disagree with the policies required by the Court's interpretation of
the Constitution, they would curb the Court's power to interpret
the Constitution. In other words, they would alter the process.
Many students of political systems, however, contend that the
stability and health of any government can be measured by how
committed its citizens are to the processes by which decisions are
made, irrespective of how much disagreement there may be about
the actual decisions. The strong government, they argue, is the
one in which agreement about decision-making processes is
deeply embedded. Such a government can tolerate considerable
disagreement about policies.

Judicial review of the acts of Congress and state legislatures, a
process most of the framers of the Constitution probably thought
was implicit in the document, has been an established practice
since Chief Justice John Marshall proclaimed it in *Marbury* v.
Madison in 1803. Yet Marshall's findings did not go entirely without criticism at the time, as the argument of Mr. Justice William
Gibson of the Supreme Court of Pennsylvania in *Eakin* v. *Raub*
in 1825 made clear. Read and ponder the following arguments,
bearing in mind however that it is the opinion of Chief Justice
Marshall and not of Justice Gibson that has achieved the status
of law and established the rule of judicial review.

I. Chief Justice Marshall [1]

The question whether an act repugnant to the Constitution can
become the law of the land, is a question deeply interesting to the
United States; but, happily, not of an intricacy proportioned to its
interest. It seems only necessary to recognize certain principles,
supposed to have been long and well established to decide it.

That the people have an original right to establish, for their future

---

[1] *Marbury* v. *Madison*, 1 Cranch 137 (1803).

government, such principles as, in their opinion, shall most conduce to their own happiness, is the basis on which the whole American fabric has been erected. The exercise of this original right is a very great exertion; nor can it nor ought it to be frequently repeated. The principles, therefore, so established, are deemed fundamental. And as the authority from which they proceed is supreme, and can seldom act, they are designed to be permanent.

This original and supreme will organizes the government, and assigns to different departments their respective powers. It may either stop here, or establish certain limits not to be transcended by those departments.

The government of the United States is of the latter description. The powers of the legislature are defined and limited; and that those limits may not be mistaken, or forgotten, the Constitution is written. To what purpose are powers limited, and to what purpose is that limitation committed to writing, if these limits may, at any time, be passed by those intended to be restrained? The distinction between a government with limited and unlimited powers is abolished, if those limits do not confine the persons on whom they are imposed, and if acts prohibited and acts allowed are of equal obligation. It is a proposition too plain to be contested, that the Constitution controls any legislative act repugnant to it; or, that the legislature may alter the Constitution by an ordinary act.

Between these alternatives there is no middle ground. The Constitution is either a superior paramount law, unchangeable by ordinary means, or it is on a level with ordinary legislative acts, and, like other acts, is alterable when the legislature shall please to alter it.

If the former part of the alternative be true, then a legislative act contrary to the Constitution is not law; if the latter part be true, then written constitutions are absurd attempts, on the part of the people, to limit a power in its own nature illimitable.

Certainly all those who have framed written constitutions contemplate them as forming the fundamental and paramount law of the nation, and, consequently, the theory of every such government must be, that an act of the legislature, repugnant to the constitution, is void.

This theory is essentially attached to a written constitution, and is consequently to be considered, by this Court, as one of the fundamental principles of our society. It is not, therefore, to be lost sight of in the further consideration of this subject . . .

So if a law be in opposition to the Constitution; if both the law and the Constitution apply to a particular case, so that the court must either decide that case conformably to the law, disregarding the Constitution, or conformably to the Constitution, disregarding the law, the court must determine which of these conflicting rules governs the case. This is of the very essence of judicial duty.

If, then, the courts are to regard the Constitution, and the Constitution is superior to any ordinary act of the legislature, the Constitution, and not such ordinary act, must govern the case to which they both apply . . .

The judicial power of the United States is extended to all cases arising under the Constitution.

Could it be the intention of those who gave this power, to say that in using it the Constitution should not be looked into? That a case arising under the Constitution should be decided without examining the instrument under which it arises?

This is too extravagant to be maintained.

In some cases, then, the Constitution must be looked into by the judges. And if they can open it at all, what part of it are they forbidden to read or to obey?

. . . it is apparent that the framers of the Constitution contemplated that instrument as a rule for the government of courts, as well as of the legislature.

Why otherwise does it direct the judges to take an oath to support it? This oath certainly applies in an especial manner to their conduct in their official character. How immoral to impose it on them, if they were to be used as the instruments, and the knowing instruments, for violating what they swear to support! . . .

Why does a judge swear to discharge his duties agreeably to the Constitution of the United States, if that Constitution forms no rule for his government? if it closed upon him, and cannot be inspected by him?

If such be the real state of things, this is worse than solemn mockery. To prescribe, or to take this oath, becomes equally a crime.

It is also not entirely unworthy of observation, that in declaring what shall be the supreme law of the land, the Constitution itself is first mentioned; and not the laws of the United States generally, but those only which shall be made in pursuance of the Constitution, have that rank.

Thus, the particular phraseology of the Constitution of the United States confirms and strengthens the principle, supposed to be essential to all written constitutions, that a law repugnant to the Constitution is void; and that courts, as well as other departments, are bound by that instrument.

The rule must be discharged.

II. Justice Gibson [2]

. . . I am aware, that a right to declare all unconstitutional acts void, without distinction as to either constitution, is generally held as a professional dogma; but, I apprehend, rather as a matter of faith than of reason. I admit that I once embraced the same doctrine, but without examination, and I shall therefore state the arguments that impelled me to abandon it, with great respect for those by whom it is still maintained . . .

The Constitution and the right of the legislature to pass the act, may be in collision. But is that a legitimate subject for judicial determination? If it be, the judiciary must be a peculiar organ, to revise the proceedings of the legislature, and to correct its mistakes; and in what part of the Constitution are we to look for this proud preeminence? Viewing the matter in the opposite direction, what would be thought of an act of assembly in which it should be declared that the Supreme Court had, in a particular case, put a wrong construction on the Constitution of the United States, and that the judgment should therefore be reversed? It would doubtless be thought a usurpation of judicial power. But it is by no means clear, that to declare a law void which has been enacted according to the forms prescribed in the Constitution, is not a usurpation of legislative power. It is an act of sovereignty; and sovereignty and legislative power are said by Sir William Blackstone to be convertible terms. It is the business of the judiciary to interpret the laws, not scan the authority of the lawgiver; and without the latter, it cannot take cognizance of a collision between a law and the Consti-

[2] *Eakin* v. *Raub*, 12 Sergeant and Rawle (Pennsylvania) 330 (1825).

tution. So that to affirm that the judiciary has a right to judge of the existence of such collision, is to take for granted the very thing to be proved. And, that a very cogent argument may be made in this way, I am not disposed to deny; for no conclusions are so strong as those that are drawn from the petitio principii.

But it has been said to be emphatically the business of the judiciary, to ascertain and pronounce what the law is; and that this necessarily involves a consideration of the Constitution. It does so: but how far? If the judiciary will inquire into anything besides the *form of enactment,* where shall it stop? There must be some point of limitation to such an inquiry; for no one will pretend that a judge would be justifiable in calling for the election returns, or scrutinizing the qualifications of those who composed the legislature. . . .

Everyone knows how seldom men think exactly alike on ordinary subjects; and a government constructed on the principle of assent by all its parts, would be inadequate to the most simple operations. The notion of a complication of counter checks has been carried to an extent in theory, of which the framers of the Constitution never dreamt. When the entire sovereignty was separated into its elementary parts, and distributed to the appropriate branches, all things incident to the exercise of its powers were committed to each branch exclusively. The negative which each part of the legislature may exercise, in regard to the acts of the other, was thought sufficient to prevent material infractions of the restraints which were put on the power of the whole; for, had it been intended to interpose the judiciary as an additional barrier, the matter would surely not have been left in doubt. The judges would not have been left to stand on the insecure and ever shifting ground of public opinion as to constructive powers; they would have been placed on the impregnable ground of an express grant. . . .

But the judges are sworn to support the Constitution, and are they not bound by it as the law of the land? In some respects they are . . . But what I have in view in this inquiry, is the supposed right of the judiciary to interfere, in cases where the Constitution is to be carried into effect through the instrumentality of the legislature, and where that organ must necessarily first decide on the constitutionality of its own act. The oath to support the Constitution is not peculiar to the judges, but is taken indiscriminately by every officer of the government, and is designed rather as a test of the political principles of the man, than to bind the officer in the dis-

charge of his duty . . . But granting it to relate to the official conduct of the judge, as well as every other officer, and not to his
political principles, still it must be understood in reference to supporting the Constitution, only as far as that may be involved in his
official duty; and, consequently, if his official duty does not comprehend an inquiry into the authority of the legislature, neither does
his oath. It is worthy of remark here, that the foundation of every
argument in favor of the right of the judiciary, is found at last to
be an assumption of the whole ground in dispute. Granting that the
object of the oath is to secure a support of the Constitution in the
discharge of official duty, its terms may be satisfied by restraining
it to official duty in the exercise of the ordinary judicial powers . . .
But the oath was more probably designed to secure the powers of
each of the different branches from being usurped by any of the
rest: for instance, to prevent the House of Representatives from
erecting itself into a court of judicature, or the Supreme Court from
attempting to control the legislature; and, in this view, the oath
furnishes an argument equally plausible against the right of the
judiciary . . .

But do not the judges do a positive act in violation of the Constitution, when they give effect to an unconstitutional law? Not if the
law has been passed according to the forms established in the Constitution. The fallacy of the question is, in supposing that the judiciary adopts the acts of the legislature as its own; whereas the
enactment of a law and the interpretation of it are not concurrent
acts, and as the judiciary is not required to concur in the enactment,
neither is it in the breach of the Constitution which may be the
consequence of the enactment. The fault is imputable to the legislature, and on it the responsibility exclusively rests.

Now consider the following hypothetical situation which illus-
trates the intimate connection between a decision-making process
(judicial review) and the content of a policy. As you read, pay
careful attention to the confusion in the minds of the participants
between these two factors.

In the first session of the Ninety-first Congress the Republicans
had a majority in both houses. The Republican party Congressional leadership, in accord with the party platform, sponsored

a series of bills intended to deal with a recognized national crisis. This proposed legislation was designed to assure American scientific, educational, and cultural pre-eminence in a continuing race with the Soviet Union, which had followed its early triumphs in space exploration with further advances, to the detriment of American prestige in the international arena.

The bills were all passed by substantial majorities in both houses of Congress, though a small number of Republicans and a few more Democrats voted against them. They provided for federal financial aid in large quantities to state, municipal, and private universities and research undertakings, including a new Institute for Space Research at Winnemac State College in Zenith and the Center for Advanced Social Science Research at the State University of Sunshine. They also provided grant-in-aid or other funds to increase teachers' salaries in elementary and secondary schools, public and private, and in state and privately supported colleges and universities. In addition they extended grants to qualified art centers and museums, music centers and symphony orchestras, and professional and community theatrical groups. In each case, however, an institution to qualify was required to satisfy the Secretary of Health, Education, and Welfare that it met certain detailed standards in terms of personnel, administration, curriculum, or program. These standards were specifically spelled out in the legislation.

Within the next year and a half cases involving all these measures reached the Supreme Court. In each case the Court, by votes of five to four, declared the legislation involved unconstitutional on the grounds that the federal government had no constitutional power to set specific standards for state institutions in the educational field, and that in so doing it was violating the Tenth Amendment, which reserves certain rights or powers to the states. These decisions brought the new scientific, educational, and cultural program to a halt, while the Soviet Union continued to make remarkable and well-propagandized progress in all these areas.

In the off-year congressional elections the Republican leaders in Congress decided to make the Supreme Court and its decisions an issue in the campaign. They charged that the Court was still living in the prespace age, and that "five justices who had barely heard of nuclear fission and spacecraft" stood in the way of a "vital program to raise American prestige in the present critical world conflict." One of their spokesmen, Senator Thaddeus Spinner of Winnemac, built his campaign around a proposal for legislation to abolish the Supreme Court's power to review lower-court decisions in which the constitutionality of legislation in the scientific, educational, and cultural areas was challenged. He described such legislation as "merely taxing and spending to promote the common defense and the general welfare of the United States," a power granted to Congress in Article I, Section 8 of the Constitution. Other Republican candidates across the nation endorsed Senator Spinner's proposal. The balloting resulted in the re-election of Spinner, and in addition the Republicans gained four new seats in the Senate for a total of 56, and twelve new seats in the House for a total of 245.

Early in the first session of the Ninety-second Congress, Senator Spinner introduced a bill to abolish the Supreme Court's jurisdiction over cases in which the constitutionality of scientific, educational, and cultural legislation was challenged. The Spinner bill was endorsed and supported by the Republican leadership in the Senate; however, the President, Winfield MacArthur, a Republican, announced that he would leave the decision on Spinner's bill entirely to Congress. Substantially all the Democrats in the Senate opposed the Spinner bill strongly, with their leaders declaring that they objected to the bill not because they were against federal aid to scientific, educational, and cultural activities, but because they believed that the Spiner bill violated the established rules of the American political system, threatened the system of separation of powers and judicial independence, and was in itself in violation of Article III of the Constitution. By the middle of March, however, the Spinner bill was passed by the Senate, 54 to 39, with only three Republicans voting nay.

With the conflict transferred to the House, opponents of the Spinner bill marshaled their forces to make a strong stand against the measure. The major opposition to the bill came from the following groups:

1. The National Chamber of Manufacturers and the Association of American Merchants, whose stand was supported by the American Lawyers' Association and other business groups. They attacked the Spinner bill as a threat to "the American way of conducting government and our Constitutional guarantees that the federal government shall be limited to its appropriate functions," and defended the Supreme Court as "our greatest bulwark" in this connection.

2. A group made up mostly of lawyers and professional people, called the Union for Constitutional Government, which had often defended individuals who claimed that their constitutional rights had been violated. The Union in a learned statement opposed the Spinner bill as "an improper way" to achieve "laudable objectives," and as a threat to "the basic American constitutional tradition, norms, and structure."

The support for the Spinner bill among organized interest group associations was not as powerful as the opposition. Such support, however, included:

1. The American Education Association, which counted among its members thousands of primary, secondary, and university teachers across the nation.

2. Several large, politically active labor unions, whose spokesmen argued that the Supreme Court had acted in a "backward, undemocratic, and irresponsible fashion," and that it was likely to do so again on such matters as labor and welfare legislation, unless "the people, through their elected representatives in Congress," made it clear that the Court could not continue in the "error of its present, five-to-four, arbitrary ways."

3. The American League to Defend World Democracy, an active citizen's group particularly concerned with foreign policy issues. Spokesmen for the League declared that the Supreme Court's decisions, if allowed to stand, threatened American ability "to maintain its position in the contest with the USSR in the form of world opinion."

The groups opposing the Spinner bill and those favoring it all engaged in widespread publicity campaigns and in active lobbying for their positions, utilizing all the legitimate means at their disposal. Reliable public opinion polls, which had shown large majorities favoring the original scientific, educational, and cultural proposals, now reported that 74 percent of all persons interviewed had an opinion on the Spinner bill, and that 58 percent of those who had an opinion favored the bill.

In the House the Spinner bill was referred to the Judiciary Committee, whose chairman was Representative Darius Greene. He soon secured a favorable committee report for the Spinner bill, unaltered. Republican leaders in the House decided that the bill should be brought up for debate as soon as possible. They felt that it was necessary to act promptly, since pressure against the bill was rapidly increasing.

The scheduled course of the bill was upset by Representative Martin Cockerell, Republican Chairman of the Rules Committee of the House. Representing a rural constituency in New York and serving his fourteenth consecutive term, he had recently become chairman of the Rules Committee following the death of the previous chairman. He had opposed the original science-education-culture legislation. He now announced in a press interview that he had "documentary evidence" that the president and the executive secretary of the American League to Defend World Democracy had formerly been members of groups which were on the Attorney General's list of subversive organizations. The next day, two more of the nine Republican members of the fifteen-member Rules Committee joined Chairman Cockerell in a public statement that there should be a "full investigation of the possible taint of Communism among the supporters of the Spinner bill," before the bill was called up for debate. Most Democrats in the House had opposed the Spinner bill from the beginning, as their fellow-partisans in the Senate had done, on the grounds that it was a threat to the American tradition and constitutional system. Now many Democratic leaders in the House joined in calling for "an investigation of possible sinister elements behind the bill."

It seemed possible, given all the forces, arguments, and pressures in the situation, that the Spinner bill might die in committee, or suffer defeat if it was called up in the House.

Review, in your text and in your class notes, materials relating to Congress, the legislative process, the judiciary and Supreme Court, separation of powers in the Constitution, and judicial review.

Assume that you are Distinguished Service Professor of Political Science at William Few University in Washington. An English acquaintance of yours, Merriman Cooke, comes to you to ask for your help. He has just been sent to the United States as correspondent for the Manchester *Defender*, an outstanding liberal, internationally minded journal of news and opinions. He shows you an editorial that has recently been printed in the *Trumpet*, an influential London weekly:

> The immediate issue before the American House of Representatives is whether to curb the irresponsible exercise of power by the Supreme Court in a critical situation. All sham stripped aside, the basic constitutional question is one that strikes at the heart of democratic government: whether the elected representatives of the people shall have the power to determine the policy of the government.
>
> The American people, after permitting the courts to veto policy decisions for many years, indicated in the last election that they do not think that a small group of men who are not responsible to the people should have that power. The intense campaign by various interest groups, and the distraction created by the present uproar over alleged Communism, do not alter the facts. They are that the Republican party, after waging a campaign on this very issue, was given a clear mandate by the people to curb the Supreme Court, if necessary, in order to enact its program.
>
> Nor should the House of Representatives let empty slogans and shibboleths, such as cries of separation of powers and judicial independence, obscure the real issue. Such notions are outmoded in the Space Age, in an era of world tension and danger in which democ-

racy must act if we are to stand up to the threat of Russian tyranny. The people have spoken: their will must be obeyed.

The Republican leadership in the House knows this, and should use the full force of its party's disciplinary machinery to thwart whatever undemocratic, obstructive plan may be in the mind of the members of the Rules Committee. The individual congressman, when faced with the pressures and diversions created by the Spinner bill's opponents, will surely realize that the source of his authority derives from the majority of his constituents who elected him to Congress, and that that majority spoke quite clearly in the elections last November.

You read and ponder this editorial. Cooke tells you that he and his paper, the *Defender,* looked favorably upon the original scientific, educational, and cultural legislation as a model Britain might follow, and that he and his paper were distressed and rather surprised that the Supreme Court could block such a fine program. He has just received a long cable from his editor. It suggests that the *Trumpet* editorial, though perhaps on the "right side," may be based on British misconceptions or erroneous assumptions about the American political tradition and political system and the way it works. It assigns Cooke to prepare a draft of an informed, thoughtful, balanced editorial-article, covering at least the following points:

1. A careful analysis of the *Trumpet* editorial, considering particularly in what ways, if any, it exhibits a misunderstanding of the nature and workings of the American political system.

2. In what ways he, Cooke, considers the Spinner bill defensible or indefensible as a means to remove the obstacles to the scientific-educational-cultural program, and his reasons in full for his judgments.

3. What the implications of the Spinner bill are beyond the immediate question of whether or not the original legislation is worthy of being passed.

4. Assuming that the Spinner bill might not pass, what other means, if any, are available within the rules of the American

political system to remove the obstacles to the original scientific-educational-cultural legislation.

But, Cooke says frankly, he does not think that he as an Englishman new to the United States has as yet sufficent understanding of American government, constitutional structure, and politics to explain the questions involved in the current complicated situation to the English readers of his paper, the *Defender;* or enough background to form an intelligent judgment on the *Trumpet* editorial or the Spinner bill. He asks you to prepare a draft of the editorial-article his editor has assigned him to do.

As a written assignment, or for class discussion, work out, in a clear, orderly, and complete way, what you would say in such a draft, covering all four of the points above.

PART III

A Nation of States

PROBLEM 9

The Nature of a Federal System

A federal system is one in which the individuals in a particular area are subject to control by *two* governments—the central or national government and the state government or (as in Canada) the provincial government. Each government has certain allocated powers. Each can exercise its own powers without the other preventing it from doing so. These powers are formally allocated to the national and state governments by the constitution of the country; and this formal allocation can be changed only by the process of constitutional amendment, a process in which both the national and state governments take part. In a nonfederal or "unitary" country such as Great Britain, there are of course local governments as well as a central government; but the authority and powers of the local governments are granted and can be taken away by the legislative action of the central government's Parliament or legislature. In contrast, in a federal union such as ours a mere act of Congress cannot increase the central government's constitutional authority or diminish the authority allocated by the constitution to the states, although either the national or the state governments may exercise more or less fully the powers that are granted, and the balance of effective powers between nation and states may shift from time to time. Of course, no state legislation can alter the scope of the national government's constitutional powers.

The Constitution of the United States spells out the powers of the national government, particularly in Article I, Section 8. The powers of the state governments are not spelled out; the states simply have all governmental powers not granted to the national government and not denied to the states (Amendment X). If a country's constitution specifically expressed all the states' powers, however, and then said that all other (unspecified) governmental powers belonged to the national government, that country, too, would have a *federal* system. It would fit the conception of a federal system given in the first paragraph.

The constitutional clauses providing the framework for federalism are the first chapter of the federal story in the United States. Many more chapters have been written since 1789, and numerous revisions and changes have characterized the developing federal system. These developments have been surrounded by some of the most bitter controversy in our political history, in particular during the period of the Civil War. The manner in which the individual states and the central government articulate their relationship and resolve their differences at any given time is determined by the expectations of the people and the nature of the problems at hand. The controversy of nation *versus* states should be examined as part of a historical context. As with any other political development, the increasing power of the national government *and* the increasing power of the state government have not taken place in a vacuum. Political developments reflect as well as influence social changes, economic happenings, technological advances, and international conditions.

In the following statement, C. Herman Pritchett briefly reviews some historical pressures influencing the growth of our federal system.[1]

---

[1] C. Herman Pritchett, *The American Constitutional System* (New York: McGraw-Hill Book Co., 1963), 29–30.

Looked at over the long reaches of United States history, there is an obvious trend toward increasing the powers and functions of the Federal government. Yet it is safe to say that Washington has never yet used all the powers it might justifiably claim under the Constitution, and there have been periods when the centralizing trend was reversed. The central-local relationship has been the product of political conflict, compromise, and consensus.

No detailed account of the politics of American federalism can be attempted here. Merely to follow the ebb and flow of centralizing trends through the major periods of our history is difficult. Of course the adoption of the Constitution was in itself a major victory of those forces favoring a strong national government, a victory which the Federalist party consolidated during the succeeding years under the astute guidance of Alexander Hamilton. But the anti-Federalist, states' rights forces were quickly rallied by Thomas Jefferson into a coalition strong enough to win the presidency in 1800 and ultimately to destroy the Federalist party itself. Once in office, however, Jefferson's Democrats by no means moved to dismantle the Federal establishment. In fact, Jefferson is particularly remembered for his bold move in purchasing the Louisiana Territory, in spite of his own expressed doubts about the constitutionality of such Federal action.

After the defeat of 1800, Federalist and nationalist ideology was kept alive by Chief Justice John Marshall on the Supreme Court. From 1801 to 1835 he devoted his immense judicial skill to broadening the constitutional interpretations of Federal power. His successor, Roger B. Taney, was of the opposite persuasion and the years up to the Civil War saw the pendulum swing back toward state powers.

Out of the Civil War the Republican party emerged as the nationalist voice of the industrial East and Midwest, and the Democratic party as the states' rights spokesman of the South. But the responsibility of government which came to the Democratic party with Woodrow Wilson's election in 1912, and the necessities of wartime organization, laid the foundation for a reversal of party positions which was fully consolidated by Franklin D. Roosevelt's New Deal. From 1932 to 1952 the general Republican position was critical of the centralization attending the government's depression, war, and cold-war programs. In 1952 a Republican president took office pledged to reverse these centralizing tides. Although President Eisenhower did largely succeed in halting further increases in Federal functions, his efforts to find services which might be discontinued or returned to the states were almost completely without result.

What this experience suggests is that shifts of power toward the central government are not the result of political ideologies or conspiracies or Supreme Court decisions, but are rather caused by the inexorable pressures of wars, depressions, new means of communication, urbanization, industrialization, technology, and all the other factors which have shrunk the size of our world and created problems so large and so urgent that of necessity they are pushed up to the national level for handling.

This process of centralization has not required the granting of new constitutional powers to the Federal government. . . . Such Federal authorizations as the commerce power and the taxing power have been fully adequate to support the greatly enlarged Federal establishment of the mid-twentieth century. For only one short period—from 1935 to 1937—did the Supreme Court construe the Constitution so narrowly as to threaten substantial Federal programs, but this crisis was soon past as the Court returned to long-established canons of broad construction of Federal powers. Particular programs of Federal centralization may be wise or unwise, but any program feasible enough politically to win the assent of Congress and the President is very unlikely to be lacking in satisfactory constitutional credentials.

Many observers of American politics have seriously misunderstood federalism because they assumed that the national government had one interest and that the states as a whole all shared another interest, and that these two interests were necessarily in opposition. Nothing in politics is quite this simple, and certainly the tremendously complex and extensive range of activities and relationships subsumed under the term "a federal system" cannot be comprehended with such a politically naive assumption. The following statement by Edward W. Weidner presents a more sophisticated perspective for viewing decision making in a federal system.[2]

[2] Edward W. Weidner, "Decision-Making in a Federal System," in Arthur W. Macmahon, ed., *Federalism Mature and Emergent* (Garden City: Doubleday & Co., 1955), *passim*.

There are countless causes for disagreement and conflict in a federal system. Personalities play a part. So do bothersome procedures, differences in the age and general background of administrators, poor communication, frequency of contact, and so on. However, all these factors are secondary in importance. They are relatively easy to deal with: procedures may be changed, frequency of contact increased, personnel shifted. This is not to say that such variables are never troublesome, for they are very troublesome on occasion. Rather, they are secondary in the sense that they are not of crucial importance to the participants in federal-state relations. The main concern of these participants, and, for that matter, most men, is to have their values [or interests] implemented to as great an extent as possible. Hence it is not surprising that the fundamental reason for disagreement and conflict in a federal system is that there is a lack of consensus as to what values [or interests] should be implemented. This is true in both the legislative and administrative spheres.

While differences on public policy or values are to be expected in a country containing as many heterogeneous elements as are to be found in the United States, it does not necessarily follow that officials in the several states will take one policy position and those of the national government another. Indeed, on an *a priori* basis it would seem surprising if this were the case, given the diversity of conditions in the several states and the fact that the union is made up of all states. "States' rights" is only one of numerous values held by state officials, and it is relatively unimportant to many of them . . . Consequently, usually national government officials can find many of their state counterparts who support national policy objectives and many others who oppose. And among the states, differences in values are the rule.

The framers of the Constitution clearly expected value or policy disagreements among the states as well as between the central government and one or more states. In his famous essay on faction . . . Madison emphasized that one of the main characteristics of the federal system would be the wide variation in the public policies that would be followed in the several states. To guard against the possible excesses of certain states the central government was given a core of power over matters deemed to be of nationwide concern. The states were expected to disagree among themselves over how the central government exercised its powers, and they were also expected to pursue different policies in matters that were reserved to them for decision.

Federalism implies that there is a variety of political values in a nation for which allowance needs to be made. It is more than a neutral centralizing or decentralizing device. Historically it has been a unifying device that took cognizance of the fact, among others, that agreement was lacking as to political goals and values, and hence single public policies for a society would be developed only in those matters over which the central government was given jurisdiction. State participation in public policy would automatically mean lack of uniformity and recognition of alternative and even competing political values. Viewed in this context, "states' rights" and the division of powers and responsibility for public services between the national and state governments become matters affecting substantive policy. They are matters upon which citizens will disagree in the proportion that their values or goals vary. . . .

Given the diverse policy objectives of the several states, it becomes unrealistic and impossible to expect of them any unified approach to important public problems. The United States learned at an early date, under the Articles of Confederation, how true this was. As a result of the experience with the Articles, the framers of the Constitution sought to vest the new central government with effective power over those matters that, in their opinion, required a single, unified policy or that required a minimum standard of performance. Foreign affairs and defense from external attacks were thought to be areas in which a single policy was necessary, while interstate commerce and the preservation of peace in the face of possible internal disturbances were thought to be areas in which minimum standards or assurances were needed.

The experience of 170 years ago is confirmed by contemporary events. The states have been unable to follow a single course even in such comparatively noncontroversial areas as are covered by the so-called uniformed state laws. If minimum standards are desired for the nation as a whole in a particular policy area such as health or welfare, it is the central government that must act to assure these ends. To leave the matter exclusively to the states means that there will be a variation in standards from very low to quite high. To set up a system of joint national-state participation means that standards and practices will vary much more than in a system of central action alone. It also means that some disagreement and conflict are inevitable because officials in various states will not all see eye-to-eye with those of the national government in terms of the objectives of the program.

This is not to blame the states in any way for their actions. . . . It would be unexpected and surprising if the several states followed identical or even similar courses of action on important public issues. The normal expectancy is that they will differ in greater or lesser degree among themselves in regard to policies they enact and in regard to the policies of the national government. . . .

The values that individuals hold are so diverse that there is no definable "state" point of view in intergovernmental relations as a whole. Even if the fifty governors were considered to be spokesmen for their entire states, there does not emerge a single state approach to intergovernmental relations. Occasionally all the governors will agree on a minor point or two but they have never agreed that a specific general reallocation of activities should take place between national and state governments. This is understandable since some of them are Democrats, some Republicans; some are liberals, others conservatives; some have national political ambitions, others do not; some come from poor states, others from well-to-do areas. These are only a few of the variables that affect the approach governors take on national-state relations. . . .

If the governors as a group cannot produce a state point of view on intergovernmental relations, there is little likelihood that it will be found elsewhere. State legislators or elected state administrators show no more tendency to agree than the governors. Political parties remain rather vague on the subject and public opinion gives no evidence of a state viewpoint. Therefore, the most that can be said is that state political officials who hold elective and/or general executive posts tend to defend state government as such more vigorously than others, but that this expediency value is often secondary to a number of other values these individuals hold.

If an analysis is made of the national government, similar conclusions are reached. Although there is only one unit of government here compared to the fifty states, a single approach to national-state relations is never found. Of course, to the extent that the President speaks for the entire government and has a clearly defined policy on relations with the several states, a "national" policy may be referred to. But such a policy is not binding on Congress, and in actual recent practice Congress, the various departments and agencies, and the President have not followed a unified policy on intergovernmental relations. No comprehensive policy has been put forth by the President or the Congress; for the most part a piecemeal approach has prevailed. The reason is not hard to find. A unified policy requires agreement or compromise on basic programmatic and expediency values and such a general agreement is difficult if not impossible to secure even when the President has a large majority in Congress. The major political parties are too diverse in composition, the interest groups too strong relative to special programs, and the determinants of values too varied. . . .

To summarize, the states disagree among themselves as to the major public policies they pursue and as to the desirability of particular national policies. They also differ even on smaller issues of national-state relations which may appear to be purely procedural in nature. The explanation is that public policies and even national-state procedures reflect particular values and on these there is lack of agreement. But it is not accurate to speak of the attitudes or policies of the several "states" or "national government." Public policies, and consequent disagreement and conflict, are not the product of entire units of government. Particular individuals, more or less associated in groups and to be found both within a unit of government and without, are the central forces behind the molding of public policy.

Even though the claim of states' rights within the federal system has depended on particular interests, which may not be the same in South Carolina or Mississippi as they are in New York or California, strong arguments have been made for states' rights as a value in itself. One of the most vigorous in recent times was offered by Frank Chodorov, from which the following excerpt is taken.[3]

States' rights sprang from fear and distrust of centralized government. It was not just a political theory worked out in an ivory tower. The 1776 Americans rose in revolt against an impersonal, self-sufficient, and arbitrary government and were in no mood to counte-

[3] Frank Chodorov, "States' Rights," *Human Events*, May 26, 1956.

nance an American Government built along the same lines. As every schoolboy should know, there were delegates to the Constitutional Convention who favored a government of practically unlimited powers, and they dropped the idea because they knew the American people would make short shrift of a constitution that embodied it. The genius of the Americans was against centralism.

But why? Why did they favor State governments as against the newly proposed government? Simply because they knew from experience, and some from history, that their freedom was less likely to be impinged upon by a government of "neighbors" than by one that was beyond their reach. One could keep one's eyes on the governor and the State legislature and, if need be, lay one's hands on them. The States cannot print money and there is a sharp limit to the deficit spending in which they can engage. Taxes could be held within reason, enforcement officers could not be arbitrary, the legislators would be more amenable to local customs.

Those early Americans knew what we have forgotten, that inherent in government, any government, is an insatiable appetite for power; that it could be contained only by the vigilance and opposition of the governed. But, how can you watch over and resist a government that is beyond reach, physically and fiscally? After all, one has enough to do to make a living. . . .

The recurring interest in States' rights in this country is but a version of the recurring struggle of the individual through history to attain a measure of freedom.

States' rights has nothing to do with sectional interests. It has nothing to do with the racial question or with the sedition laws of Pennsylvania. It has everything to do with freedom. It is a device invented by our forefathers to prevent the centralization of power, to the detriment of the individual. If the present enthusiasm for this doctrine is to be galvanized into a political movement, a movement to restore Article 10 to the Bill of Rights, it will be only because the spirit of freedom is not dead in this country.

Review in your text and class notes materials relating to federalism, the Articles of Confederation and the Constitution, and relations between the national and state governments. Then assume the existence of the following two situations:

A. You are a member of a Convention assembled to draft a constitution for a new nation composed of people living on four large islands, each about 100 miles distant from another. You have instructions from your Island legislature to establish a federal system for this imaginary country. The drafting committee has presented the following proposals:

1. There shall be a National Parliament, consisting of six representatives from each Island.
2. The National Parliament shall choose a Prime Minister, who shall be the Chief Executive and shall serve at the pleasure of the National Parliament.
3. There shall be a National Supreme Court, which shall decide controversies between the Islands, but shall not have power to hold acts of the National Parliament unconstitutional.
4. The National Parliament shall have authority to request each Island to furnish men, ships, and airplanes to compose the National Armed Services.
5. The National Parliament shall have the power to levy taxes, but no act of the National Parliament levying taxes shall be effective in any Island if the Island legislature passes a resolution prohibiting the collection of such taxes.
6. Each Island legislature shall have power within its Island to (a) establish public institutions of learning; (b) prevent crime; (c) promote sanitation and health, and preserve order; (d) impose taxes, including import taxes on any goods brought into the Island; (e) establish courts of justice; (f) regulate industry and labor.
7. The National Government shall have exclusive power to make treaties with foreign nations.
8. The enforcement of all National and Island laws, treaties, and regulations in each Island shall be the duty, exclusively, of the government of that Island.
9. All proper governmental powers not specifically mentioned

heretofore in this Constitution shall be vested in the National Parliament.

As a written exercise or for class discussion prepare a report to the Convention, indicating what changes must be made in this draft in order to establish a federal system.

B. Assume that you are a Professor of Government in one of the island universities. A former student who has been serving on the drafting committee writes you a letter about his experiences at the convention. His letter includes the following paragraphs:

Knowing your interest in federal systems, I am sure that you have been watching the developments at the convention. You may have read that I am the chairman of a subcommittee on "The Political Implications of the New Constitution." Our task is to specify the types of conflicts which might be generated among the Islands, and between each of the Islands and the National Government, if the present proposal is accepted. I have been looking over some of your lecture notes and ran across your thoughts on federal systems. Your argument, if I understand it correctly, went something as follows: the way in which a government distributes power among the various units which constitute the system has an impact on the kinds of political conflicts which may arise and on the methods by which conflicts are resolved. The passage as I copied it down read: "We should never forget a fundamental axiom in politics. The structure of government in a given society and the nature of that society's policy and procedural disagreements are closely connected. For example, when a federal system permits constituent units or states semi-independence, you can expect differences *among the units* as well as *between the individual states and the central authority.* When, for instance, the local units can nullify decisions of the central unit, the local unit which receives less benefit from a policy than one of its sister states is likely to veto that policy. However, there is a countervailing tendency in federal systems which modifies disagreement. Giving all units a share in ruling themselves reduces local resentment when things are not going according to the wishes of a particular locality. This is like the point often made about democracy—that participation in the acts of ruling and of being ruled results in acceptance by persons even of those laws which they feel run counter to their own interests."

These notes seem applicable to our situation and in particular to the sub-committee report for which I am responsible. I wonder if I might bother you for an extension of your ideas and for your thoughts on the proposal now before our convention. I need answers to the following questions:

1. If the proposal as it now stands is adopted, what kinds of conflicts are likely to occur between the National and Island governments, and among the Island governments?

2. What changes would you suggest in the present proposal which might eliminate or moderate these conflicts? Are these changes likely to create other kinds of problems?

3. If we accept the proposal exactly as it now reads, what kind of political developments would you predict for the next decade or so as they might involve relation between the National and Island governments?

If I could have your thoughts in a form which could be distributed to delegates, I am sure the entire convention would appreciate it.

Prepare a carefully argued statement about the political problems you think will be linked to the structure of the government as it is outlined in the proposal, in terms of answers to each of your former student's three questions.

PROBLEM 10

Nation and States: Cooperation
or Conflict?

WHAT should be the proper relationship between the national
government and the governments of the fifty states? This issue
has been debated and, on occasion, fought over, since independence was declared. It was at the heart of the controversies over
the Constitution, helped generate the Civil War, and it continues
to emerge in much of the American political dialogue. *"Centralization versus Decentralization"* is one way of putting the
question, and *"States' Rights"* is another slogan often employed.
But more than rhetoric is involved. The relationships between
nation and states affect many matters of public policy, and we
may best approach the many-faceted issue in terms of a policy
dispute.

*Read carefully the following statements in which opposing
points of view are presented concerning the desirability of federal grants-in-aid to help finance state governmental activities.
The first statement is from the report of an official government
commission set up by President Dwight D. Eisenhower; the
other two are instances of unofficial analysis or commentary.*

Statement I [1]

The National Government has used the grant-in-aid primarily to achieve some National objective, not merely to help States and local governments finance their activities. Specific objectives have been as varied as getting the farmer out of the mud, assisting the needy aged, providing lunches for school children, and preventing cancer. As a condition of financial assistance the National Government establishes requirements and provides administrative supervision.

The trend has been toward sharper definition of objectives, closer attention to conditions and requirements, more extensive administrative supervision, and recently, greater attention to relative State fiscal capacity. . . .

As a result of many developments, the grant has become a fully matured device of cooperative government. Its elements are well established: the objectives are defined; apportionment and matching formulas are laid down; conditions, minimum standards, and sanctions are prescribed; and provisions are made for administrative supervision. The maturing of the grant as a means of stimulating and shaping particular programs, as distinct from a subsidy device, is reflected not only in increasing legislative attention to conditions, standards, sanctions, and methods of supervision, but also in the evolution of National administrative machinery and procedures. The conditions attached to grants have not remained mere verbal expressions of National intent; National agencies have generally had funds and staff to make them effective.

In establishing grants-in-aid programs, the Congress has apparently regarded the disparities in fiscal capacity among the States as a matter of secondary importance. Almost all grants are available to all States, even the wealthiest; the formulas for allotting funds among the States and prescribing their matching expenditures do not usually reflect differences in State resources; and, further, many programs offer relatively small amounts of money.

During the past decade, however, the grant structure has been modified to recognize varying State fiscal capacity. In grants for

[1] The Commission on Intergovernmental Relations, *A Report to the President for Transmittal to Congress* (Washington, D.C.: Government Printing Office, 1955), 118–31, *passim*.

hospital construction, school lunches, and public health, for example, the National Government assumes more of the financial burden in States of lesser fiscal capacity than in more prosperous ones. Thus Mississippi, with the lowest per capita income, receives for hospital construction four and one-half times as much per capita as New York does. . . .

While the traditional type of grant-in-aid is to be preferred to the subsidy, substantial improvement is desirable in determining both when and how to use it. The Commission advances the following broad principles for guidance:

1. A grant should be made or continued only for a clearly indicated and presently important national objective. This calls for a searching and selective test of the justification for National participation. The point has been made . . . that existence of a national interest in an activity is not in itself enough to warrant National participation. Related questions are the relative importance of the national interest and the extent to which it may be served by State and local action. Consequently, where the activity is one normally considered the primary responsibility of state and local governments, substantial evidence should be required that National participation is necessary in order to protect or to promote the national interest.

2. Where National participation in an activity is determined to be desirable, the grant-in-aid should be employed only when it is found to be the most suitable form of National participation. It is important to compare the strong and weak points of the grant-in-aid device with those of other forms of National-State cooperation as well as with those of other forms of direct National action. It is likewise important to consider the types of objectives and situations for which the grant is best adapted. The probable effect on State or local governments is an important consideration.

3. Once it is decided that a grant-in-aid should be made, the grant should be carefully designed to achieve its specified objective. This requires careful attention to the shaping of apportionment formulas and matching requirements, the prescription of standards and conditions, and the provision for administrative machinery and procedures. Objectives as varied as cancer control, old-age assistance, highway construction, and forest fire prevention call for imaginative use of varied types of standards, controls, and fiscal formulas. . . .

Where used effectively, the grant not only has increased the volume of State and local services, but also has promoted higher standards both in service and in administration. These gains have come through the conditions attached to the grants and from the administrative leadership and supervision of National agencies. . . .

Notwithstanding its obvious usefulness, the grant-in-aid is not a panacea. Its limitations should be recognized along with its potentialities.

When only a few States are not providing reasonably adequate services, the grant-in-aid may be a costly way to stimulate these States. The National Government has not as yet developed a method of making grants that is flexible enough to meet such a limited objective. In this situation it remains to be explored whether National contractual services or loans, or direct National action on a limited basis, may be preferable alternatives to a grant.

Other limitations of the grant-in-aid are inherent in its complexity. It divides responsibility and offers ample opportunity to dodge it. There is joint provision of policy, finances, and administration, but National and State action do not mesh perfectly. The States must wait for Federal appropriations to plan their budgets for grant-aided activities; State policy must be geared to National standards and conditions; and State administrators must accept National supervision. In such a situation some friction cannot be avoided.

The Commission notes with concern that a number of State budget officers believe that grants-in-aid have distorted State budgets. Neither the nature nor the extent of the distortion, however, is entirely clear.

Almost of necessity, grants-in-aid in their early stages will induce State and local governments to adopt a pattern of expenditure in which the emphasis is somewhat different from that which would prevail in the absence of grants. Such an effect is indeed one of the major objectives of grants-in-aid, for the grant is intended to stimulate States and their localities to exert greater effort in aided programs than they presumably would exert without financial inducement from the National Government.

To say that States are not required to accept grants-in-aid is not a completely satisfactory answer. Although State authorities are not legally required to accept grants, they are under strong practical compulsion to do so. . . .

Mr. Burton (former Budget Director of New York State) observes: "The Commission has not emphasized sufficiently an inherent danger in the grant device. By this device the National Government spends money and exercises controls for programs which might not be supported if the National Government proposed to spend the money directly and exercise the control. In other words, the National Government does things indirectly which the public might not support if it attempted to do so directly." Governors Driscoll (New Jersey) and Thornton (Colorado) join in this view.

Governor Driscoll adds the following comment: "Woodrow Wilson once observed that we ought not to pit power against weakness. In the relationship between the National Government and the States, it is important that we maintain, as nearly as circumstances will permit, a reasonable balance between the collective powers and responsibilities of the States on the one hand and the National Government on the other.

"A grant-in-aid program should be the exception rather than the rule. Federal grants are not cloaked in magic. They derive their support from the same taxpayers that provide the wherewithal for all levels of government. If grants should become a part of every governmental activity, there is good reason to believe we would lose some of the substance of our present republican form of government and federal system. . . .

"It is conceded that grants-in-aid have upon a number of occasions performed a useful service. This fact, however, does not invite indiscriminate expansion. It has been suggested that grants to support specific programs may be made without strings and that controls need not be a conspicuous feature of these grants. An examination of the facts discloses that the grant has frequently been used to establish the authority of the National Government over State policies. . . .

"I do not question the right of the National Government to attach reasonable controls to its grants-in-aid. I do question the wisdom of adopting the costly and frequently confusing grant device as standard practice in government. A grant-in-aid program of all States, irrespective of relative need and ability to pay, is a cumbersome and expensive method of administration which negates many of the values of our American system of political decentralization.

"I find that grants-in-aid in practice result in a much greater impact of National policy on State budgets, administration, and policies than the Commission report indicates." Governors Battle (Virginia), Thornton, and Peterson (Nebraska) and Mr. Burton join in this view.

Statement II [2]

Sometime ago it appeared that the old controversy over the wisdom and validity of grants-in-aid was about over, and that future debate would center on the wisdom of specific programs; however, in the last few years the issue has been revived by a propaganda campaign which is lambasting indiscriminately all federal grants. This campaign is emanating from two major sources: some politicians and officials, particularly state officers, and business organizations—the trade associations, the chambers of commerce, and various organizations like the Committee for Constitutional Government, the Tax Foundation, and taxpayer groups.

The criticism from state officials proceeds from mixed motives. Partially it is constructive criticism intended to remedy specific defects in grant distribution formulae and administrative procedures. Often, however, it is tinged with parochialism and official self-esteem and self-interest. It is interesting to note that an ex-state politician sometimes acquires a national outlook when he migrates to Washington. Finally it should be noted that many state officials, in every state, are not hypercritical. In general, the professional administrators directly concerned with the operation of joint state-federal programs are favorable to federal grants, even staunch advocates. Unbridled criticism generally proceeds from elective political officials who have little first hand contact with grant programs. Indeed, there is a distinct inverse correlation between the volume of criticism and the amount of contact with and knowledge of federal programs. . . .

This propaganda would appear to be motivated by considerations more tangible than esoteric federalist theory. The basic objectives are: to reduce the level of government services in general and specifically to cut those services financed by federal grants, and

[2] Howard A. Hamilton, *Political Institutions* (Boston: Houghton Mifflin Co., 1962), 160–63.

finally, it is fervently hoped, to end the trend to expanding government functions. The strategy is based on the correct assumptions that if many of these functions can be divested of federal financial support they will languish from lack of funds. Furthermore a strong precedent will thereby be established against federal government "meddling" in such "local" matters. If it were likely that any reduction of federal grants would be fully offset by increased states and local expenditures for these government services, there would be less effort expended in anti-federal aid propaganda.

These assumptions are correct, because the taxing capacity of state and local governments is so inferior to that of the national government. Also, the influence of business groups on governmental policy is greater at the state and local levels than nationally. Reforms or new government services can be blocked more readily in fifty legislatures than in one Congress. Also, on occasion a state government can be bought. . . .

There is a close relationship between the grant-in-aid device and the development of government services in the United States, and to the "New Deal," the "positive state," the "social service state," or the "welfare state." These functions are vital to our domestic welfare and, if the grants are not suspended, are functions for which the public is likely to demand more rather than less expenditures in the future.

Those who criticize the "myth of grants-in-aid" are vigorously cultivating an assortment of myths, including:

1. The growth of federal aid is a manifestation of the insatiable appetite of federal bureaucrats for power. This myth is oblivious to the fact that grant-in-aid programs are established and their levels of operation are determined by Congress.

2. Federal-aid programs are administered by wasteful Washington bureaucrats. Actually 90 per cent of the administration, and any waste is by state government agencies.

3. Local and state governments are democratic, responsive to public opinion, and efficient, while the national government is irresponsible, tyrannical, wasteful, and inefficient. Actually there is little basis for such generalizations and this myth is irrelevant, since the grant programs involved all levels of government.

4. Federal grant programs are wasteful. The available evidence points to the contrary. Students are generally agreed that the

federal influence has improved the quality of state administration. For example, many states ignored civil service until they were obliged to apply merit principles in certain state agencies as a prerequisite for federal aid. Even today in about half the states civil service covers only those agencies administering federal aid.

5. All federal grants-in-aid produce centralization, wasteful duplication, and top-heavy bureaucracy. Although some centralization is inherent in the grant program, this generalization is untenable, because (a) the alternative to the grant pattern in some cases would be direct and exclusive federal administration, and (b) some grant programs represent distinct efforts to decentralize and to avert duplications.

The employment security and federal highway grant programs illustrate the utility of the grant-in-aid as a decentralizing instrument. Under the Constitution, the federal government has the specific responsibility "to establish post offices and post roads." Given the current scope of rural mail service, this would justify direct federal administration of nearly every road in the nation. However, the federal government has elected to achieve a national system of highways by the use of grants to states. Similarly Congress used the grant-in-aid device, coupled with the tax offset, to induce states to establish employment security programs, rather than establish such programs under direct federal administration.

6. Federal grants have led the national government to greatly increase its taxes, thereby making it difficult for states to raise revenue, and thus ham-stringing state and local government. The fallacy in this argument is that federal aid has not been a significant cause of the increase in federal taxation. Except in the period of the depression, grants have never constituted more than 8 per cent of the national budget. Actually, World War II expenditures and the postwar defense program have been responsible for high federal taxation. As Senator Paul Douglas has remarked, this isn't the welfare state; it is the warfare state.

7. Federal grants-in-aid are a hoax, a "losing game," because federal tax collections in X state exceed X state receipts for "so-called grants-in-aid." This favorite theme of newspaper editorials is ludicrously absurd. Aggregate federal grants could equal federal tax collections only if the federal government did nothing but distribute federal grants. The federal government has other and far

more expensive functions. This type of arithmetic has no validity, because federal grants, except for highway construction programs, are appropriated from the general fund rather than from dedicated revenues.

8. Federal grants help to destroy state and local government. On this point, Professor Joseph P. Harris states: "There is a good deal of misinformation and misconception about the alleged decline of the states and the usurpation of state and municipal functions by the federal government. The facts are that the state governments have never before played such an active, vital role in the life of the states. The whole character of state government has been radically changed during the last quarter of a century. Prior to the first World War, the states had only rudimentary departments or agencies, dealing with highways, health, welfare, education, labor, agriculture, and the regulation of utilities and business. Unemployment compensation, public employment offices, old-age assistance were unknown. In all these fields today, the state is rendering vital services to its citizens."

Statement III [3]

Local and state governments are beating so incessant a handout path to Washington, they are grabbing off more than a tenth of the national budget.

During the last decade, rising Federal aid to states and localities has increased from $2,700,000,000 in 1954 to $10,000,000,000 this year, according to computation by the *U. S. News and World Report.* Cash crutches to municipal and state administrations have multiplied almost four-fold within 10 years!

Every now and then Governors hold a conference where they talk heatedly about states' rights and the waning influence of their governments. Then they dash home, many of them cudgeling their brains for new ways to sidle up to the Washington trough.

With scarcely an exception, state regimes vie furiously to siphon more and more Federal funds to their "sovereign" commonwealths. They are bartering away this "sovereignty" as fast as they latch on to new hunks of Federal bounty.

The thickening trend toward Washington support of state and

[3] *St. Louis Globe-Democrat,* September 18, 1964.

local government is inexorably taking states' rights and self-determination down the low road to monolithic national government.

Regional self-reliance is steadily sloughing away. Now we have a major move in the Administration for a Cabinet-size urban department—just about as desperately needed as Uncle Sam needs another left hand. The "gimme march" on Washington goes on apace, a constantly increasing pace.

The biggest single subsidy, of course, goes to help build roads, which is not objectionable since highways are used by motorists from all over the country.

The second largest wedge of Potomac cake goes to public assistance for the needy—approximately $2,700,000,000 this year. About 7,000,000 persons are on these relief rolls, some receiving more than they ever made, or could make if they were able to work.

Other Federal funds are parceled out to hospital construction, school lunch programs, education, slum clearance, wildlife, even draining coal mines.

It is perhaps natural for a Governor, Mayor, or County Supervisor to maneuver a pipeline into the national Treasury which gathers enormous tax sheaves from everybody—certainly easier than to plaster local tax levies higher on burdened voters' backs.

Somehow most citizens have a miasmic conviction Washington's moneybags are bottomless. And even if they aren't, federalia isn't bothered by hundreds of billions of debt.

Too many of us fail to realize that no government can give anything for nothing. We are paying steeply; our taxes one way or another will go up; and that debt must eventually be paid—from the pocketbooks of us all.

There is no money-tree necromancy about Washington largesse.

The amount states, cities, hamlets dig annually from the Washington wallet is just about the size of the annual deficit. In effect we are living, states and cities, on Uncle's cuff.

The worst aspect of this Federal purse snatching is that states and municipalities are becoming more heavily subservient to Washington.

Many states, even big city exchequers would be bogged in the red now, if they didn't get a multi-million divvy from the central government.

Washington is perfectly willing. Recent administrations have increasingly been dedicated to the welfare state thesis—a soothing euphemism for mushrooming Federal control.

If things continue as they are, states will become mere political subdivisions of Washington government, Governors proconsuls of the Washington administration.

We are moving steadily, narcotically toward a one-state nation.

In your text and class notes, review materials concerning federal grants-in-aid and intergovernmental cooperation. Then assume the existence of the following situation:

In the near future a new and disabling disease appears in the United States. It attacks chiefly tiny infants and people in the age group from twenty-five to forty-five. Little is known about its transmission, but in different areas at different times it assumes epidemic proportions. Some distinguished doctors announce the discovery of a vaccine which, they say, will protect most individuals from infection or at least mitigate the effects of the disease. Other doctors express doubts as to the vaccine's effectiveness, and still others say that it will be fully effective only in cases where the people inoculated are less than thirty-five years of age. Limited experiments in mass inoculations give all three medical groups some evidence to support their different positions; but the most extensive experiment, on the Pacific Coast, has had such apparently good results that a widespread public demand has arisen for a national inoculation program. The arguments for a *public* and *national* program are that: (1) the vaccine is expensive, and unless it is provided by the government, poor people cannot afford it; and (2) the spread of the disease is not checked by state boundaries, so the problem is a national one.

MEANWHILE:

A. California has enacted a compulsory inoculation law, applicable to all persons thirty years of age and older; to finance this program, the state has increased its income tax 2 percent.

B. Wisconsin has enacted a voluntary inoculation law which provides that people in the age group twenty-one to thirty-five may be inoculated at state public health centers on payment of a $5 fee. People with low incomes are excused from paying any fee.

C. Inoculation bills introduced in the legislatures of New York, New Jersey, Massachusetts, Connecticut, and Pennsylvania have been badly defeated. There have been few cases of the disease in that area. All those states (let us assume) have recently tripled their budgets for mental hospitals and clinics, and have sharply increased their tax rates accordingly. Many of the leading physicians in that region are openly dubious about the effectiveness of the new vaccine.

D. Two southern governors have issued a joint statement as follows: "The people of each of the states can meet this crisis themselves, and have a right to do so without dictation from Washington."

E. A bill has been introduced by Representative Carl Claggett in the United States House of Representatives, providing that the United States should offer to match state appropriations up to $1,000,000 a year for any state for a state inoculation program.

To qualify for such a "matching grant" a state program, compulsory or voluntary, must (1) include free inoculation for all babies before the age of six months and all adults from twenty-five to thirty-five years of age; (2) provide for full monthly reports of health statistics to the United States Public Health Service on forms prescribed by the Public Health Service; and (3) provide that all nonmedical personnel employed in the program will be selected under a civil service or merit system approved by the Public Health Service.

Now assume that you are Assistant Secretary of the United States Department of Health, Education, and Welfare. Your chief, the Secretary, says to you: "The President has decided to make a televised address on this inoculation business. As you know, there's a grant-in-aid bill pending in the House. However, our party's leader in the House, Barney Keenan of Connecticut, just telephoned me to urge that the Administration go slow on this. He says that there is considerable opposition to the bill in

Congress, and it may not pass even though it has some strong support.

"Now what the President wants to do is to propose something that will be practical, will be consistent with our scheme of government, and will get this disease stopped if that's at all possible. Moreover, he wants to say something that will contribute to ending the whole nation-versus-states argument, if he can. He wants to point the way toward what he is calling a happier federalism.

"Please prepare a memorandum that I can give to the President to help him in writing his speech. Indicate the alternative possibilities, select the one that is most appropriate, and justify your choice of it. Explain why your plan meets most of the objections that may be raised. Be sure to provide at least a sketch of a broad approach to be taken toward the federalism issue in the future. How ought we to look at it? Also be sure to show the connection between the broad approach and the specifics of the Claggett bill."

Draft a memorandum for the Secretary to give to the President, covering all the points involved as clearly and fully as you can.

PART IV
Liberty and Equal Rights

PROBLEM 11
Freedom of Speech and Association

*Congress shall make no law . . . abridging the freedom of speech . . .
or the right of the people peaceably to assemble. . . .*

THESE words of the First Amendment appear to recognize that
everyone in the United States has a right to say whatever he likes
and join in whatever peaceable assemblies or associations he
likes. The Amendment prohibits Congress from interfering with
these rights, and, by judicial interpretation of the Fourteenth
Amendment, the individual's rights of free speech and association are likewise protected against interference by state or local
governments.

Yet the question remains, what *is* the freedom of speech and
association that cannot be "abridged" by government? It is not
absolute liberty of expression. No person has the right to slander
his neighbor with impunity or to utter obscenities even though
these activities involve "speech," or to meet together to conspire
to commit a felony. In cases such as these, courts have had no
difficulty in deciding that the rights are limited. The really difficult cases are those in which the "speech" or "assembly" is not

slanderous, or obscene, or conspiratorial, but where it is alleged to be "subversive" or "seditious." One of the basic reasons underlying the First Amendment is the belief that freedom to criticize the government is a necessary safeguard against tyranny. And it is fairly easy to claim that severe criticism is itself "subversive" or "seditious." Therefore, laws punishing alleged subversive or seditious utterances have been attacked as violating the very heart of the First Amendment. On the other hand, such laws have been defended as necessary to protect the country from foreign aggression or domestic violence. The right to freedom of speech or assembly, this argument contends, does not include the right to say things that weaken or endanger the national security.

In deciding such difficult cases, the courts have started with the assumption that freedom to criticize—even to dissent vehemently and to urge drastic changes in government—should be protected, unless there is a clear necessity for suppressing such speech or association. The problem is to decide when such a "clear necessity" exists. In trying to meet this problem the courts have been faced with a difficult and never-ending problem of drawing lines; of deciding from case to case that this speech or association is protected or that speech or association may be restricted. These lines have come to be phrased in verbal formulae, which the courts then use to guide them in making future decisions.

Read carefully and thoughtfully the statements below in which are quoted five often cited principles for deciding cases concerning free speech or association.

1. Justice Holmes [1]

We admit that in many places and in ordinary times the defendants in saying all that was said in the circular would have been within their constitutional rights. But the character of every act depends upon the circumstances in which it is done. . . . The ques-

[1] *Schenck* v. *U.S.*, 249 U.S. 47 (1919).

tion in every case is whether the words are used in such circumstances and are of such a nature as to create a clear and present danger that they will bring about the substantive evils that Congress has a right to prevent. It is a question of proximity and degree. When a nation is at war many things that might be said in time of peace are such a hindrance to its effort that their utterance will not be endured so long as men fight and that no Court could regard them as protected by any constitutional right.

II. *Justice Brandeis* [2]

Those who won our independence by revolution were not cowards. They did not fear political change. They did not exalt order at the cost of liberty. To courageous, self-reliant men, with confidence in the power of free and fearless reasoning applied through the processes of popular government, no danger flowing from speech can be deemed clear and present, unless the incidence of the evil apprehended is so imminent that it may befall before there is opportunity for full discussion. If there be time to expose through discussion the falsehood and fallacies, to avert the evil by the processes of education, the remedy to be applied is more speech, not enforced silence. Only an emergency can justify repression. Such must be the rule if authority is to be reconciled with freedom. Such, in my opinion, is the command of the Constitution. It is, therefore, always open to Americans to challenge a law abridging free speech and assembly by showing that there was no emergency justifying it.

III. *Chief Justice Vinson* [3]

In this case we are squarely presented with the application of the "clear and present danger" test, and must decide what that phrase imports. We first note that many of the cases in which this Court has reversed convictions by use of this or similar tests have been based on the fact that the interest which the State was attempting to protect was itself too insubstantial to warrant restriction of speech.

[2] Concurring, in *Whitney* v. *California*, 274 U.S. 357 (1927).
[3] *Dennis* v. *U.S.*, 341 U.S. 494 (1951).

. . . [But] overthrow of the Government by force and violence is certainly a substantial enough interest for the Government to limit speech. Indeed, this is the ultimate value of any society, for if a society cannot protect its very structure from armed internal attack, it must follow that no subordinate value can be protected. If, then, this interest may be protected, the literal problem which is presented is what has been meant by the use of the phrase "clear and present danger" of the utterances bringing about the evil within the power of Congress to punish. . . .

Obviously, the words cannot mean that before the Government may act, it must wait until the *putsch* is about to be executed, the plans have been laid and the signal is awaited. If Government is aware that a group aiming at its overthrow is attempting to indoctrinate its members and to commit them to a course whereby they will strike when the leaders feel the circumstances permit, action by the Government is required. The argument that there is no need for Government to concern itself, for Government is strong, it possesses ample powers to put down a rebellion, it may defeat the revolution with ease needs no answer. For that is not the question. Certainly an attempt to overthrow the Government by force, even though doomed from the outset because of inadequate numbers or power of the revolutionists, is a sufficient evil for Congress to prevent. The damage which such attempts create both physically and politically to a nation makes it impossible to measure the validity in terms of the probability of success, or the immediacy of a successful attempt. In the instant case the trial judge charged the jury that they could not convict unless they found that petitioners intended to overthrow the Government "as speedily as circumstances would permit." This does not mean, and could not properly mean that they would not strike until there was certainty of success. What was meant was that the revolutionists would strike when they thought the time was ripe. We must therefore reject the contention that success or probability of success is the criterion.

[With respect to the "clear and present danger" test] . . . Chief Judge Learned Hand, writing for the majority below, interpreted the phrase as follows: "In each case (courts) must ask whether the gravity of the 'evil,' discounted by its improbability, justifies such invasion of free speech as is necessary to avoid the danger." . . . We adopt this statement of the rule. As articulated by Chief Judge

Hand, it is as succinct and inclusive as any other we might devise at this time. It takes into consideration those factors which we deem relevant, and relates their significances. More we cannot expect from words. . . .

IV. *Justice Harlan* [4]

The essence of the Dennis holding was that indoctrination of a group in preparation for future violent action, as well as exhortation to immediate action, by advocacy found to be directed to "action for the accomplishment" of forcible overthrow, to violence "as a rule or principle of action," and employing "language of incitement," is not constitutionally protected when the group is of sufficient size and cohesiveness, is sufficiently oriented towards action, and other circumstances are such as reasonably to justify apprehension that action will occur. . . . Mere doctrinal justification of forcible overthrow, if engaged in with the intent to accomplish overthrow . . . even though uttered with the hope that it may ultimately lead to violent revolution, is too remote from concrete action to be regarded as the kind of indoctrination preparatory to action which was condemned in Dennis. . . . The essential distinction is that those to whom the advocacy is addressed must be urged to *do* something, now or in the future, rather than merely to *believe* in something.

V. *Justice Goldberg* [5]

This case is the culmination of protracted litigation involving legislative investigating committees of the State of Florida and the Miami branch of the National Association for the Advancement of Colored People. . . . [A] committee of the Florida Legislature . . . held hearings and sought by subpoena to obtain the entire membership list of the Miami branch of the NAACP; production was refused . . . the committee chairman . . . declared the hearings would be "concerned with the activities of various organizations which have been or presently are operating in the State in the fields of . . . race

[4] *Yates* v. *U.S.*, 354 U.S. 298 (1957).
[5] *Gibson* v. *Florida Legislative Investigation Committee,* 372 U.S. 539 (1963).

relations [and] would be directed to Communists and Communist activities, including infiltration of Communists into [such] organizations . . ." [The President of the Miami branch refused] to produce his organization's membership lists . . . on the ground that [to do so] would interfere with the free exercise of Fourteenth Amendment associational rights of members. . . . "It is beyond debate that freedom to engage in association for the advancement of beliefs and ideas is an inseparable aspect of the 'liberty' assumed by the Due Process Clause of the Fourteenth Amendment, which embraces freedom of speech." The First and Fourteenth Amendment rights of free speech and free association . . . "need breathing space to survive." . . . This Court has recognized the vital relationship between freedom to associate and privacy in one's associations. . . . Inviolability of privacy in group association may in many circumstances be indispensable to preservation of freedom of association, particularly where a group espouses dissident beliefs . . . We hold that groups which themselves are neither engaged in subversive or other illegal or improper activities nor demonstrated to have any substantial connections with such activities are to be protected in their rights of free and private association. . . . To permit legislative inquiry . . . would be to sanction unjustified and unwarranted intrusion into the very heart of the constitutional privilege . . .

Review carefully the materials in your text and lecture notes relating to problems of free speech and association.

You are a justice of the United States Supreme Court. The cases listed below have come before the court on appeal. In each of them the defendant was convicted as charged. Each defendant argues that the activities for which he is being punished are protected by the First or Fourteenth Amendment of the Constitution. You must decide whether to uphold the convictions or reverse them and set the defendant free. The statements quoted above are the legal rules you are to follow in determining what the First Amendment means.

A. The little town of Valleyville lies on the banks of the Blake River just below a large dam. Behind the dam is a reservoir large enough to flood the entire valley and easily wash Valleyville off the face of the earth. One evening James Jones raced through the town shouting "The dam is bust !" Appropriate sound effects were heard coming from the dam, and the frightened people ran for the hills without stopping to investigate. Before they could return, thieves looted the houses and made off with a sizeable haul. Jones thought all this was a huge joke, which apparently was what he was after in the first place. There was no evidence linking him to the thieves. However, he was arrested and convicted of disturbing the peace, in violation of the following local law: [6]

Any person who with intent to provoke a breach of the peace, or whereby a breach of the peace may be occasioned, commits any of the following acts shall be deemed to have committed the offense of disorderly conduct:

1. Uses offensive, disorderly, threatening, abusive or insulting language, conduct or behavior;

2. Acts in such a manner as to annoy, disturb, interfere with, obstruct, or be offensive to others; . . .

B. The United States has recently been having repeated diplomatic difficulties with the new but large and potentially powerful nation of Graustark. In a public meeting a lecturer, one Orville Lyceum, reports that on a recent visit to Graustark he observed enormous strides being made in the economic and social development of that country. Lyceum suggests that the "Graustarkian way" is admirably suited to the rapid development of new nations. He concludes with the observation that Congressional government is not well suited to the conditions of modern life, and that the United States could learn much from the methods of the new nation. Graustark is an absolute monarchy in which the king rules by divine right. The king owns all the property in the country, with which he may and does do exactly as he pleases. Many observers have disagreed with Lyceum's estimate of Graustarkian accomplishments, and since the diplomatic conflicts began, those

[6] Sec. 722 of the Penal Law of New York, quoted in Thomas Emerson and David Haber, *Political and Civil Rights in the United States* (Buffalo: Dennis & Co., 1952), 666.

who spoke in praise of Graustark have found themselves highly unpopular.

Lyceum is indicted and convicted under the following federal legislation: [7]

And be it further enacted, that if any person shall write, print, utter or publish, or shall cause to procure to be written, printed, uttered, or published, or shall knowingly and willingly assist or aid in writing, printing, uttering, or publishing any false, scandalous and malicious writing or writings against the government of the United States, or either house of the Congress of the United States, or the President of the United States, with intent to defame the said government, or either house of the said Congress, or the said President, or to bring them, or either of them, into contempt or disrepute; or to bring excitement against them, or either or any of them, the hatred of the good people of the United States, or to stir up sedition within the United States, or to excite any unlawful combinations therein, for opposing or resisting any law of the United States, or any act of the President of the United States, done in pursuance of any such law, or of the powers in him vested by the Constitution of the United States, or to resist, oppose, or defeat any such law or act, or to aid, encourage or abet any hostile designs of any foreign nation against the United States, their people or government, then such person, being thereof convicted before any court of the United States having jurisdiction thereof, shall be punished by a fine not exceeding two thousand dollars, and by imprisonment not exceeding two years.

C. John Alden, an elderly man of old New England family, has recently taken to making speeches on the causes and cures of the decline of New England. The essence of his argument is that New England has declined in economic and social influence because "the system" is rotten to the core. Otherwise, argues Alden, New England would have retained its dominance. Obviously the way to cure this evil is to destroy "the system." Alden is never very clear about what constitutes "the system," but he has made reference from time to time to "rascally rulers, state and national." He has advocated seizing property "owned by outsid-

[7] 1 *Statutes* 570, Sec. 2; cited in *ibid.*, 369.

ers." Doctors have attested that Alden is not insane. Although he has often found his audiences sympathetic, particularly in mill towns and other places suffering from unemployment, Alden has no organized backing and he himself has always operated entirely on his own. There have been rumors of financial and moral support from abroad, but nothing more is known about this aspect of the case.

Alden is convicted under the following federal legislation: [8]

It shall be unlawful for any person to knowingly or willfully advocate, abet, advise, or teach the duty, necessity, desirability, or propriety of overthrowing, or destroying any government in the United States by force or violence, or by the assassination of any officer of any such government.

D. The Lysistrata Society for the Advancement of Women's Rights, an association devoted to the cause of full political equality for women, has been especially active in the midwestern states, and particularly in the state of Winnemac. They have undertaken a campaign to boycott and picket every merchant in the state who does not pledge his support to female candidates who have been entered in the primaries of both parties for every statewide office. The Lysistrata Society has demanded that every businessman give prominent display to their candidates by setting up posters or signs in their places of business or suffer the consequences of Society pressure. The Retail Merchants Association has become very upset about this campaign. They charge that the Lysistrata Society is a front group financed by a few chain stores who hope through this pressure to drive many of the small merchants out of business. The merchants are convinced that a public investigation will reveal this background, and they have brought pressure on the Winnemac state legislature to conduct such an inquiry. The legislature establishes an investigating committee and gives it the power to compel testimony, and to punish those who refuse to testify. Hearings are held, and the first witness before the committee is Emmiline Woodhurst. Miss

[8] 54 *Statutes* 670–671, Sec. 2 [A(1)]; cited in *ibid.*, 461–62.

Woodhurst refuses to testify. She declines to answer any questions concerning the officers, finances, membership, past activities, or future plans of the organization. In a rather florid speech she denounces the committee and its inquiry and claims that it has no right to question her. She says that the First and Fourteenth Amendments justify her refusal to answer. She is convicted of contempt of the legislature.

For each of the cases described:

1. Decide whether the defendant has violated the statute in question. Has he or she really done things that the law forbids?

2. Decide in each case whether the law can be applied to the facts without overstepping the limits of the First or Fourteenth Amendments.

3. As you reach your conclusions in 2, carefully and explicitly compare your decisions with *each* of the five precedent cases quoted.

Does your decision "square" with each of these statements of principles? If not, why not?

PROBLEM 12

The Equal Protection of the Laws

EQUALITY of all men before the law is one of the cardinal principles of justice as that word has come to be defined and applied in the United States. "Equal rights for all, special privileges for none," and other similar aphorisms by which American government has traditionally been characterized, convey that no rules of a society that calls itself free can impose prejudicial restrictions on some of its people or reserve special privileges for others. Thus when the Fourteenth Amendment provided that no state shall *"deny to any person within its jurisdiction the equal protection of the laws,"* the Constitution was made consonant with such concepts of justice.

Of course, equal protection does not require that all men be treated with literal equality by government. Persons are constantly being classified by governmental actions for one purpose or another, from taxation to farm price supports, from military service to welfare benefits. Few men receive exactly the same treatment from public officials because few men find themselves in exactly similar circumstances of life. But the great significance of the equal protection clause is that it permits only "reasonable" classifications to be made. Rich men are required to pay higher taxes than poor men on the maxim that there is a reasonable connection between the ability to pay and the obligation to pay. Therefore, government may choose to classify men on the basis of income for purposes of allocating the tax burden. On the other hand, there is no reasonable relation between the color of a man's hair and any legitimate purpose of government, so a state could not impose special literacy requirements for voting on all red-headed men.

Not only must the classification meet the test of "reasonableness," but the purpose of the classification must be one properly within the authority of government. Thus while a reasonable classification for purposes of taxation is permitted, even a reasonable classification for the purpose of suppressing newspapers would be invalid.

Read carefully the following judicial statements of the meaning of the equal protection clause:

I. Chief Justice Vinson [1]

These cases present for our consideration questions relating to the validity of court enforcement of private agreements, generally described as restrictive covenants, which have as their purpose the exclusion of persons of designated race or color from the ownership or occupancy of real property. Basic constitutional issues of obvious importance have been raised. . . .

It cannot be doubted that among the civil rights intended to be protected from discriminatory state action by the Fourteenth Amendment are the rights to acquire, enjoy, own and dispose of property. Equality in the enjoyment of property rights was regarded by the framers of that Amendment as an essential pre-condition to the realization of other basic civil rights and liberties which the Amendment was intended to guarantee . . . the present cases . . . do not involve action by state legislatures or city councils. Here the particular patterns of discrimination and the areas in which the restrictions are to operate, are determined, in the first instance, by the terms of agreements among private individuals. Participation of the State consists in the enforcement of the restrictions so defined. The crucial issue with which we are here confronted is whether this distinction removes these cases from the operation of the prohibitory provisions of the Fourteenth Amendment . . . the principle has become firmly embedded in our constitutional law that the action

[1] *Shelley v. Kraemer*, 334 U.S. 1 (1948).

inhibited by the first section of the Fourteenth Amendment is only such action as may fairly be said to be that of the States. That Amendment erects no shield against merely private conduct, however discriminatory or wrongful. . . .

That the action of state courts and judicial officers in their official capacities is to be regarded as action of the State within the meaning of the Fourteenth Amendment, is a proposition which has long been established by decisions of this Court. . . .

These are not cases, as has been suggested, in which the States have merely abstained from action, leaving private individuals free to impose such discriminations as they see fit. Rather, these are cases in which the States have made available to such individuals the full coercive power of government to deny to petitioners, on the grounds of race or color, the enjoyment of property rights in premises which petitioners are willing and financially able to acquire and which the grantors are willing to sell. The difference between judicial enforcement and non-enforcement of the restrictive covenants is the difference to petitioners between being denied rights of property available to other members of the community and being accorded full enjoyment of those rights on an equal footing. . . .

We hold that in granting judicial enforcement of the restrictive agreements in these cases, the States have denied petitioners the equal protection of the laws and that, therefore, the action of the state courts cannot stand.

II. Chief Justice Warren [2]

In the instant cases . . . the Negro and white schools involved have been equalized, or are being equalized with respect to buildings, curricula, qualifications and salaries of teachers, and other "tangible" factors. Our decision, therefore, cannot turn on merely a comparison of these tangible factors in the Negro and white schools involved in each of the cases. We must look instead to the effect of segregation itself on public education.

In approaching this problem, we cannot turn the clock back to 1868 when the [Fourteenth] Amendment was adopted, or even to 1896 when *Plessy* v. *Ferguson* was written. We must consider pub-

[2] *Brown* v. *Board of Education,* 347 U.S. 483 (1954).

lic education in the light of its full development and its present place in American life throughout the Nation. Only in this way can it be determined if segregation in public schools deprives these plaintiffs of the equal protection of the laws.

Today, education is perhaps the most important function of state and local governments. Compulsory school attendance laws and the great expenditures for education both demonstrate our recognition of the importance of education to our democratic society. It is required in the performance of our most basic public responsibilities, even service in the armed forces. It is the very foundation of good citizenship. Today it is a principal instrument in awakening the child to cultural values, in preparing him for later professional training, and in helping him to adjust normally to his environment. In these days, it is doubtful that any child may reasonably be expected to succeed in life if he is denied the opportunity of an education. Such an opportunity, where the state has undertaken to provide it, is a right which must be made available to all on equal terms.

We come then to the question presented: Does segregation of children in public schools solely on the basis of race, even though the physical facilities and other "tangible" factors may be equal, deprive the children of the minority group of equal educational opportunities? We believe that it does.

In *Sweatt* v. *Painter, supra,* in finding that a segregated law school for Negroes could not provide them equal educational opportunities, this Court relied in large part on "those qualities which are incapable of objective measurement but which make for greatness in a law school." . . . Such considerations apply with added force to children in grade and high schools. To separate them from others of similar age and qualifications solely because of their race generates a feeling of inferiority as to their status in the community that may affect their hearts and minds in a way unlikely ever to be undone. The effect of this separation on their educational opportunities was well stated by a finding in the Kansas case by a court which nevertheless felt compelled to rule against the Negro plaintiffs: "Segregation of white and colored children in public schools has a detrimental effect upon the colored children. The impact is greater when it has the sanction of the law; for the policy of separating the races is usually interpreted as denoting the inferiority of the negro group. A sense of inferiority affects the motivation of a child to learn. Segregation with the sanction of law, therefore, has a tendency to [retard] the educational and mental development of negro children and to deprive them of some of the benefits they would receive in a racial[ly] integrated school system." Whatever may have been the extent of psychological knowledge at the time of *Plessy* v. *Ferguson,* this finding is amply supported by modern authority. Any language in *Plessy* v. *Ferguson* contrary to this finding is rejected.

We conclude that in the field of public education the doctrine of "separate but equal" has no place. Separate educational facilities are inherently unequal. Therefore, we hold that the plaintiffs and others similarly situated for whom the actions have been brought are, by reason of the segregation complained of, deprived of the equal protection of the laws guaranteed by the Fourteenth Amendment.

III. Chief Justice Warren [3]

One must ever be aware that the Constitution forbids "sophisticated as well as simple-minded modes of discrimination." . . . Representative government is in essence self-government through the medium of elected representatives of the people, and each and every citizen has an inalienable right to full and effective participation in the political processes of his state's legislative bodies. Most citizens can achieve this participation only as qualified voters through the election of legislators to represent them. Full and effective participation by all citizens in state government requires, therefore, that each citizen have an equally effective voice in the election of members of his state legislature. . . . Since the achieving of fair and effective representation for all citizens is the basic aim of legislative apportionment, we conclude that the Equal Protection Clause guarantees the opportunity for equal participation by all voters in the election of state legislators.

Review materials in your text and in your lecture notes dealing with equal protection of the laws.

In each of the following cases a claim is made that a person is suffering from discrimination which is unjust and which denies

[3] *Reynolds* v. *Sims,* 12 L. ed. 2d 506 (1964).

to the individual the equal protection of the laws as guaranteed by the Fourteenth Amendment.

A. Jay Hanna claims that his eighteen-year-old son has failed a civil service examination with a score four points under the minimum passing mark set by the Catawba State Civil Service Commission. As a result of failing the examination, young Hanna has not been able to secure a job as a file clerk with the State Department of Finance, on which his heart was set. Young Hanna says that the reason for his failure was his inability to handle higher mathematics, but upon investigation it appears that the questions were fairly simple arithmetic problems.

B. J. A. Jakasian, president of the Armenian American Federation, claims that his son's application for admission to Winnemac State University has been turned down along with the applications of every other prospective student of the past several years whose name ended in the letters "ian," the usual ending for Armenian names. In each case the University has claimed that lack of housing facilities was the reason for denying the applications, but Jakasian has data showing that the rejected applicants' grades on the entrance examinations were satisfactory and that other male applicants have invariably been admitted provided their grades were adequate. Jakasian also has some press clippings in which the president of the University Board of Trustees is reported as having made insulting remarks about Armenians.

C. The State University of Catawba provides that all undergraduate male students must take military training if physically able to do so. Any prospective students who claim religious scruples against such training are admitted to the University but are required to attend an extension branch in another city during their first two years. The extension branch offers only a two-year program, and its academic standing is far below that of the world-famous Catawba U. William Penn, a Quaker and a pacifist, claims that he has been "shunted off to a second-rate school" in violation of his constitutional rights.

D. John Wright, a Negro, has been refused admission to the examination given by the State of Winnemac for the licensing of architects. The state board of examiners claims that Wright's academic preparation is inadequate for admission to the examination. Wright graduated in 1946 from Winnemac A. & I., then a state-supported college for Negroes, where he took all the courses available that related to architecture. Admittedly, however, these courses were not on a par, in quantity or quality, with those of other colleges providing architectural training. At the time Wright attended it, Winnemac A. & I. was the only state-supported college in Winnemac that Negroes were allowed to attend.

E. Leonard Vinci has graduated from Eli University with the highest honors in physics, despite the fact that he has just celebrated his eighteenth birthday. His IQ has been measured at 197. His published poetry has won several prizes, a philosophical essay has received international acclaim, and he has composed several pieces of chamber music. He has supported his wife and year-old child by writing and working part-time as a truck driver. Leonard is deeply interested in politics and wants to participate fully in the political process. He contends that the Fourteenth Amendment guarantee of equal protection of the laws includes the right for him to vote and to run for political office. He claims that state laws denying him these rights because he is not yet twenty-one violate the Federal Constitution.

As a written exercise or for class discussion, for each of the five cases:

1. Outline all the arguments that might be used to support the claim made in each case. Show in what respects it may be argued that the person is suffering an injustice, and in what ways this injustice violates his constitutional right to equal protection of the laws.

2. Outline the counterarguments that might be used.

3. Decide whether the equal protection clause of the Fourteenth Amendment has or has not been violated. Explain fully the reasons for your decisions, and be sure to relate them to the relevant portions of the Supreme Court decisions quoted above.

PART V

Actors in the Political Arena

PROBLEM 13

Interest Groups in the Political Process

BROADLY speaking, a political interest group may be thought of as a number of people who share some sense of identity with one another and make some common claims or demands on government. Thus manufacturers, wheat farmers, factory workers, Italo-Americans, teachers, Negroes, cotton growers, or doctors may all be thought of as constituting interest groups in American politics today. In the twentieth century most such loose groupings have come to be represented by organized associations, and have taken on the status of organized interest groups or pressure groups. Associations like the National Association of Manufacturers, the American Farm Bureau Federation, the American Federation of Labor-Congress of Industrial Organizations, the National Association for the Advancement of Colored People and the Congress on Racial Equality, or the American Medical Association, all attempt to articulate the interests they represent and devise techniques to make their demands on government as effective as possible. Many techniques of strategy and tactics have become standardized in the American pressure-group system, but it must be borne in mind that in certain situations less conventional techniques may seem more useful. Thus in a revolutionary situation a revolutionary movement might use force outside of the rules of the existing political system. In another kind of situation still other kinds of interest groups might use mass demonstrations or similar techniques, perhaps partly within or partly outside of the rules or conventional procedures of politics. The choice of techniques depends heavily on the kind of interest group involved, its situation, its goals and resources of power or influence, its leadership, and the techniques the group thinks will bring it success.

Review in your text and in your lecture notes materials relating to interest-group activity, and then read carefully the following statement.[1]

Individual interest groups generally function in a pragmatic and opportunistic fashion, using any method or technique which they believe will serve their purpose effectively. Undoubtedly dictating most pressure group activity is the criterion: what action will produce the maximum desired result with the minimum expenditure of time and resources. The techniques and tactics which any particular group employs will be determined largely by such factors as size and geographic distribution of the membership, cohesion of membership, financial resources, prestige position of the organization, quality of leadership and staff, and relations with the political parties and other organized groups.

Where are pressures applied? Depending on the aims and characteristics of the individual organization, an interest group may attempt to influence its own membership; other pressure groups; the electoral process; the legislative, executive, and judicial branches of the government; and public opinion.

One characteristic of virtually every large organization is the tendency for a few individuals to gain effective control of the group. In some associations the officers may enjoy near permanent tenure, and in others they may be selected from a relatively small elite.

[1] Henry A. Turner, "How Pressure Groups Operate," *Annals of the American Academy of Political and Social Science,* 319 (1958), 64–69, 71.

These officers and the paid bureaucracy in many instances literally run the organization. Hence, from the standpoint of origination of policy, they become the organization.

In some organized groups, a considerable portion of the time and energy of the staff may be expended to influence the members of the group and potential members. Most associations wish to retain and enlarge their membership—if for no other reason—in order to increase the political strength of the group. In group meetings, publications, and direct communications to the membership, efforts are also directed toward producing greater group cohesion, to "educating" the membership to accept and support the policies of the organization, and to inducing the members to engage in desired political activity. Types of activity urged on group members include: registering and voting; working in political campaigns and making financial contributions; and communicating via personal conversations, letters, telegrams, and telephone calls to public officials and those who control the media of mass communication.

In a sense, pressure groups lobby other pressure groups. Organized interest groups seek the active support of their allies or potential allies, the endorsement of groups less directly interested, and the neutralization of their opponents. Such co-operation may be achieved by one group merely activating another, by promising future assistance, or by making concessions or compromises. In some cases co-operating groups develop only informal working arrangements, but there are instances in which organizations have signed formal agreements to pool their political efforts in working for a program. Examples may also be cited of groups co-operating through interlocking directorates. . . .

By definition, pressure groups are non-partisan organizations which attempt to influence some phase of public policy. They do not, themselves, draft party platforms or nominate candidates for public office. Pressure associations do, however, appear before the resolutions committees of the political parties to urge the endorsement of their programs as planks in the parties' platforms. They often attempt to secure the endorsement of both major parties and thus remove their program from the arena of partisan controversy. Many groups are also active in the nomination and election of party members to political offices.

Most interest groups which are active in election campaigns will support a candidate of either party if his general outlook is similar to that of the group. Thus organized labor has followed the policy, first prescribed by Samuel Gompers, of "rewarding friends and punishing enemies" by support or opposition in campaigns and at the polls. Apparently, however, some labor, business, farm, professional, and other organizations have found most of their "friends" in one party and most of their "enemies" in the other, for they have tended to align themselves with one or the other of the two major parties.

The most common method of aiding in a campaign is through financial contribution. Labor unions and corporations are prohibited by law from making "a contribution or expenditure in connection with any election" at which a member of Congress or the President and Vice-President are selected; but they have devised means for evading the spirit, if not the letter, of the law.

Testimony before the Senate subcommittee investigating the 1956 election campaign revealed that both labor unions and corporations pay salaries to officers and employees working full time for a party or candidate, publish political arguments in their house organs, and purchase television and radio time and newspaper space to present political views. In addition, the subcommittee was informed that corporations make political contributions by permitting party officials or candidates to use offices and equipment without charge and pay bonuses and permit expense accounts to be padded with the understanding that political contributions will be made from the bonuses and padded accounts . . .

The major organized interests maintain permanent staffs of professional lobbyists, research personnel, press agents, and secretaries in Washington throughout the year and have similar but smaller staffs in most state capitals during legislative sessions. Associations which have only an incidental interest in legislative proposals customarily do not have a full-time lobby staff, but may employ a lobbyist to represent them on occasions when legislative issues of interest to their members arise.

Some interest groups have "stables" of legislators who will work closely with them either because they owe their election largely to those groups or because they are themselves members of those groups. Pressure organizations with like-minded spokesmen in the legislature, or "inside lobbyists," naturally have an advantage over other groups.

Available information indicates that pressure associations originate a large percentage of the bills introduced in Congress and the state legislatures. Many organizations have their staff members read all bills introduced to determine which they wish to support, which to oppose, and which to attempt to have amended. As would be expected, lobbyists customarily watch the bills which they have sponsored to help expedite their movement through the various stages of the legislative process to enactment.

Committee hearings on bills provide the various organizations with opportunities to present their information and arguments and also to show how strongly the members of the group favor or oppose a given proposal. Officers of the association, their lobbyists, or lay members will testify before committees, often with charts and graphs to show statistical data. Sizeable delegations may be organized to attend committee hearings. At crucial times—such as when a committee is considering a bill or when the measure is being debated by one of the houses of the legislature—pressure associations often have their members write, telegraph, or call their legislators. Some groups attempt to flood the legislators with messages, while others concentrate on having communications sent by the principal supporters of each legislator and other key persons in each district.

Basically, lobbying consists of communicating with the legislators. Organized groups utilize every available opportunity to inform legislators of their wishes; to provide them with facts, information, and arguments; and to impress upon them the ability of the organization to reward or punish the legislator by giving or withholding support at the polls, campaign contributions, or gifts and items of value to the legislator. In spite of the pressures brought upon them, most legislators agree that private groups perform a valuable function in presenting information regarding the multitude of bills—many of them of a highly technical nature—introduced in each legislative session.

Any survey of pressure group operations would be incomplete that omitted reference to the social lobby and the use of unethical or illegal methods. There is widespread agreement that both types of practices still exist, but that they are of much less importance than in the days of the "old lobby." It should also be noted that these methods are undoubtedly employed as much today to influence administrators as legislators. Although the social lobby, minor favors, and practices of a distinctly corrupt nature may influence some public officials, their total impact on the political process is probably not great today.

One of the most noteworthy changes in pressure-group activity during this century is the increased effort to influence the executive branch of the government. Pressures are applied on executive and administrative personnel who are in the position to render decisions or take action of interest to organized groups. As in earlier years, after a bill has been passed by the legislature, interest groups may inundate the Chief Executive with statements, letters, telegrams, and memorials; and they may appeal to him personally to veto or sign the measure. Well aware of the importance of the Chief Executive's recommendations regarding legislative policies and budgetary matters, organized interests urge the President or governors to incorporate or omit specific proposals from their legislative programs and to increase or decrease budgetary requests for particular administrative departments or agencies.

The vast expansion of governmental regulation of economic life and the tendency of the legislatures to grant administrative officials broad discretionary powers have caused pressure associations to evince more interest than in the past in the selection of administrative personnel. Moreover, it is apparent to most groups that administrators may forcibly execute a statute or virtually nullify it. For these reasons it is not uncommon for groups to seek the appointment of their members or of individuals friendly to their group to administrative posts of particular interest to them. Pressure organizations with friends in top administrative positions have found that they have advantages not available to other groups in securing permits, licenses, contracts, subsidies, favorable adjustments of tax problems and antitrust suits, and various other types of privileges and favors.

Administrative agencies which have been granted quasi-legislative powers find that representatives of interest groups commonly appear before them to oppose or support rules and regulations. On the national level, the Administrative Procedure Act requires most administrative agencies to hold public hearings on proposed rules and permits interested individuals to request the issuance, repeal, or amendment of rules. Pressure associations have availed themselves of these rights and lobby the administrators in much the same fashion as they lobby Congress or the state legislatures.

Interest groups may importune the legislature to amend the statutes under which an agency operates and to increase or decrease its appropriation in order to expand or curtail its operations. In some instances, organized interests have been able to get legislators to investigate administrative agencies in an effort to punish administrators for unco-operative or unfriendly action. It is incorrect, however, to assume that the relationship between private associations and governmental agencies is typically one of antagonism. On the contrary, it is not uncommon to find pressure organizations, legislators, and administrative agencies working together harmoniously for their mutual benefit.

Although pressure organizations expend considerably less energy and time attempting to influence the judicial branch of the government than either the executive or legislative branch, reference should be included to their efforts to influence the courts. Whether judges are elected or appointed, organized interests often participate in their selection.

Occasionally groups seek to advance the cause of their members by initiating litigation to test the constitutionality of legislation or the action of public officials. For a number of years the National Association for the Advancement of Colored People has relied on litigation as a principal means for upholding Negro rights. Some organizations also file briefs as friends of the court to support other groups involved in litigation, or they have articles prepared for publication in law reviews with the expectation that they will be used as briefs or may be read by judges and possibly influence their decisions.

The continual increase in the efforts of interest groups to win support for their organizations and programs by using the mass media of communication to influence public attitudes is perhaps the most significant recent development in pressure-group activity. Among factors contributing to this development are: the increasing awareness on the part of interest-group leaders that public opinion is an entity which must be considered; the development and refinement of new propaganda techniques and devices; and the revolutionary changes in communication media which make it possible for literally millions of Americans to be reached daily via television, radio, the motion pictures, newspapers, and periodicals.

The rise of the public-relations counsel has occurred concomitantly with the growth of pressure groups and the extraordinary development of the communication media. To advise their highest officials on public relations and to direct propaganda programs many business organizations, labor unions, farm groups, professional associations, government agencies, and other organizations now employ public-relations counsels—some on a full-time basis in the top-echelon-planning and strategy group; others only occasionally to direct specific campaigns . . .

Pressure groups use propaganda both as a tactical means of accomplishing specific short-term goals and as a part of their long-range political strategy. From a tactical standpoint, a well-organized public-relations campaign may have either of two results. It may give the impression that there is such broad public support for a proposal that the campaign itself will result in the effectuation of the desired policy. Or, the campaign may activate the citizenry to the extent that they will demand through letters, telegrams, and other means that the officials make the decision wished by the organized group. In either event, the basic aim is to make the program of the group appear synonymous with the general welfare.

The strategic or long-term goal of a public-relations campaign tends to be ideological. Groups employing propaganda for strategic purposes often have as their aim selling the public a particular philosophy of government. In effect, they wish to condition the attitudes of the people so that a state of public opinion will be created in which the public will almost automatically respond with favor toward programs desired by the group and reject programs opposed by the group.

The dynamic nature of interest-group activity may perhaps be seen most vividly by noting a new type of pressure organization, the oldest of which was established slightly over two decades ago. These organizations have as their primary purpose the publication and dissemination of leaflets, pamphlets, and books which present a particular viewpoint on current political and economic problems. . . .

To these organizations "the dissemination of literature is both the reason for the group's existence and a primary means by which it exists." Much of the success of these organizations in raising funds may be due to the fact that they have succeeded in getting the United States Treasury Department to classify them as educational foundations with contributions to them deductible for income-tax purposes . . .

The efforts of organized interests to propagandize the public have caused some concern regarding the future of the American democratic system. The very fact, however, that pressure groups believe it necessary to make extraordinary expenditures of time and resources to shape public attitudes may be evidence of the fundamental strength of American democracy; although interest groups can on occasion manage public sentiment, they are aware that they court defeat if they flout it.

Now read carefully the following cases:

A. You are executive secretary of the Winnemac State Fuertes Association. Your group is composed of some 12,000 members, two-thirds of whom live in Zenith County, which is the largest urban center in the state, containing about one-third of the state's three million people. The Fuertes Association is devoted to birdwatching. Its members are, for the most part, little interested in politics. During the last session of the legislature, however, a few of the group's leaders became alarmed over the menace of the growing cat population, and they sponsored a bill to require that all cats wear bells. The bill passed both houses of the legislature but was vetoed by the governor. In part because of the absence of Zenith legislators, neither house could muster the necessary two-thirds majority to override the veto. The president of the Fuertes Association is absolutely determined to get the bill passed at the next session, to be held one year hence. He asks your advice.

B. You are executive secretary of the National Oil and Gas Association, composed of 84 percent of the nation's oil producers. Several well-known Congressmen from both parties have recently made speeches urging the president and their legislative colleagues in Congress to support an increase in federal taxes on oil and gas. The board of directors of the National Oil and Gas Association is alarmed and instructs you to "get to work."

C. You are executive secretary of the Society for the Prevention of Waste. Your group is composed of some ten thousand members living in every state in the union. The Society has been well supported in the past through the generosity of a few large givers, but beginning with the year after next the prospective income will be cut in half. The Society is devoted to the cause of conservation of all natural resources, and has particularly concentrated on eliminating litter and noxious industrial wastes. You must make your annual report to the Society with recommendations for future action to strengthen the Society and its influence on public policy.

D. You are executive secretary of the Winnemac State Council for Equal Rights. Since 1883 there has been a statute on the books of the State of Winnemac guaranteeing every citizen equal and nondiscriminatory access to all places of public accommodation in the state. Althought outright racial discrimination is relatively rare in the metropolitan center of the state, it is common elsewhere. In most of the rural areas and in many small and medium-sized cities and towns Negroes are still denied service in hotels, motels, restaurants, theaters and the like. Federal law now supplements state law to guarantee equal access, but in outstate Winnemac no effort has so far been made to enforce either state or federal law. You have been assigned to secure full cooperation in enforcement from state and local officials.

As a written exercise or for class discussion prepare a report indicating for each of the four cases above:

1. What steps you would recommend that the organization undertake and in what order.

2. What major obstacles you would expect to meet and what specific means you believe would be most effective in surmounting them.

3. What specific reasons you would give to support your recommendations in 1 and 2.

PROBLEM 14

Building Political Party Organization

CANDIDATES for public office in the United States have to depend on political party organization to help them conduct their campaign in the states, counties, and towns in which they may be running. Patterns of local organization vary immensely, however, from place to place, from time to time, in the purposes they serve, and in effectiveness. There is no standard scheme of organization, although certain recurring features of organization may be discerned. Much depends on who is doing the organizing, what attracts him or them to politics, what goals or functions the organization is expected to serve, and the particular circumstances within which organization is undertaken. While we are often told that "organization wins elections," there is no single assured formula for success.

Review in your text and your lecture notes materials relating to political parties and party organization. Then read carefully the following statements discussing the nature and functions of local party organization.

Statement I [1]

Since the Second World War a new kind of politician has appeared in large numbers in several of the biggest American cities. Although they are nowhere in complete control of their parties,

[1] James Q. Wilson, *The Amateur Democrat* (Chicago: University of Chicago Press, 1962), 1, 3–4, 9–10.

these new politicians have played a crucial part in the defeat of the boss of Tammany Hall and have contributed to the election of several important officials: a governor in California, a mayor in New York City, and a state's attorney in Chicago. Their ambitions extend far beyond these offices, however, for they intend to alter fundamentally the character of the American party system, and accordingly of all governing institutions . . .

An amateur is one who finds politics *intrinsically* interesting because it expresses a conception of the public interest. The amateur politician sees the political world more in terms of ideas and principles than in terms of persons. Politics is the determination of public policy, and public policy ought to be set deliberately rather than as the accidental by-product of a struggle for personal and party advantage. Issues ought to be settled on their merits; compromises by which one issue is settled other than on its merits are sometimes necessary but they are never desirable . . .

The amateur takes the outcome of politics—the determination of policies and the choice of officials—seriously, in the sense that he feels a direct concern for what he thinks are the ends these policies serve and the qualities these officials possess. He is not oblivious to considerations of partisan or personal advantage in assessing the outcome but (in the pure case) he dwells on the relation of outcome to his conception, be it vague or specific, of the public weal. Although politics may have attractions as a game of skill, it is never simply that.

The professional, on the other hand—even the "professional" who practices politics as a hobby rather than as a vocation—is preoccupied with the outcome of politics in terms of winning or losing. Politics, to him, consists of concrete questions and specific persons who must be dealt with in a manner that will "keep everybody happy" and thus minimize the possibility of defeat at the next election. The professional politician rarely broods about his function in society, the larger significance of the issues with which he deals, or the consistency of his procedures with some well-worked-out theory of democracy. Although he is not oblivious to the ends implied by political outcomes, he sees (or, since he is rarely given to theorizing, acts as if he sees) the good of society as the by-product of efforts that are aimed, not at producing the good society, but at gaining power and place for one's self and one's party.

The principal reward of politics to the amateur is the sense of having satisfied a felt obligation to "participate," and this satisfaction is greater the higher the value the amateur can attach to the ends which the outcomes of politics serve. The principal reward of the professional is to be found in the extrinsic satisfactions of participation—power, income, status, or the fun of the game. The ideal amateur has a "natural" response to politics; he sees each battle as a "crisis," and each victory as a triumph and each loss as a defeat for a cause. The professional tends, by contrast, to develop a certain detachment toward politics and a certain immunity to its excitement and its outcomes. . . .

[T]he ethic of the machine persists, in modified form, in the habits of professional politicians for whom the value of organization and leadership are indisputable, personal loyalties and commitments remain indispensable, and the lower-class basis of the big-city electorate is unchanging. Similarly, contemporary amateur politicians are critical of the naïveté of older reform efforts which sought to capture elective offices without first capturing the party organization. Nonetheless, the essence of the reform ethic persists: the desire to moralize public life, the effort to rationalize power with law, and the insistence that correct goals will be served only if goals are set and officials selected by correct procedures.

The political ethic of the followers of the professional politician places constraints on him entirely different from those placed on the amateur. He is not expected to reflect on theories of government, take positions on controversial and abstract problems of public policy, or help club members devise organizational procedures which will give them control over his behavior. He is expected to win elections and, by winning them, provide the stream of inducements which the followers require as a condition of their contributing time, effort, and money. In some professional political organizations, notably those found in Chicago, the inducements are primarily material—jobs, payoffs, and political income. Should a city's political system be such that these material incentives are not readily available in sufficient quantity to "take care" of everybody, then other, less tangible inducements must be used. In Manhattan, for example, Tammany clubs have become more and more vehicles for the expression of neighborhood, ethnic, or tribal solidarity and for social action among old acquaintances.

In such organizations, the extrinsic rewards of politics may be intangible, but they are by and large unrelated to issues, the ends of government, the abstract desirability of citizen participation, or the need for the "better element" to control the party. Rather, the intangible rewards of the professional arise from the prestige, sociability, and personal loyalties which politics can provide: being a "big man" to one's neighbors, placing voters under an obligation to one's self, expressing one's gratitude to a district leader from whom a favor was received, taking pride in the congratulations from the leader when one has "delivered" his district or precinct, or simply being able to meet regularly with one's neighbors and friends as one canvasses for votes or petition signatures and thus overcome loneliness or boredom.

Statement II [2]

The reports of the death of the American urban machine may be somewhat premature, but the news of its decline over the last 30 years is not. More than any other signal its demise symbolizes the changes afoot in American party organization. As a measure of its decline the defeat of Carmine De Sapio and the Tammany tiger by the reformers in the fall of 1961 may stand as one of the great turning points in American politics.

The city machine as a type of political organization dominated the great cities of the northeastern quarter of the United States in the early decades of the 20th century. Rooted in the immigrant and first-generation populations of these industrial centers, it developed a mode of organization that for sheer discipline and mobilization of efforts may never have been equalled in the party system of any democracy. It was built around a swarm of ward and precinct workers who maintained a systematic, block-by-block contact with the voters of the area. From the local worker, the party developed upward (with a fine bureaucratic sense of "channels") to the central political leader, the "boss," of vast political cunning and virtually unlimited party power. The machine performed a broad array of services for its clientele, asking in return only its unwavering thanks

[2] Frank J. Sorauf, *Political Parties in the American System* (Boston: Little, Brown and Co., 1964), 53–57.

at the polls. Through control of the electorate it often controlled access to candidacy and, indeed, the entire governmental apparatus, often including the courts of the city.

The fabled machine centered its life and attention on the election function. It cared little for ideologies and ideas. It specialized, in fact, in an issueless politics of immediate and tangible reward. Its only excuse for winning elections and holding power was to keep available a supply of patronage and favors with which to fill the demands of its workers and voters. The key to its success was its ability to maintain an electorate that could be "turned out" and "delivered" to the candidates and tickets of its choice. And to do that it had to deliver the goods to its insatiable followings.

The American political culture, however, no longer easily accepts either the patronage ethic that recognizes "merit" other than qualification for the job or the unthinking and unswerving loyalty (and often imperceptible abilities) of the machine's candidates. Its decline derives also from other causes. The machine created a good deal of its own supportive political culture, but now public education, the news media and opinion formers, and assorted interest groups promote other political values and perceptions. Rising levels of prosperity and relatively full employment undercut the value of the old patronage incentives. The social-service state has also preempted the machine's help for the poor, the sick, the unemployed, strangers to the ways of the city, the troubled, and the rejected. The fading of old ethnic and religious ties and the absorption of what were minorities into the mainstream of American life denied the machine its monopoly of avenues of social mobility and economic advancement. The old-style urban machine thrives today chiefly where there are unintegrated minorities, high unemployment, and urban poverty and misery—in areas of heavy Negro and Puerto Rican concentration, for example. . . .

The American parties have faced a crisis in adapting to new political conditions over the recent decades, and they have not fared well in it. The traditional party organization of the states rests on the electoral constituency; it presupposes an electoral party in door-to-door and face-to-face campaigning. But it is much less necessary in media- and candidate-centered campaigns, and it is poorly adapted to the increasingly ideological orientation of the American electorate. That function falls more easily to the business association, the trade union, the ADA, or the conservative club. The older party organization also suffers a lack of respectability because of its earthy political style and its blunt incentive system. Neither comports well with middle-class views about the well-mannered, selfless citizen. Indeed, the paternal tone and rigid hierarchy of the usual statutory organization strike a strangely ancient note in the informal, mobile homogeneity of the suburb. Indeed, the conventional organizational forms reflect a conviction that in politics it's the party rather than the candidate that counts. But for many Americans, it *is* the candidate who counts. They will work selectively in special campaign organizations for this candidate or that, but they will not make a blanket commitment to a political party. Thousands who would balk at joining a party do not hesitate to join the Volunteers for Nixon or the Citizens for Kennedy.

But in even more direct ways the machinery of many parties is wrong for today's politics. Chosen at primaries of inflexible intervals, it resists a quick turnover in leadership, the often-necessary changing of the guard. It fails to recognize that one set of men and women may involve themselves in a presidential election, whereas quite another might become excited over a school-board campaign. It is entirely local in its orientation, representing every possible local constituency, but American political attention focuses more and more on national politics. Even the emphasis on the locality presupposes residential patterns and cohesive social neighborhoods that may no longer prevail. The individual's friendship, kinship, and occupational groups are also less and less likely to be his immediate neighbors.

For the moment, then, we see in American politics a fragmentation of political organization. Politically conscious interest groups, civic associations, candidate and officeholder followings, informal social and economic elites—and the political parties—form an unstable and ever-changing reservoir of politically informed and politically oriented individuals with a strong disposition to political activity. They move, as individuals and groups, in and out of alliance with each other for specific tasks and limited goals. Trade union joins Democratic party to elect a slate of candidates at a municipal election; civic association and community elite join Republican party leadership to support home-rule legislation; and citizens ordinarily wary of a political party join with one another to work for the election of a particularly attractive candidate. In brief, the parties find it progressively more difficult to keep within their formal organizations the recruitment and election of candidates to public office. They find it even harder to meet growing demands that they concern themselves with the statement of ideas and issues and with the management of their representatives in office.

Now consider carefully the following situation:

The community of Greenacres is nearly 200 years old. Until World War II it never had more than 7,000 residents, some of whom worked in the city of Caterham, five miles to the east, and some of whom served the town and surrounding countryside. After the war more and more people from Caterham moved to Greenacres, and in the 1950's the town that had been semi-autonomous became tightly linked to the metropolis. In 1957 a large new automobile assembly plant was built just outside Greenacres, and this produced a rapid spurt of growth in the town's population. The 1960 census showed a population of 37,000 and the estimated total for 1970 is 60,000. You are one of the many people who have moved to Greenacres in the last few years.

A considerable portion of these "newcomers" work in the assembly plant and in other manufacturing plants that have been constructed in the suburbs of Caterham. Most of these people live on the South Side of town, primarily in modest single-family homes built since the war. In the northeast part of Greenacres are the older and often rather lavish homes of the "old families." Some of these houses go back to pre-Revolutionary days, and many a house has been owned by the same family since it was built. The "old families" comprise most of Greenacres' local professional and business class; the merchants, doctors, lawyers, and real estate dealers are mostly from this group. The "old families" are far from completely homogeneous, of course, but politically they tend to be strongly Republican. The "newcomers" on the other hand, are largely Democratic, and many of them belong to the United Auto Workers or other unions with strong Democratic leanings.

There is considerable social and political tension between these two groups, the "old families" and the "newcomers." In the most recent city elections, two years ago, the "old families" maintained a majority of the seats on the nonpartisan Greenacres city council, and they retained the city manager who had been under fire from the "newcomers" for allegedly neglecting streets and parks on the South Side. In last year's elections for the school board on the other hand, the "newcomers" ousted the "old guard" and forced the resignation of the superintendent. Very little of this antagonism has yet been manifested in party contests for county, state, or national offices, however.

Still a third group lives in Greenacres, primarily in University Heights in the Northwest section. These are people associated with Caterham University, a major private institution of higher learning, which twenty years ago built a new campus on the edge of Greenacres. At first, the faculty and staff found it too expensive to live in Greenacres, but in recent years more and more of them have moved in, and this group now accounts for perhaps one-sixth of the population. The "eggheads" are still inactive politically, however. They tended to vote with the "old families" in the last city election, and with the "newcomers" in the school board election. They thus seem to act as an unorganized balance of power. So far, there is little contact between the University people and either of the other main sectors of the community.

Greenacres is located in Comstock County which, except at its east end where Greenacres is located, is still largely agricultural. There are numerous small villages to the west of Greenacres, but the whole population of the county in 1960 was only 97,000, and Greenacres is by far the largest city. Comstock County, in turn, is one of twenty counties in the State of Ayrshire. Caterham County, consisting mainly of the City of Caterham, contains 420,-000 people. No other county in the state except for Comstock has a population of more than 40,000, and the entire population of the state of Ayrshire is just over one million.

State law prescribes that any city in excess of 25,000 must be divided into wards for purposes of electing party committeemen and committeewomen, and Greenacres has four wards. Only two of the eight party committeemen and committeewomen in your party, however, are at all vigorous in pursuing the party's work. Nor is there a larger proportion of effective workers among the other sixteen people who make up the twenty-four member Comstock County Committee. Nevertheless, partly by law and partly by custom, the county committee members control the selection of many party officials, such as delegates to state and national conventions; and they appoint all precinct captains. The ward leaders distribute whatever patronage and perquisites of political office may arise. Most of these benefits come from the state level, however, not from the county or city, and they therefore go to the party holding the governorship.

You are a lawyer. Nine years ago, having recently been admitted to the bar, you moved to Greenacres and built up a thriving practice, and you now have four associates in the firm. In addition, because you enjoy teaching, you give one course at the Caterham University Law School. You grew up in a politically active family in what used to be a "machine" city, and you have been amazed at the apparent absence of effective political organization in Greenacres. You yourself have campaigned for friends on two occasions but have had no association with the official party structure.

Last week an old college friend, Wilson Barbour, who lives in Caterham, told you that he wants to become governor. In part he is interested in running because of normal personal ambition, but he is also very much committed to the task of rebuilding the fortunes of his, and your, party in the state. Although many of the votes have been close, your party has lost almost every statewide election in the past decade. Moreover, the candidates your party has nominated have not represented what you both believe to be the best elements of your party's tradition. Thus, you are being asked not only to assist a friend but to build political strength for the values you believe in.

Actually Barbour does not expect to make a successful race until the election after next, six years from now. He wants you to organize Caterham so that he can receive a sizable plurality in any primary contest he might have to face to gain the party nomination and also, of course, get as many votes as possible in the general election. Remember, you will have to maintain your law practice. You do not have very much money, and your party does not control the state.

As a written exercise or for class discussion prepare a plan of action, to be undertaken over the course of the next six years, which is feasible and likely to succeed in terms of the goals outlined above. Be as specific as possible, and weigh carefully the advantages of each step you propose to undertake. Be sure to relate your program to the particular features of Greenacres, Comstock County, and Ayrshire described above. Think in terms of the numbers of votes involved.

Would your party affiliation have an important effect on your planning? That is, would you proceed differently depending on whether you were a Democrat or a Republican?

PROBLEM 15

Toward More Responsible
Political Parties?

FOR decades American political parties have been criticized on
the grounds that they have failed to serve as efficient instruments
of national policy making in government. Their loose, heterogeneous, federal structures and their lack of discipline over their
members in Congress and elsewhere, the argument runs, have
made them the spokesmen of local and special interests rather
than of meaningful national majorities. Despite the wide variety
of functions they have undertaken in the electoral arena they have
been prone to internal division and deadlock in government, the
critics maintain, and therefore are ill-equipped to perform the
crucial functions of carrying out a consistent pattern of national
policy. The result is that policy making is a product of a helter-
skelter of pressures, bargaining, and compromises rather than of
responsible party action. The electorate is in consequence denied
the opportunity of a clear and consistent national choice between
the parties on policy issues. Most such critics have maintained
that the only answer lies in more cohesive, responsible, and disciplined national political parties in a more meaningful, programmatic two-party system.

Meanwhile, other students of our political parties have argued
that they are not nearly so ineffectual as they have been painted;
that many of the suggested reforms are either impracticable or
not politically feasible; or that the proposed reforms would do

more harm than good. Within these general terms, the debate continues.

Review in your text and class notes materials relating to inter-est groups, political parties, recent developments in the American party system, constituency and other pressures in Congress, and the role of parties in policy making. Review also the readings con-cerning party origins and party functions in Problem 3, "Demo-cratic Functions and Political Parties," above, and the readings about pressures on members of Congress in Problem 19, "The Legislator's Choice," below.

One of the sharpest criticisms of American parties has been made by James M. Burns, who sees them in a chronic state of deadlock. This is the case, he maintains, because they have fallen into the "Madisonian" pattern of the fragmentation of powers and balancing off of special interests rather than the "Jefferson-ian" model of majority rule acting through strong leadership and a competitive, responsible two-party system. As he sees it, we have in effect a *four*-party rather than a *two*-party system in the United States today, with nationally oriented "Presidential Demo-crats" and "Presidential Republicans" on the one hand and locally oriented "Congressional Democrats" and "Congressional Repub-licans" on the other, representing different kinds of interests, and all acting virtually as parties. He summarizes his conclusions as follows: [1]

I have tried to describe the four parties today with some objec-tivity—even more, to put myself in the positions of their leaders, to share their aims and outlook, to see the political world through their eyes. But I shall not pretend neutrality or detachment. The chief results of the ideas and institutions embraced by the Madisonian model are, I believe, as follows:

1. We have been captured by that model, which requires us to

[1] James MacGregor Burns, *The Deadlock of Democracy: Four-Party Poli-tics in America* (Englewood Cliffs, New Jersey: Prentice-Hall, Inc., 1963), 323–27, 332–33, 334.

await a wide consensus before acting, while we have neglected, except furtively and sporadically, the Jeffersonian strategy of strong leadership, majority rule, party responsibility, and competitive elections. Hence, government action has been unduly delayed, whether measured by the progress of other comparable nations, such as Britain; or by the ascertainable needs of people, such as the jobless of the 1930's or the civil rights of minorities today; or by what the voters wanted or would accept, as reflected in the national platforms of both major parties and in the campaign promises of their presidential candidates.

2. Our four-party system requires coalition government, which is notoriously unable to generate strong and steady political power. To act, American leaders have had to gain the concurrence not simply of a majority of the voters, but of majorities of different sets of voters organized around leaders in mutually checking and foot-dragging sectors of government. The price of this radical version of checks and balances has been enfeebled policy, as major concessions have been made to gain the necessary support.

3. Hence as a nation we have lost control of our politics. We cannot collectively settle the elementary question of who may vote in national elections and hence we cannot extend the vote to millions of our fellow Americans, especially Negroes. We cannot exercise the primitive right of controlling congressional and presidential election arrangements, especially gerrymandering, rural over-representation, and one-party districts. We have lost control of political money and its misuse.

4. We lack popular control of the policy-making process. Our splintered parties set up barriers between the people and their national government rather than simplifying the alternatives, clarifying competing party doctrines, and allowing the victorious majority to govern.

5. Our government lacks unity and teamwork or, when it exists, it is often the integration of drift. Ideally, the winning party under a two-party system pulls together the executive and legislative branches in order to deliver on the party's (and candidates') promises to the people. But a fragmented party system cannot do this because the winning party is split into factions warring with each other.

6. We oscillate recklessly between deadlock and a rush of action.

Congress fails to act on crucial long-term problems; inevitably crisis comes, and the President uses his emergency powers. The Senate kills a bill to control harmful drugs; then a drug causes babies to be born without limbs; the Senate passes the same bill unanimously. Congress slashes vital foreign aid appropriations, then passes mammoth arms bills with little debate and without a single dissent.

7. We can choose bold and creative national leaders without giving them the means to make their leadership effective. Hence we diminish a democracy's most essential and priceless commodity—the leadership of men who are willing to move ahead to meet emerging problems, but who are also sensitive to the rights of the opposition and subject to the results of a free and competitive election.

8. We cannot define our national purpose and mobilize our strength to move vigorously against the problems that beset us at home and abroad, or to exploit the enormous possibilities of urban man and world man in the last third of the 20th Century.

"If you ask me—as a historian, let us say—whether a country in the state this country is in today," George F. Kennan has said, "with no highly developed sense of national purpose, with overwhelming accent of life on personal comfort and amusement, with a dearth of public services and a surfeit of privately sold gadgetry, with a chaotic transportation system, with its great urban areas being gradually disintegrated by the headlong switch to motor transportation, with an educational system where quality has been extensively sacrificed to quantity, and with insufficient social discipline even to keep its major industries functioning without grievous interruptions—if you ask me whether such a country has, over the long run, a good chance of competing with a purposeful, serious, and disciplined society such as that of the Soviet Union, I must say that the answer is 'NO'!"

We need a new kind of bipartisanship. The two presidential parties should join forces in Congress and elsewhere just long enough to work out the rules of the game for a fair, orderly, and competitive battle between the two national parties for the decades to come. The presidential parties must singly and jointly overcome the arrangements that thwart political competition, that prevent them from broadening their electoral support, and keep them from dealing with the way-of-life issues that increasingly dominate the nation's future. This means that each presidential party must convert its congressional party into a party wing exerting a proper, but not controlling or crippling hold on party policy.

The overcoming of the congressional parties requires the curbing of the institutional buttresses of their power: the seniority system in Congress, the other minority devices such as Rules Committee veto and the filibuster, mal-apportionment and one-party districts in the states, and, if feasible, midterm elections for the House. It means the shaping of new party structures and procedures. Above all, it means that the parties must protect themselves as organizational entities. Today . . . they are holding companies for numberless state and local and "candidate" organizations over which they have little control. But some of these organizations—especially those built around officeholders—have a divisive and stultifying impact on the national parties. Other party organizations—especially those oriented around governors who share the national party's style and outlook—could serve as foundation blocks for the national party.

This uneasy relation between the national and local parties poses a severe intellectual and organizational problem. Most of those who favor stronger parties want the national parties to combine more closely with state and local parties for the sake of more party coherence, discipline, and responsibility. Certainly this is desirable when the presidential and state parties are enough akin in doctrine and policy to strengthen each other. But other state and local parties are so different in outlook and doctrine that the presidential party must disentangle itself from them and set up its own separate independent party, at least in the states and congressional districts, with its own officers, finances, and communications channels . . .

Members of the presidential parties can resolve this problem only if they keep in mind what end must be sought. The aim is to draw the congressional and presidential party leaderships to each other by drawing the two party electorates more closely together— more specifically, by combining the smaller congressional party electorates with the bigger, more inclusive presidential party electorates in the states. As far as possible the President and his party majorities in Congress should be elected by substantially the same electoral groupings, for the sake of clarity of policy, unity in government, and responsibility to the majority. To do this the parties must pay a price: they cannot be allowed to be all things to all men. In some states a nationally oriented Republican party might not be able to win; but it could still field candidates who would stage vigorous campaigns, put over the message of national Republicanism, and build toward the day when the Republicans would have a fighting opportunity in that area. Such candidates could "bend" the national platforms a bit toward local political needs but what they must not do—what the national party leaders should be in a position to prevent them from doing—is so to distort Republicanism that its national meaning and appeal is perverted and impaired.

Once the Democratic and Republican parties agreed on such assumptions, the specific elements of party consolidation would fall into place. . . .

I list these proposals in a mixed spirit of conviction and skepticism. Conviction, because I am sure we must adopt them for a more orderly, relevant, and effective politics. Skepticism, because I am well aware that I am only the latest in a long line of Americans, celebrated and obscure, who have urged changes to achieve that kind of politics. "The Constitution is not honored by blind worship," Woodrow Wilson wrote 80 years ago. "The more open eyed we become as a nation, to its defects, and the prompter we grow in applying with the unhesitating courage of conviction all thoroughly tested or well-considered expedients necessary to make self-government among us a straightforward thing of simple method, single, unstinted power, and clear responsibility, the nearer will we approach to the sound sense and practical genius of the great and honorable statesmen of 1787." Since then, A. Lawrence Lowell, Henry Jones Ford, Herbert Croly, Walter Lippmann, William Yandell Elliott, Thomas K. Finletter, and a host of others, including many working politicians, have dealt with the central problem in one fashion or another. Aside from a little fixing and patching, the results have been small. Why?

Americans have had the cushion of time. We have never been so close to the abyss, in domestic affairs (except when we went over it in 1861), that we felt much urgency about strengthening our political system. If that government could not cope with economic crises, if it could not deal with even as primitive a social problem as child labor, if it was a generation or two behind other modern nations in welfare programs, if it could not meet its international obligations, if Negroes were still segregated and discriminated against a century after Emancipation—we could wait until a large enough popular consensus could be achieved to allow our divided government to act. There is grave doubt now that history still allows us this cushion.

We have also suffered from a gimmick approach to political problems. Our genius at tinkering and improvising leads us to think that the most serious political problems can be solved by mechanical devices. In the old days it was the initiative, referendum, and recall; the party primary and proportional representation; nonpartisan ballots and honest election administration. Today there are proposals to solve executive-legislative deadlock and friction by question-hours, joint cabinets or councils, or mechanical changes in Congress. There may be nothing wrong with these proposals in themselves, but they have little bearing on the real problems of President and Congress, which are problems not of misunderstanding or of faulty communication but of who gets what—and who does not. . . .

But the main reason, I think, that we have not come to grips with our political problem is *intellectual:* we have been so enamored by one model of government, the Madisonian, that we have failed to comprehend the legitimacy and possibilities of what I have called the Jeffersonian strategy of politics. We have not called the Madisonian model by that name; we have called it the Constitution (forgetting that the Constitution can accommodate the Jeffersonian model) and during most of our life as a nation we have, indeed, as Wilson said, dishonored the Constitution by blind worship. We have complained about government by barter, government by fits and starts, government by minorities, and so on, but as a people we have never squarely faced the philosophical assumptions on which that government is built. . . .

A defense of American political parties has been offered by Edward C. Banfield, who sees them as subtle instruments which "fit" the American social and political systems. While it is easy to criticize their internal functioning or structure and suggest reforms, he argues, they should be judged not by the abstract standards of ordered responsibility and discipline their critics often suggest, but by their compatibility with the pluralistic American political system as a whole and by the results they produce. Evaluated in these terms, he maintains, American political parties as they have developed over the centuries have served the nation well. With these standards in mind he summarizes some of the main points in his argument in the following passages: [2]

The American party system has been criticized on four main grounds: (1) The parties do not offer the electorate a choice in terms of fundamental principles; their platforms are very similar and mean next to nothing; (2) they cannot discipline those whom they elect, and therefore they cannot carry their platforms into effect; (3) they are held together and motivated less by political principle than by desire for personal, often material, gain, and by sectional and ethnic loyalties; consequently party politics is personal and parochial; and (4) their structure is such that they cannot correctly represent the opinion of the electorate; in much of the country there is in effect only one party, and everywhere large contributors and special interests exercise undue influence within the party.

These criticisms may be summarized by saying that the structure and operation of the parties do not accord with the theory of democracy or, more precisely, with that theory of it which says that everyone should have a vote, that every vote should be given exactly the same weight, and that the majority should rule.

"It is a serious matter," says Maurice Duverger, a French political scientist who considers American party organization "archaic" and "undemocratic," "that the greatest nation in the world, which is assuming responsibilities on a world-wide scale, should be based on a party system entirely directed towards very narrow local horizons." He and other critics of the American party system do not, however, base their criticisms on the performance of the American government. They are concerned about procedures, not results. They ask whether the structure and operation of the parties is consistent with the logic of democracy, not whether the party system produces— and maintains—a good society, meaning, among other things, one in which desirable human types flourish, the rights of individuals are respected, and matters affecting the common good are decided, as nearly as possible, by reasonable discussion.

If they were to evaluate the party system on the basis of results,

---

[2] Edward C. Banfield, "In Defense of the American Party System," in Robert A. Goldwin, ed., *Political Parties, U.S.A.* (Chicago: Rand McNally and Co., 1964), 21–23, 24–26, 34–36.

they would have to conclude that on the whole it is a good one. It has played an important part (no one can say how important, of course for innumerable causal forces have been at work along with it) in the production of a society which, despite all its faults, is as near to being a good one as any and nearer by far than most; it has provided governments which, by the standards appropriate to apply to governments, have been humane and, in some crises, bold and enterprising; it has done relatively little to impede economic growth and in some ways has facilitated it; except for the Civil War, when [the party system] was, as Henry Jones Ford said, "the last bond of union to give way," it has tended to check violence, moderate conflict, and narrow the cleavages within the society; it has never produced, or very seriously threatened to produce, either mob rule or tyranny, and it has shown a marvelous ability to adapt to changing circumstances.

Not only has the American party system produced good results, it has produced better ones than have been produced almost anywhere else by other systems. Anyone who reflects on recent history must be struck by the following paradox: those party systems that have been most democratic in structure and procedure have proved least able to maintain democracy; those that have been most undemocratic in structure and procedure—conspicuously those of the United States and Britain—have proved to be the bulwarks of democracy and of civilization. . . .

The critics of the party system tend to value democratic procedure for its own sake, that is, apart from the results it produces. There is no reason why they should not do so. But they are in error when they do not recognize that other values of equal or greater importance are often in conflict with democratic procedure, and that when they are, some sacrifice of it is essential in order to serve the other values adequately. If they faced up to the necessity of assigning priorities among *all* of the relevant ends, they would not, it is safe to say, put "democratic procedure" first. Probably they, and most Americans, would order the ends as follows:

1. The party system must above all else provide governments having the will and capacity to preserve the society and to protect its members. Any sacrifice in other ends ought to be accepted if it is indispensable to securing this end.

2. The party system must insure periodic opportunity to change

the government by free elections. Any sacrifice of other ends (except the one above) ought to be accepted if it is indispensable to securing this one.

3. The party system should promote the welfare of the people. By "welfare" is meant some combination of two kinds of values: "principles," what is thought to be good for the society, described in rather general terms, and "interests," the ends individuals and groups seek to attain for their own good, as distinguished from that of the society. The party system should produce governments that assert the supremacy of principles over interests in some matters; in others it should allow interests to prevail and should facilitate the competitive exercise of influence.

4. The party system should moderate and restrain such conflict as would threaten the good health of the society. Other conflict it should not discourage.

5. The party system should promote and exemplify democracy, meaning reasonable discussion of matters affecting the common good in which every voice is heard.

These ends have been listed in what most Americans would probably consider a descending order of importance. In devising a party system, we ought not to try to serve fully each higher end before serving the one below it at all. The first two ends are exceptions to this rule, however: each of them must be attained even if the others are not served at all. With respect to the remaining three, the problem is to achieve a proper balance—one such that no reallocation from one end to another would add to the sum of value.

Finally, we must realize that we can rarely make important social changes by intention. The most we can do is to make such minor changes as may be consistent with, and more or less implied by, the fixed features of the situation in which we are placed. Even to make minor changes in an institution like a political party requires influence of a kind and amount that no group of reformers is likely to have or to be able to acquire. It is idle to propose reforms that are merely desirable. There must also be some possibility of showing, if only in a rough and conjectural way, that they might be carried into effect.

With respect to the American party system, it seems obvious that the crucial features of the situation are all fixed. The size of our country, the class and cultural heterogeneity of our people, the number and variety of their interests, the constitutionally-given fragmentation of formal authority, the wide distribution of power which follows from it, the inveterate taste of Americans for participation in the day-to-day conduct of government when their interests are directly at stake—these are all unalterable features of the situation. Taken together, they mean that the party system can be reformed only within very narrow limits. . . .

The hope that the two-party system might be made to offer a choice betweeen distinct alternatives is illusory for at least two reasons. One is that a party which does not move to the middle of the road to compete for votes condemns itself to defeat and eventually, if it does not change its ways, to destruction. But even if this were not the case, the parties could not present the electorate with what reformers think of as "a valid choice." The reason is that the issues in our national life are such that there does not exist any one grand principle by which the electorate could be divided into two camps such that every voter in each camp would be on the "same" side of all issues. The idea of "left" and "right" is as close as we come to having such a grand principle, and it has little or no application to many issues. The logic of "left" and "right" does not, for example, imply opposite or even different positions on (for example) foreign policy, civil liberties, or farm subsidies. Without a grand principle which will make unities—opposed unities—of the party programs, the electorate cannot be offered "a valid choice." A choice between two market baskets, each of which contains an assortment of unrelated items, some of which are liked and some of which are disliked, is not a "valid" choice in the same sense that a choice between two market baskets, each of which contains items that "belong together" is a "valid" one. In the American party system, most items are logically unrelated. This being so, "valid" choice would become possible only if the number of parties was increased to allow each party to stand for items that *were* logically related. . . .

The hope that the parties might commit themselves to carry out their programs is also illusory. A party could do this only if its leaders were able to tell the President and the party members in Congress what to do, and could discipline them if they failed to do it. Therefore, unless . . . we were to have two sets of national leaders, one in governmental office and another much more important one in party office, it would be necessary for our elected leaders—in effect, the President, since only he and the Vice President are elected by the whole nation—to control the Congressmen and Senators of their party. This would be possible only if the President could deny re-election to members of Congress who did not support the party program. Thus, instead of merely bringing forward and electing candidates, as they do now, "responsible" parties would have to govern the country. We would have a parliamentary system with the President in a position somewhat like that of the British Prime Minister, except (a very important difference) that, not being a part of the legislature, he could not use it as a vehicle through which to exert his leadership. The legislature would in fact have no function at all.

This great shift of power to the President would remedy another "defect" in the party system: its receptivity to the demands of interest groups. With the President in full control of Congress, logrolling would cease or virtually cease. It would do so because no one could any longer make the President pay a price for assistance in getting legislation passed; the traders who now sell their bits and pieces of power to the highest bidders would have to lower their prices and would probably go out of business. With their opportunities for exercising influence vastly reduced, interest groups would be less enterprising both in their efforts to anticipate the effects of governmental action and in bringing their views to the attention of the policy makers. . . .

The destruction of political traders and of local centers of power would mean also that the President's power would derive from somewhat different sources than at present. Instead of relying upon logrolling and patronage to get the votes he would need in Congress, he would have to rely upon direct appeals to the electorate. To some extent he might manipulate the electorate by charm and personality; TV and the arts of Madison Avenue would become more important in politics. But in order to get elected he would have to depend also, and to a greater extent, upon appeals to political principle or ideology. Whereas the political trader maintains his control by giving and withholding favors to individuals . . . the President would have to maintain *his* by the uncertain and costly expedient of offering to whole classes of people—the farmer, the aged, the home owner, and so on—advantages that they would have only at each other's expense. If charm and the promise of "something for everybody" did not yield the amount of power he required to govern the country, the President might find it necessary to exploit whatever antagonisms within the society might be made to yield more power. Class and ethnic differences might in this event serve somewhat the same function as logrolling and patronage do now.

Now read and analyze carefully the following recommendations concerning political parties, proposed by a special Committee of the American Political Science Association as part of a report on possible avenues of party reform: [3]

We propose a Party Council of 50 members. Such a Party Council should consider and settle the larger problems of party management, within limits prescribed by the National Convention; propose a preliminary draft of the party platform to the National Convention; interpret the platform in relation to current problems; . . . consider and make recommendations to appropriate party organs in respect to congressional candidates; and make recommendations to the National Convention, the National Committee, or other appropriate party organs with respect to conspicuous departure from general party decisions by state or local party organizations. . . .

Establishment of a Party Council would do much to coordinate the different party organizations, and should be pressed with that objective in mind. . . . Local party organizations should be imbued with a stronger sense of loyalty to the entire party organization and feel their responsibility for promoting the broader policies of the party. This can be done by fostering local party meetings, regularly and frequently held, perhaps monthly. The national organization may deal with conspicuous or continued disloyalty on the part of any state organization. Consideration should be given to the development of additional means of dealing with rebellious and disloyal state organizations. . . . .

[3] Committee on Political Parties, American Political Science Association, *Toward a More Responsible Two-Party System* (New York: Holt, Rinehart and Winston, Inc., 1950), 5–7.

There has been much difference of opinion as to the exact binding quality of a platform. All of this suggests the need for appropriate machinery, such as a Party Council, to interpret and apply the national program in respect to doubts or details. When that is done by way of authoritative and continuing statement, the party program should be considered generally binding [on party leaders and on party members in Congress and other government offices] . . . . Party platforms should be formulated at least every two years. National platforms should emphasize general party principles and national issues. State and local platforms should be expected to conform to the national platform on matters of general party principle or on national policies.

This proposal for a coordinating, directing party council is aimed at bringing about one major purpose. This goal is what the APSA Committee called "more responsible" political parties in the United States—that is, parties that would commit themselves to relatively clear-cut positions of program or policy on national issues; support this national program in a relatively united or cohesive way at both national and local levels; and bind their leaders and their members in government office, especially Congress, to work for the national program. The proposal raises two questions. The first is whether, given the way in which the American political system as a whole generally operates, merely setting up a Party Council as a piece of party machinery would *in fact* result in "more responsible," more "programmatic," more "disciplined" parties, as the APSA Committee believes it would. This question entails a *prediction*, based on a factual analysis of American political life. To answer in the affirmative is to agree with the proposition that structural revision can substantially affect the distribution of political influence. Next, *assuming* that the proposed party council *would* produce "more responsible" parties, the second question is whether such a development would be considered desirable or undesirable. This question involves the *value judgments* that various participants in American politics might make concerning the assumed results of the proposal, and the *grounds* on which these judgments of "good" or "bad" would rest.

Next read and digest the following summaries of salient facts about two important American interest group associations.

A. The National Association of Manufacturers, an influential business interest group, claims a membership of 15 percent of all manufacturing firms in the United States employing eight or more workers. It depends particularly on large firms, which tend to dominate its policy, although not all large firms subscribe to the NAM position. It has been interested in a minimum of government regulation of the economy and in government policies to regulate, limit, or diminish the power of organized labor, and has become a major spokesman for a "conservative" point of view in American politics. Its political tactics include the expenditure of large sums of money aimed at molding public opinion in a direction generally favorable to business objectives in the hope that such opinion will have an impact on government. The NAM has also worked through skilled lobbying, emphasizing direct contacts with Congressmen and other government officials, testimony before congressional committees, and written statements or briefs for its position. It does not directly endorse candidates for Congress or other government offices, though it has provided its member firms with congressional voting records and other information about the actions of government officials. Officials of its member firms are often very influential in their communities, or nationally.

B. The American Federation of Labor-Congress of Industrial Organizations encompasses some 13,500,000 members in various trades and industries. Its members thus comprise more than one-fourth of all nonfarm workers currently employed in the United States. Although there are sometimes internal divisions within the AFL-CIO, its leadership is generally active in behalf of "liberal" political objectives. The AFL-CIO is interested in considerable government intervention in the economy, particularly in relation to regulation of business and to wages and hours standards, and in government policies to improve working conditions, uphold labor union organization, and promote union bargaining power. It is also interested in promoting social security measures, public housing programs, medicare, and other welfare policies. It seeks to mobilize its mass membership, through local unions and in election districts, to register, to work and canvass actively in election campaigns, and to vote. It may directly endorse and often contribute to the campaign expenses of the candidates it favors, usually through its local branches but often on the basis of information from the national headquarters, both in primary and in general elections. Thus its political tactics stress mass public action, although it also engages in direct lobbying and in some general propaganda.

Now, bearing in mind the arguments and data presented above, prepare as a written exercise or for class discussion thoughtful answers to the following:

1. Decide, on the basis of what you know about American politics, interest groups, and parties:
    (a) whether you think the APSA Committee proposal to include a Party Council as a part of the formal machinery of American major parties is one which *in fact* could be put into effect in the near future; and
    (b) whether you think the establishment of such Councils would *in fact* result in a "more responsible," more "programmatic" party system in the United States.

Present the *evidence* and *analysis* upon which you base your predictions in (a) and (b).

2. Now, regardless of your own conclusions in Question 1, above, *assume* that the establishment of a Party Council along the lines of the APSA Committee proposal would *in practice* result in "more responsible," more "programmatic" American parties. On the basis of this assumption, decide whether you would favor

or oppose the APSA Committee recommendations *if* you were an intelligent, well-informed person who is:

(a) a state *Democratic* party leader in South Carolina;

(b) a local *Republican* party leader in a working-class district in a major northern city, like New York or Chicago;

(c) a *Democratic* Congressman from a northern city district in which the population is approximately half Negro;

(d) a national official of the National Association of Manufacturers;

(e) a national official of the AFL-CIO.

For each of these five roles consider carefully the particular *grounds* on which, in each case, you would base your support for or opposition to the APSA Committee proposal for a Party Council. Give attention both to the probable relevant facts which would be involved in each case, and to the special group, party, or factional interests you would probably, in each position, like to see served.

3. Would you, yourself, *favor* or *oppose* the establishment of Party Councils in the major parties as proposed by the APSA Committee recommendations? State carefully the grounds and analysis on which you would base your own personal judgment.

PROBLEM 16

Presidential Nominations and Electoral Strategy

THE nomination of candidates for president of the United States takes place amid the colorful and sometimes spontaneous, sometimes contrived hoopla of the national party conventions. But behind the flamboyant oratory, the frenetic demonstrations of enthusiasm and confidence, and the probing of the television cameras, lies much careful calculation. The main objective of the party in convention assembled is usually to nominate the man, fit for the presidency, who is most likely to win the election. The various interests to which the party leaders look for support and the principles to which they subscribe cannot be ignored, but the primary concern of the delegates is usually the desirability of electoral victory, and the choice of the man they think is most nearly able to bring it to them. Thus presidential nominating conventions generally operate within certain assumptions or informal rules of the game of politics. Some possible exceptions may be noted, such as the Democrats' nomination of William Jennings Bryan in 1896 or the Republicans' choice of Barry Goldwater in 1964, but generally the rules hold.

From the point of view of the convention delegates the candidate should be the man with the widest and most powerful positive appeal to voters and with the fewest drawbacks or negative attributes. He must be able to pull wavering adherents away from the opposition and win a large bloc of the uncommitted voters to his banner without alienating any large groups that usually support his party. If a candidate is too closely identified with a particular interest, he may alienate another competing interest whose support is necessary to win the election. Identification with a racial or religious minority has often been regarded as a severe handicap in seeking an electoral majority. Political eminence itself may be a handicap, however, because a man in political office must constantly make decisions; and while these decisions may win support from some groups they may also alienate others. Thus many Republicans feared that Senator Robert A. Taft could not win election as president in 1952, largely because the definite positions he had taken in the Senate had made him too many enemies; and the convention turned to Dwight D. Eisenhower as a potential winner. This seems to have been one factor that, for decades, made it more difficult for senators—who must vote on many issues of national controversy—to win the nomination than it was for governors, whose unavoidable commitments take place in one state only, and who seldom if ever have to make actual decisions on national issues. For a number of reasons, however, including the general nationalization of politics in an era of critical national and international concerns as well as the difficulties many governors have faced in their states in recent years, the balance may now be shifting so that it is more favorable for senators and less so for governors.

The process of nominating a presidential candidate involves the strategic commitments and tactical choices of all the participants. Day after day the candidates and their advisors must decide whether to take this stand, support that program, meet with this state or pressure-group leader, call a press conference, or shake still another hand. The judgments must be made in a context of uncertainty, since no one can tell in advance just how things will turn out. This is one reason that politics is regarded as an art form which, at the presidential level at least, calls for the virtuoso performance.

Read the following passages describing the patterns and practices of the presidential nominating process.

1. Presidential Primaries [1]

Primaries are important largely because the results represent an ostensibly objective indication of whether a candidate can win the election. The contestants stand to gain or lose far more than the small number of delegate votes which may be at stake. Thus a man situated as was Richard Nixon in 1960 would be ill-advised to enter a primary unless the information at his disposal led him to believe that he was quite certain to win. This stricture applies with special force to any candidate who is well ahead in delegate support. All he can gain is a few additional votes, while he can lose his existing support by a bad showing in the primary since this would be interpreted as meaning that he could not win in the election. The candidate who is far behind, or who has to overcome severe handicaps, however, has little or nothing to lose by entering a risky primary. If he wins, he has demonstrated his popularity; if he loses, he is hardly worse off than if he had not entered the primary at all. Such was the case when John Kennedy quieted the apprehensions of Democratic politicians about the religious issue by winning in Protestant West Virginia. The man who is ahead needs more certain information about how primaries are likely to turn out because he takes the greater risk.

The man who is behind in securing convention support or whose ability to win is in doubt engages in strategies of enticement in which he issues siren calls inviting the leading contenders into a primary. He suggests that they are cowardly, lacking in fighting spirit, afraid to face the public. By luring them into a primary, he hopes to deal a severe blow to their chances and thereby boost his own. In order to avoid this trap, it may be necessary for candidates to publicize their disdain for primaries, to specify in advance all the reasons why such a contest would be unnecessary, unfair, and a waste of time. The candidate who finds himself in a primary (and wishes to live and fight again another day) does well to have alibis ready to explain away seemingly disadvantageous results.

In a primary in which there are many contenders a defeated

[1] Nelson W. Polsby and Aaron B. Wildavsky, *Presidential Elections: Strategies of American Electoral Politics* (New York: Charles Scribner's Sons, 1964), 72–75.

candidate may attempt to gain advantage from what may be regarded as an ambiguous result by claiming that the man who
actually won was allied to him ideologically. The results may
then be viewed as a victory for the ideology rather than defeat
for the candidate. After La Follette had won an overwhelming
victory in the 1912 Republican primary in North Dakota, Theodore
Roosevelt issued a statement "claiming an immense progressive
victory." He even went beyond this to count the La Follette delegation as part of the Roosevelt camp once it had cast "a compli-
mentary vote for La Follette."

One strategy for primaries, the write-in, offers the maximum
possibility of gain with the minimum possibility of loss. If a candidate gets virtually no votes, he can easily explain this by saying that he did not campaign and that it is difficult for people
to write in names. If he receives 10 percent of the vote, he can
hail this as a tremendous victory under the circumstances. And
if he should win, he can build it up to the sky, stressing the extraordinary popularity required to get people to go to all the
trouble of writing in a name. But the man who is behind cannot
rest content with being able to explain away a poor showing; he
must win to establish himself as a contender. The strategy of the
write-in, consequently, is most accessible to the man who is ahead
and hopes to solidify his position while minimizing his risks.

The foregoing discussion should help us to understand why
those who win primaries sometimes do not win the nomination.
Part of the reason is that there are not many primaries and not
all of those actually commit delegates to vote for a candidate. Of
greater significance, however, is the fact that primary activity
is often (though by no means always) a sign that a candidate has
great obstacles to overcome and must win many primaries in order
to be considered for the nomination at all. The image communi-
cated to political professionals by a few primary victories, unless
they are overwhelming, may be less that of the conquering hero
than that of the drowning man clutching at the last straw.

Thus, entering and winning primaries may be of little value
unless the results are widely interpreted in such a way as to
improve a candidate's chances. The contestant who "loses" but
does better than expected may reap greater advantage from a
primary than the one who wins but falls below expectations. It

is, therefore, manifestly to the advantage of a candidate to hold his claims down to minimum proportions. Kennedy tried in 1960 to follow this advice in Wisconsin—he claimed Humphrey had been Wisconsin's third Senator—but the press, radio, and TV took note of his extensive organization and of favorable polls, and in advance pinned the winner-by-a-landslide-label on the Senator from Massachusetts. The public media have taken some of the control over "expectations" from the candidates.

Yet there is more to the strategy of primaries than mere calculation of chances on the candidate's part. The desires of the existing state organizations may also have to be taken into account. The state organization may be sponsoring a favorite son who, it hopes, may be nominated in case of deadlock. It may wish to remain uncommitted in order to increase its bargaining power by making a claim on the winner in return for throwing last minute support to him. The party may be divided and fear internecine warfare over rival candidates which would leave it in a shattered condition. For all of these reasons, the state leadership may request candidates to stay out and may threaten to work against them in the primary and at the convention if they disobey. Presidential aspirants may have to rest content with second or third choice support unless their position is so desperate that they have little to lose by antagonizing the state party.

Paradoxically, the candidate who can show that he has no choice but to enter a primary may gain a bargaining advantage. The state leaders may then decide that it is worth making concessions to him to avoid the internal strife that would be caused by a primary contest. This is more or less what happened when John Kennedy, fortified by a poll claiming that he would win, insisted that he absolutely had to have Ohio's votes to have a chance at the national convention. Ohio Governor Michael DiSalle, who wanted to run as a favorite son, had to back down in order to avoid a primary fight that could have been extremely embarrassing to him, and so he ran on a slate pledged to Kennedy. The Governor's decision was prompted by the knowledge that the Cuyahoga County (Cleveland) party faction, which was hostile to him, would run a slate pledged to Kennedy and use this as a weapon to reduce the Governor's stature within the state. The struggle for power within a state may have much to do with its action at the convention.

II. Presidential Availability [2]

Popular writing in every presidential election year always includes efforts to define the personality characteristics and other qualifications of "the perfect President" or "the ideal nominee." The data we have presented do not lend themselves easily to this kind of judgment—except to suggest that there *is* no single pattern of characteristics that the conventions will invariably choose. A convention may be guided to some extent by an unconscious ideal that has already screened out those clearly unavailable, but it is mainly seeking to choose among those who are still available. The system seems to throw up a wide range of types for choice, although not always very wide in any one year.

The early Presidents from Washington to John Quincy Adams were all well known from their previous participation in national affairs, and had many qualities in common. The congressional nominating caucus in most cases stayed within the circle of its own observation and acquaintanceship. When Andrew Jackson came to power as a people's hero, the earlier channels of advancement were disregarded and the convention system soon effectively prevented their restoration. Within a decade the field was open to state officials as well as federal, to legislators as well as executives, and to persons with no governmental experience who had somehow developed that intangible quality known as availability.

A sort of cumbersome "natural selection" has always gone on in the determination of initial availability—resulting in various standards that are essentially negative, but that sometimes change as national or sectional mores change. For instance, up to 1960 all women were still excluded and all Negroes, and aspirants with conspicuous marital difficulties or with close identification to a specific economic interest group were essentially excluded . . .

[T]he conventions have not easily solved the problems of defining the standards for final choice among the still fewer aspirants who will be actual candidates. For the observer, the patterns of preference from convention to convention are difficult to under-

[2] Paul T. David, Ralph M. Goldman, and Richard C. Bain, *The Politics of National Party Conventions*, rev. condensed ed. (Washington, D.C.: The Brookings Institution, 1964), 158–65.

stand. Largely as a guide to what has been clearly untypical and to what is perhaps becoming more typical, the information in this chapter may be helpful in suggesting the kind of person a party is more likely to nominate.

Among the eight first-time Democratic nominees for President from 1896 through 1956, for instance, Bryan, Parker, and Davis all seem notably untypical in major respects. Bryan was young, inexperienced, and from a small, predominantly Republican state. Parker, a high court judge long withdrawn from active politics, was a vigorous supporter of the gold standard opposed earlier by majorities of his party. Davis was a Wall Street lawyer, who had previously been elected twice to the House of Representatives from West Virginia and held appointive positions under Wilson.

Each of the other Democrats—Wilson, Cox, Smith, F. D. Roosevelt, and Stevenson—was the active and able incumbent governor of a populous, hard-fought, two-party state. Their ages respectively were 55, 50, 55, 50, 52. Relatively new to the national scene, each had already achieved distinction in a public-service type of career. Cox was somewhat untypical in being a businessman and publisher, and Smith was certainly untypical in being highly urban and of the Roman Catholic faith. But all five were typical of much that has seemed best in the American political system; the rapid elevation, through elective executive office in states where politics is vigorous and competitive, of able leaders still in the prime of life who have not necessarily yet taken on the characteristics of a "father image." This appears to be the type recently preferred by the Democratic party in its first-time presidential nominations, when the type was available. And the two elected—Wilson and Roosevelt—were highly exemplary of that preference.

The Republican party seems to have had a fondness for "untypical" nominees—of whom Willkie was probably the most outstanding example, with his total lack of governmental experience. Eisenhower, with his eminence as a five-star general, was a reversion to an earlier pattern of American politics—and thus one of the most untypical of the choices offered. Hughes, remote and Olympian, was untypical—despite his experience as a successful governor of New York State—as the only Supreme Court Justice in history nominated for President. Harding, the only nominee from the Senate between Douglas in 1860 and Kennedy in 1960, was untypical in a sufficient number of other respects.

Of the other five Republican nominees of 1896–1956, McKinley, Landon, and Dewey were incumbent governors, and [William H.] Taft and Hoover served in the Cabinets of the Presidents that they succeeded. They seem to offer a composite pattern of the Republican preference in first-time presidential nominees. All were able executives, well known to be closely affiliated with the business community. Their ages respectively were 53, 49, 42, 51, and 54. Their careers had included distinguished public service and evidence of capacity to cultivate the electorate. With the exception of Landon, their origins were the populous, two-party states that often decide presidential elections. None of them, except perhaps Dewey, was characterized by the kind of dynamism in approaching public problems that appeared to be a collective characteristic of the five Democrats deemed typical. They were therefore less likely to become the kind of "strong" President that, since Lincoln, seems to have been regarded by the Republican party as objectionable in the White House.

One must remember that either party at any given time can choose only from among those who are available. If the preferred type, especially in a party out of power, is a vote-getting governor with a distinguished record in an important two-party state the number is seldom large. There have been times in out-party history when no such candidate was available, and some of the odd nominations that have been made were the result.

The picture given in this chapter has been one based mainly on the long historical record. It remains to be seen whether the nominations of 1960 reflect some permanent change. Kennedy was an incumbent senator when nominated, as Nixon had been before becoming Vice President. Neither had ever been a governor and neither had ever headed a large executive organization. In other respects, however, both men conformed to the type that has been identified: both had risen rapidly and with great distinction in a public service career, both were relatively young—43 and 47— and each was the product of vigorous competition in the campaigns and elections of a populous, two-party state.

It is possible that the Senate may become the most important source of presidential candidates in the future; the growing im-

portance of the issues of national policy and of American involvement with the world at large are shifting the political spectrum in
that direction. But it is much too early to conclude that governors
are finished as presidential candidates, and especially so on any
permanent or long-term basis.

Now assume that in a preconvention campaign four men have
been mentioned as the leading candidates for the presidential
nomination of their party. In order to simplify the task, even
though it greatly oversimplifies what a real convention situation
would be like, assume that six states where party strength is approximately equal appear to hold the key to success in the election. In this particular election, for one reason or another, other
large states that are often thought of as pivotal as well as many
smaller ones are regarded as reasonably safe for one party or the
other; and each party can count on receiving just about half of
these safe electoral votes. Thus the delegates to the convention
will try to nominate the man who, in the November election,
seems most likely to win a majority (seventy-one or more) of the
total electoral votes of six key states. These six states and the
number of electoral votes in each state are:

California, 40	Massachusetts, 14	Ohio, 26
Illinois, 26	Minnesota, 10	Texas, 25

Consult your text and lecture notes for any material relating to
the general patterns of politics in these states. Pay particular attention to the interests that might affect the political decisions of
residents of these states. Additional data may be obtained in *The
Encyclopedia Americana, The Congressional Quarterly Almanac,*
and *The World Almanac.* Your instructor may be able to direct
you to more extended treatments of the politics of these states.

The four most likely nominees and the known relevant facts
concerning each are as follows:

A. *Joseph O'Keefe:* Fifty-four years old, Catholic, married, six
children; first-term Governor of Massachusetts, having won an
upset victory over the previous incumbent; formerly head of the

state AFL-CIO; state senator for several years and national committeeman from Massachusetts before becoming governor, early supporter of previous party nominee for President; as governor has actively promoted expansion of school construction and public housing and has vigorously enforced existing legislation designed to eliminate racial discrimination in employment; in speeches during preconvention campaign has placed most emphasis on attacking foreign aid, advocating higher protective tariffs, arguing that the United States must follow a more self-sufficient foreign policy. He has urged taking more aggressive action in the Cold War, especially in the Far East.

B. *Robert Ballard:* Fifty-five years old, Episcopalian, bachelor; president of Ballard Electronics, a comparatively small manufacturing company in Ohio which under Ballard's leadership has been highly successful; has never run for elective office or been closely identified with the party organization; recently served as chairman of the President's Bipartisan Commission on Governmental Reorganization and was widely acclaimed in newspaper editorials for his impartial public service; has fostered friendly relations with the union in his company; has taken no pronounced stands on any of the leading controversial questions of the day, except to plead for greater cooperation between the United States and other nations of the free world and urge that foreign aid be increased.

C. *Peter Hansen:* Forty-six years old, Lutheran, married, no children, severely wounded in World War II; Governor of Minnesota in second term, having won large majorities in each election; former Congressman who served on Agriculture Committee in House of Representatives; an outspoken advocate of high price supports for farm commodities, especially for wheat and dairy products; as governor permitted a "right-to-work" bill to become law without his signature, thus making it more difficult for labor unions to maintain their memberships; has concentrated all his preconvention fire on the farm issue; is regarded as somewhat independent of his state party organization, preferring to act in his own name rather than that of his party; frequently ignores his party's candidates during election campaigns and rejects the party organization's patronage requests in the state government.

D. *James Jonas:* Sixty-four years old, Presbyterian, married, two grown sons and six grandchildren, handsome and gifted orator; Senator from Washington, former professor of economics at the state university, author of several books on world economic problems; first man of his party to win election to the Senate from his state in several decades; emphasized in his senatorial campaign the need for massive federal construction of electric power facilities in the Northwest and the need to increase expenditures for air power and aircraft carriers; in the Senate has continued to stress these issues and has been very critical of the leadership of both parties on these matters; has made dozens of speeches to meetings of state and local organizations of his party during the past two years and is regarded as the party's best fund-raiser; during four years in the Senate has become a leading spokesman on questions of economic policy and taxation and is regarded by many senators of both parties as the leading expert in public life on the intricacies of these problems; has generally opposed large-scale tax reduction, particularly in the upper-income brackets, but would reduce taxes on low incomes in time of recession; has recently become a member of the Senate Foreign Relations Committee and has attracted favorable international publicity for his speeches on foreign policy problems, in which he has advocated greater international efforts to control thermonuclear weapons.

Now, as a written exercise or for class discussion:

1. Assume that you are campaign manager for each of the four candidates, and that each is seeking the *Democratic* nomination for president. Advise your candidates, in turn, as to whether they should enter the leading primaries and specify the advantages and disadvantages to his candidacy of your recommendation. Would some primaries be more significant than others? Find out from

your text or instructor which states hold primaries, when they are held, and whether the results bind the delegates.

2. Perform the same tasks assuming you are the campaign manager for each of the four candidates seeking the *Republican* nomination.

3. Assume that you are a newspaper columnist assigned to cover the preconvention campaign which is about to begin in earnest. On the basis of the available information, you are to predict whom the delegates will nominate as they seek to name the man most likely to win a majority (seventy-one or more) of the electoral votes in the November election from the six key states indicated. Make your predictions first on the assumption that the candidates are Democrats. Then repeat the operation assuming the rivals are Republicans. In so doing, follow these procedures:

A. As accurately as you can—complete confidence is not possible—assign each key state to the candidate with the greatest positive appeal to the interests in that state, explaining fully your reasons for each assignment. Remember that the electoral votes of each state must be assigned as a bloc and no state's electoral vote can be divided among two or more candidates.

B. If, at first, no candidate seems able to win a majority, some compromises and second choices will have to be made. Take the votes of the candidate receiving the least support in your first calculation and assign these votes to the remaining candidate or candidates with the next greatest appeal to the interests in the state or states involved. Continue this process until one candidate has a majority. Explain your reasons for each assignment of votes.

PROBLEM 17

Choosing a President: An Experiment in Voting Behavior

BECAUSE elections perform such vital functions in American politics, political scientists have exerted considerable effort to explain why people vote as they do. We have accumulated a great deal of information about some of the conditions and reasons that lead people to vote, and lead them to vote for one party rather than the other. Students of American politics found very early in their research that many citizens develop a stable identification with one or the other of the major parties. Being able to identify a person as a Democrat or Republican helps in explaining many things about his political behavior. We know, of course, how he is *likely* to vote: in about eight out of ten cases, persons who identify themselves with one of the parties vote for that party in presidential elections. We also know how the individual is likely to evaluate candidates, stand on issues, and judge policies. The ways in which an individual's partisan loyalties can serve as a "mental shortcut" have been summarized by Robert E. Lane in a discussion of voting decisions.[1]

> Parties may be central forces in organizing political attitudes and behavior. Over the long run party identification has more influence over a person's vote decision than any other single factor, although in any one election this may not be true. Moreover, in general, party identifiers tend to vote more than those with no

[1] Robert E. Lane, *Political Life: Why People Get Involved in Politics* (Glencoe, Ill.: The Free Press, 1960), 300–302.

party loyalties at all; and those with strong identifications tend, in each party, to participate more in the election campaign than those with weak identifications. As for their attitudes on policy matters, party identifiers "not only vote the party line; within limits they also think the party line," and they do this regardless of socio-economic status. In foreign policy, when the rival party leaders adopt positions similar to each other, party loyalty naturally doesn't affect a person's views on American policy; but when the party leaders take different stands . . . then party loyalty seems to have a very strong effect on public opinion regarding foreign policy.

It isn't always the case that attitudes on policies, candidates, and parties are congruent, although the tendency of party loyalty to serve as a central organizing attitude encourages such congruence. When the most important of these attitudes are in harmony with each other, a person is much more likely to go to the polls and be otherwise active in a campaign. . . . When the party position on an issue is not known, or when there is none, the party obviously does not serve as a reference group in opinion formation. Further-more, when the party leaders are found performing acts which are generally disapproved of, such as engaging in graft, but when these do not affect the satisfactions which flow from party membership, membership in the party does not influence behavior or belief; members behave in no way different from non-members. Party identification, then, is broadly distributed in the population, im-portant in many, although not all, political situations. . . .

The satisfactions to be derived from an appropriate use of political parties as reference groups include, among others, a sense of orientation in a confused situation, identification with the symbols of higher status, legitimization of aggression against other ethnic or class groups and a sense of solidarity with other people in a family, neighborhood, or factory. The search for social solidarity is expressed in politics . . . in the adjustment of opinions and party preferences so as to avoid offense and to receive the rewards of social unity against an opposing group.

What sort of things lead one man to become a Democrat and the next a Republican? Review in your text and in your class notes materials relating to partisan attachments and voting behavior. Then consider the following propositions adapted from a summary in Bernard R. Berelson, Paul F. Lazarsfeld, and William N. McPhee, *Voting: A Study of Opinion Formation in a Presidential Campaign* (Chicago: University of Chicago Press, 1954), Appendix A, which relates certain situational factors to voting behavior.

FACTORS	PROPOSITIONS
1. Family Background	1.1 In 80 percent or more of all cases, voters and their immediate family agree in the way they vote, i.e., agree in favoring one candidate rather than another.
	1.2 Young people tend strongly to vote in the way their parents did.
2. Personal Associations (Friends and Co-workers)	2.1 People generally agree in their voting behavior with their friends, and with the people they work with (co-workers); and this tendency to agreement is slightly higher among friends, who are self-chosen, than it is among co-workers.
3. Age	3.1 A higher percentage of younger people vote Democratic in comparison with older people.
4. Region	4.1 There are no appreciable differences in voting behavior tendencies from region to region in the United States, except for the strong Democratic vote in the South.
5. Education	5.1 Well-educated persons are more likely to vote Republican than Democratic.
6. Ethnic or Religious Background	6.1 Protestants tend to vote Republican in higher proportions than do Catholics or Jews.
	6.2 Persons of German, Scandinavian, and Scotch-or-English descent tend to vote Republican in higher proportions than persons of Irish, Italian, and Polish origins, and Negroes.

7. Socioeconomic
Status—Social
Standing, or
Class Position

7.1 The higher a person's social or class status or position is, the more likely he is to vote Republican.

7.2 The higher a person's or family's income is, the more likely that person or family is to vote Republican.

7.3 The "higher" a person's occupation or occupational standing is, the more likely he is to vote Republican.

8. Residence
(Size of
Community)

8.1 Urban residents, or city-dwellers, tend to vote Democratic in higher proportions than rural residents do.

8.2 However, residents of metropolitan areas and of open country (farms), tend to vote Democratic in higher proportions than residents of small or middle-sized towns or cities do.

There is a tendency for these factors to be cumulative. For example, coming from a favored economic class increases the possibility of getting a college education. The more of the factors operating in the same direction, the more likely is the individual to attach himself to the party indicated. On the other hand, a moment's thought will reveal that different factors in voting behavior may operate in different directions. For example, an individual might be a Catholic, an Italo-American, and live in a metropolis like Chicago, factors which would indicate a Democratic vote; but at the same time, he may be a high business executive, who earns $25,000 a year, and whose friends and co-workers are mostly Republican, all factors which would indicate a Republican vote. Such a person is said to be subject to *cross-pressures*. The following statements adapted from Berelson, Lazarsfeld, and McPhee relate to the important factor of cross-pressures.

1. The more the members of a family disagree in their political views, the more a member of the family is likely, during a campaign, to be uncertain about whom to vote for.

2. The more he and his friends or co-workers agree about politics, the stronger an individual's conviction in support of a particular candidate will be; conversely, the more such personal associates disagree in their political views, the more an individual is likely, during a campaign, to be uncertain about whom to vote for.

Propositions suggesting possible results of being cross-pressured:

3. The more cross-pressures a voter is subject to, the longer he is likely to delay his final decision as to whom to vote for.

4. The more cross-pressures and inconsistencies a voter is subject to, the more likely he is to be uncertain about his voting preference during a campaign.

Early voting behavior studies tended to stress what we may call *situational* factors, that is to say, aspects of the social environment or social situation in which the voter lives and behaves. The propositions above refer almost entirely to such situational factors. A pioneering voting behavior study, Paul F. Lazarsfeld, Bernard R. Berelson, and Hazel Gaudet, *The People's Choice* (New York: Columbia University Press, 1944), placed particular emphasis on situational elements:

There is a familiar adage in American folklore to the effect that a person is only what he thinks he is, an adage which reflects the typically American notion of unlimited opportunity, the tendency toward self-betterment, etc. Now [in voting behavior in the presidential election of 1940] we find that the reverse of the adage is true: *a person thinks, politically, as he is, socially. Social characteristics determine political preference.*

Adding to studies identifying the situational components of voting behavior, more recent investigators have stressed a slightly different, though closely related set of factors. The work of the Survey Research Center of the University of Michigan has been summarized in Angus Campbell, Gerald Gurin, and Warren E. Miller, *The Voter Decides* (Evanston, Ill.: Row, Peterson and Co., 1954), and Angus Campbell, Philip Converse, Warren E. Miller, and Donald Stokes, *The American Voter* (New York: John Wiley and Sons, 1960). The emphasis in these studies is on the ways in which an individual *perceives* and *responds* to his environment. Three factors are found to be particularly relevant for explaining the outcome of the election:

(a) party identification—that is, the way in which a person thinks of himself or identifies himself as "a Democrat" or "a Republican";

(b) issue orientation—a person's ideas about, attitudes toward, or reactions to current domestic or foreign policy issues which he sees as being involved in the election contest; and

(c) candidate orientation—a person's perceptions of, attitudes toward, or feelings about the personality of a particular candidate or candidates.

We have already noted that social considerations aid in accounting for why one individual perceives political objects through a set of lenses called the Democratic party and another prefers to interpret and evaluate political events from the perspective of the Republican party. Thus, it is undoubtedly true that perceptual explanations and situational explanations of the vote are each dependent to some degree on one another.

Like situational factors, the factors of perception and response may also develop cross-pressures within an individual. For example, a person may identify himself with the Democratic party and agree with Democratic policy stand on most issues, but at the same time be so strongly and favorably oriented toward the personality of a Republican candidate like Dwight D. Eisenhower that he votes Republican. He may do this despite the fact that situational factors would indicate a Democratic vote.

The difference between the situational and perceptual approaches to analysis may be summed up in a pair of diagrams. The former approach seems to assume a causal connection between social situation and political behavior, thus:

Social Situation| ——————————————→ |Political Behavior

The perceptual approach, on the other hand, stresses the importance of individual factors such as identifications, orientation, evaluations, and perceptions between the situation and the behavior.

Explanations of political behavior which draw on both sets of factors are probably more accurate than attempts stressing only one. We can draw a second diagram as follows:

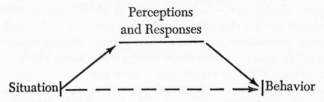

Explanations drawing on both situational and perceptual factors (solid lines) are more comprehensive than explanations which depend only on information about someone's social characteristics (dashed line). Still, to some degree, explanations which follow the path of situational analysis are possible.

It must also be borne in mind that patterns of voting behavior may change through time, from election to election. Thus during the 1930's and to a lesser degree during the 1940's, when economic and "rich-man/poor-man" issues seemed central in the minds of many voters, "social characteristics" may have determined "political preference" to a high degree. In the 1950's, with economic, occupational-group, and class issues less dominant, such factors as candidate orientation and concern with different issues played a larger part in ultimate behavior. In the 1952 and 1956 presidential elections a movement toward Eisenhower was apparent in substantially *all* economic and social groupings or groups, including, for example, wage-earners and labor union members. In 1960 economic and religious cleavages probably had a greater effect than they did during the Eisenhower years, and in 1964 the liberal-conservative issue was an important element in the campaign. Thus, factors that might seem to provide an adequate basis for prediction in one period might clearly fail to do so in another.

A short Voting Profile designed by Eugene Burdick to provide some prediction of voting behavior is reproduced here in revised and adapted form, with a form for Tally Sheets and a Scoring

Chart. This simple twenty-question schedule was not designed for refined professional use, but was presented as part of a popular article discussing the possibilities of prediction in voting behavior. Furthermore, while efforts at prediction in professional studies are concerned with statistical tendencies in large numbers or aggregates of voters, this Voting Profile is aimed at predicting the probable vote of a *particular individual*—a considerably riskier business. Again, asking the Voting Profile's twenty questions of a dozen quite unscientifically selected persons is by no means the same as interviewing a much larger number of persons in a scientifically designed sample. These warnings and qualifications should be kept in mind. The twenty questions, however, are based on many of the findings of voting behavior research, and should provide a usable and useful tool in an informal experiment aimed at achieving some understanding of voting behavior and of the possibilities and difficulties of prediction in this area.

In this informal experiment, the Voting Profile itself is subject to testing as to its usefulness as a predictive instrument and to subsequent analysis of its strengths and weaknesses.

Undertake the following informal experiment and prepare the results for class discussion or a written report:

1. Analyze carefully the Voting Profile, to see what factors associated with voting behavior it includes, what factors it stresses, and what possibly important factors it fails to include.

2. Give the Voting Profile to twelve people, if possible people whose voting intentions you do not know in advance. Half of your respondents should be students; the other half should be non-students, not more than two of them teachers or members of your immediate family. Review the questionnaire thoroughly before you start interviewing, to make sure that you can ask the questions smoothly and clearly. Never express any approval or disapproval of answers you get during an interview. Make up a Tally Sheet for each interview, based on the form given after the questionnaire.

3. After you have given the Voting Profile, ask each person how he voted, or would have voted, in the most recent presidential election. On the basis of this information, you will be able to judge how successful the Profile was in predicting how the people you interviewed voted, or would have voted.

4. Where the Profile failed to predict voting accurately, question the respondent further to find out why he voted or would have voted as he indicated, in order to find out why the Voting Profile failed in that case—what factors it left out, overemphasized, or underemphasized, and so on. On the back of your tally sheets, make notes of the answers to these additional questions.

5. If the Voting Profile was more successful in predicting the behavior of the nonstudents of voting age you interviewed than it was in predicting the behavior of fellow students, analyze the possible reasons for this result.

6. On the basis of your findings in Steps 3, 4, and 5, make what general statements you can about the strengths and weaknesses of the Profile as a tool for prediction. Relate your generalizations to what you have discovered from your reading and this experiment about the factors involved in voting behavior.

Voting Profile [2]

INSTRUCTIONS. Items in Roman type are questions to ask respondent. Items in *italics* are instructions for the interviewer. Ask respondents to answer questions quickly. Use separate tally sheet for each respondent, following the Form indicated after the questionnaire. If an item is not appropriate, or the respondent cannot give an answer, leave space on tally sheet blank.

1. Is (*if living*) Was (*if deceased*) your father a Democrat or a Republican? *Put 5 points under column of father's party, if father voted or identified self regularly or usually with one party.*

2. Is (*if living*) Was (*if deceased*) your mother a Democrat or a Republican? *Put 5 points under column of mother's party, if mother voted or identified self regularly or usually with one party.*

[2] Adapted and reproduced by permission from Eugene Burdick, "How You'll Vote This Fall," *This Week Magazine*, May 16, 1956.

3. *If respondent's father and mother are (were) of the same party, put 5 additional points under that party.*

4. *If father and mother are (were) of different parties,* CROSS OUT *the figures entered after Questions 1 and 2.*

5. (*If married*) Is your (*wife*) (*husband*) a Democrat or a Republican? *Put 15 points under the party which respondent's spouse usually supports.*

6. Just quickly and "off-the-cuff," do you think most of your friends are Democrats or Republicans? *Put 10 points under the party which most of respondent's friends support or favor.*

7. Now as to your age; are you thirty or younger, or are you over thirty? *If respondent is thirty or younger, put 4 points in the Democratic column.*

8. *If respondent is older than thirty years of age, put 4 points in the Republican column.*

9. *If respondent is regularly a resident of one of the following states, put 6 points in the Democratic column: Alabama, Arkansas, Florida, Georgia, Louisiana, Mississippi, North Carolina, South Carolina, Virginia.*

10. Which party do you think will win the next presidential election, regardless of which party you prefer? *Put 2 points in the column of the party respondent thinks will win.*

11. Do you read a foreign language newspaper regularly? *If* YES, *put 3 points in the Democratic column.*

12. Are you of Scandinavian, German, or Scotch-or-English ancestry? *If* YES, *put 2 points in the Republican column. If* NO *ask:*

13. Are you of Irish, Italian or Polish ancestry? *If* YES, *put 2 points in the Democratic column.*

14. What is your occupation, or the kind of work you do? *List occupation briefly on tally sheet. If respondent is a factory worker, put 4 points in the Democratic column, or 6 points if he is also a union member.*

15. *If respondent is regularly a resident on a farm, or in a suburb, or in a town smaller than 40,000, put 3 points in the Republican column.*

16. *If respondent is regularly a resident in a city larger than 50,000, put 3 points in the Democratic column.*

17. Regardless of which party you prefer, under what party do you think you personally, or your immediate family, will be better

off in an economic sense? *Put 10 points under the column of the party respondent names.*

18. Can you quickly and "off-the-cuff" think of a person older than yourself whom you know, and whom you respect very highly? Which party do you think this person belongs to or supports? *Put 10 points under the column of that party.*

19. Can you recall the last time you talked about politics with a group, whether large or small, as long as it included people outside your own family? Did you have the impression that the group was mostly Republican or mostly Democratic? *Put 4 points under the appropriate column.*

20. Is (your) (your family) income more, or less, than $6,000 per year? *If* LESS *than $6,000 per year, put 4 points in the Democratic column.*

Scoring Chart

On Tally Sheet for each respondent, figure for Net Voting Preference will appear in either Republican or Democratic column, or at 0. Locate Net Voting Preference for respondent at appropriate point on "continuum line," below.

Net Voting Preference
Republican

Net Voting Preference
Democratic

80 70 60 50 40 30 20 10 0 10 20 30 40 50 60 70 80

Between 60 and 80—almost certain to vote for party indicated.
Between 30 and 60—ten-to-one will vote for party indicated.
Between 20 and 30—better than even chance will vote for party
indicated.
Ten or less either way—an Independent or Undecided voter.

Form for Tally Sheets

REPUBLICAN		DEMOCRATIC
Question 1		5
2		5
3		5
4		15
5	10	4
6		2
7		3
8		2
9		4
10	10	10
11	4	
12	4	
13		
14		
15		
16		
17		
18		
19		
20		
Add columns: Totals	28	55
Subtract smaller total from larger		
Result—Net Voting Preference		

PROBLEM 18

Strategy in a Congressional Campaign

EVERY year countless would-be public officials, some for the first time and others for as much as the fifteenth or twentieth time, submit themselves to the trials of a campaign as a necessary step for achieving public office.

These campaigners, whether they are seeking the presidency or a position as county coroner, must operate within several major working assumptions. The American politician feels that it is his constitutionally protected right to criticize his opponent and to project himself as the more worthy candidate. Moreover the campaigner realizes that he must work to build a political following. He assures potential supporters that he understands and represents their best interests, and this task often requires building alliances among groups with somewhat different political goals. A successful campaign begins, in large measure, with an accurate assessment of the potential support and strength of various interests and segments of opinion in the constituency. Finally, the campaigner must usually convince foe and friend alike that he stands firmly in the American tradition and that he plays the game of politics according to acceptable rules. His personal characteristics and his political candidacy must "fit" the image held by the voters of the "American way of doing things."

These are not easy requirements and the difficulty is compounded when one of them contradicts another. For example, building a following from one group may alienate a different section of the voters. We speak of the "art of campaigning" as the means by which the hopeful public servant attempts to fulfill and reconcile the demands placed upon him. The art of campaigning is spoken of with distaste as often as it is with devotion; the campaign maze is viewed by some as an insult to Americans and by others as the great protector of democracy. In academic and popular journals particularly, considerable attention has been focused on the weaknesses of our own brand of campaigning. Around election time we hear accusations of "oversimplification," "mud-slinging," "slander by innuendo," "distortion of the issues," and so forth. In a discussion of the basic character of American political campaigns, Professors Austin Ranney and Willmore Kendall summarize much of this discussion and attempt to answer some of the critics.[1]

> Much of the existing literature on American political parties assumes that their campaigning activities are essentially "propagandistic" rather than "educational," and describes in greater or lesser detail the "propaganda techniques" used by the parties in campaigns. In the opinion of the present writers, however, American campaigns are at least as "educational" as they are "propagandistic." They are, be it remembered, a characteristic activity of American political parties, which, we contend, faithfully reflect the character of American society. They are planned and executed . . . by the sort of men who have achieved leadership in the American party systems. These leaders are neither propagandists nor educators, but—because they make nominations and contest elections—a little of both, but not much of either. Considered in general terms, the campaigns they run show the following characteristics:
>
> (1) American campaigns do not provide a sober canvass of the major political, economic, and social issues of the day, calculated to give the voters anything comparable to what a university professor would regard as knowledge about and understanding of these issues. This is so partly because the system requires that the major issues—the ones on which the most crucial decisions will be made between this campaign and the next one—either be

[1] Austin Ranney and Willmoore Kendall, *Democracy and the American Party System* (New York: Harcourt, Brace & Co., 1956), 356–59.

avoided or be touched upon only marginally by the campaign strategists on both sides. And it is partly because their mood and manner—like that of American advertising campaigns, American religious campaigns, and even American "educational" campaigns —is not that of the classroom. In short, one of the rules . . . is this: Don't overtax the intellectual capacity of the masses of voters. Or, variously, don't assume that the voters, insofar as they pay attention to you at all, do so out of a desire to be instructed (some may, but not enough to affect the election results). But not over-taxing the intellectual audience is as sound a rule in education as in propaganda.

(2) American campaigns do oversimplify even the issues they deal with, and in doing so indeed hew close to the classic rules of propaganda as laid down by such experts as Adolf Hitler and Joseph Goebbels. But we must not conclude from this that they over-simplify out of any intent on the part of the strategists to patronize or manipulate the voters. For one thing, the oversimplification is clearly a matter not of strategy in the Hitler-Goebbels sense, but of tacit and spontaneous agreement by *two* sets of strategists, who as the campaign proceeds tacitly negotiate with one another as to which not-very-relevant and not-very-urgent issues to treat as "the" issues. The problem, as the strategists on both sides neces-sarily see it, is not the Hitler-Goebbels problem of how to impose an ideology and a program despite the best efforts of the opposi-tion to impose theirs, but how to square off to opponents whose ideology and program are almost identical with their own—how to keep on saying for weeks and weeks what the opposition is saying, and yet give it a sufficiently different twist and sound to keep the campaign interesting. The parties, in short, are actors in one and the same show; each needs the other to perform well, lest the audience get bored and stay home on election day. And for another thing, there is every reason to believe that the oversimplification reflects, as much as anything else, an honest effort on the part of both sets of strategists to explain what the election is about to *themselves*. They, hardly less than the voters, are overwhelmed by the scale and complexity of the problems to be dealt with by the government they seek to control. And to suppose that they say to each other in their midnight councils: "The real issues are these, but the voters wouldn't understand them, so let's

keep quiet about them," is to overlook both the rapport between American party leaders and American voters and the deep respect with which the former regard the latter. The rule, if conscious rule there be, is: Choose issues appropriate to the American political system, and discuss them in such a way as to capture and retain the interest of the American people and to bring some of them, who might not otherwise have done so, to vote for our side.

(3) Even the previously mentioned rule about "pork chops"— [voters . . . try to cast their votes in such a manner as to protect and advance their own economic interest]—must be grasped in the context of the system. It means neither that the strategists regard the voters as motivated exclusively or even primarily by economic considerations, nor that American party leaders so conduct campaigns as to subordinate other issues to economic issues, nor, finally, that they are prepared to contemplate any drastic redistribution of pork chops. Here, as in other respects, the parties are as careful as, say, Ford and General Motors to approach their "customers" each with approximately the same commodity; and neither deceives itself, any more than do Ford and General Motors, as to whether total sales are going to be greatly affected by what is said via the mass-communications media. The rule is: Don't go after new supporters with appeals that might lose you many old ones.

(4) The same considerations as in the foregoing paragraph apply to the strategists' handling of America's many delicate conflicts of interest and aspiration between ethnic groups. One party may, over a number of years, gradually win from the other party a considerable proportion of the voters belonging to a particular ethnic group, as the Democrats appear, in recent years, to have taken away from the Republicans a sizable part of the Negro vote. But the process by which this is accomplished does not reflect itself recognizably and as such in the party's campaign appeals, where the rule is: Avoid issues between ethnic groups.

(5) To picture American campaigns as the unfolding of the plans of the master strategists at the top flies in the face of what we know about the internal organization of American parties. A propaganda machine is *ipso facto* centralized; it cannot, given the character of its mission, tolerate improvisation in its lower echelons; the "line," *because* it constitutes a carefully devised assault upon

the less rational susceptibilities of the recipients, must originate at the top and descend to the bottom with the obligatory force of a command. An American national party, on the other hand, is *ipso facto* decentralized; given the character of its organization, it cannot prevent improvisation in its lower echelons; and any "line" adopted at the top will be effective at the bottom just to the extent that those at the bottom recognize it as meeting *their* standards of appropriations, honesty, and fair play; commands . . . play no role in the process.

(6) One who views an American campaign as a chess game between two teams of high-powered general-staff officers armed with the latest know-how about manipulating the masses not only misses the point; he also misses the fun. An American party campaign is, in the nature of the case, a comedy of errors, which stands in the same relation to a genuine propaganda operation as, say, the annual congressional baseball game to the first game of a World Series. The catcher has no way of signaling for a low one inside, and the chances are that the pitcher—assuming there's only one in the box, and that the bat boy is willing to let him have the ball for a moment—doesn't know how to throw one. No one knows, when he hits the ball over the fence, whose score the run will be added to; so in general the players economize their energies, and seem to prefer foul tips to home runs. Since the real score is going to be chalked up—on another day, and in another ball park— in a popularity contest, the players worry very little about their batting and fielding averages—which, in consequence, run pretty low. And the fun of watching the spectacle consists precisely in understanding that this is the kind of game it is.

(7) The general impact of each campaign *is* educational, in the sense that it does focus public attention for a few brief weeks each quadrennium (and, to some extent, each biennium) on public affairs, and does involve the communication of a certain amount of more or less opposite information and argument about those affairs. If its mood is not that of the university classroom, it is also not that of Nuremberg and Red Square—and, since there are two sets of loudspeakers, each of which is prepared to call the other a liar if it strays too far from the truth, it *cannot* be that of Nuremberg and Red Square. "Slogans" and "symbols"—irrational symbols if

you like—figure prominently in it, but so do facts about the national debt, and reasonably sober reflection about American foreign policy. And—what is most important from the standpoint of our inquiry—it educates the American people with respect to the special character of their politics, and instructs them in the special character of their own role in those politics.

A defense of the campaign art from one who has run for election is illustrated by the following selection by John C. Cort, a candidate for the Massachusetts state legislature in 1958.[2] In reading this account, pay attention to those things which Cort felt were accomplished by his campaigning as well as examining the particular campaign techniques he used.

I've learned what it feels like to run for public office. There was the day early in the campaign when I went down to Goodenough Street to find a friend. I had the wrong address and, seeing this group of people sitting on the lawn across the street, I approached them to ask directions.

They gave me directions and then I said, "As long as I'm here, have one of my cards. I'm John Cort, running for state representative."

An elderly lady said, "Sorry, but we're committed to Paul Kinsella."

"But you have two votes," I said. (It was a two-seat ward.) "You can always give me the other one."

"No," she said, "Joe Cusack's relatives live down the street."

Confronted by this hopeless situation, I said the first thing that came into my head. It was not one of my more felicitous remarks. "Well," I said, "if either one of them drops dead, remember me." The reaction was not good.

Afterwards—in fact, almost immediately—I thought of something more tactful to fit this situation. In fact, as I covered the ward ringing door bells, I developed a set of stock answers for almost any situation.

I was not, however, a match for the old Polish lady who didn't want to vote for me because I had too many children.

[2] John Cort, "My First Hurrah," *Commonweal*, November 7, 1958.

"Too much money," she said.

"You mean I'd have to take too much graft to support my children?"

"That's right," she said.

"Do I look dishonest?" I said, a little indignant. And then, in a reference to a local scandal in the Department of Public Works, I went on: "After all, I don't believe in $140 a week for a station wagon."

"What's the matter?" she said. "Not enough?" She was a sharp one.

It was only fair, though, that I should have lost a vote because of the children. I certainly got enough because of them and I used the family picture shamelessly. I discovered that it is an article of faith among many of the Boston Irish that a man who has a large family must be a good man. I almost came to believe it myself. There was also a big sympathy vote for any candidate who had a lot of mouths to feed. "If he has that many kids," was the feeling, "he *needs* the job". . . .

To counteract this sympathy vote, however, there was a tendency to circulate various data, real or imagined. One such was the glad news that my wife was related to the DuPonts. When confronted with this intelligence she would confess only to the fact that her cousin sells paint. Another one was that I came from Texas, presumably from a big oil or cattle family. There was also a vicious whispering campaign to the effect that I was born and raised in New York. This happens to be true and hurt me among the element who feel that coming from New York is little better than coming from Moscow. . . .

From such experiences I picked up a few lasting impressions. One is a grudging admiration for politicians as a class. Sometime in their lives they must have sweat. From my own experience I can say that there is no more gruelling job in the world than running for office where there is any kind of a contest. . . .

Another lasting impression was this: the average voter is a profoundly cynical man, or woman. One young lady was so disgusted with politicians that she told me she intended never to vote again. Again and again I ran into the conviction that politics and dishonesty were synonyms . . . .

As a matter of fact, the cynicism is by no means justified. Both the district and the city have produced honest officials, and even more who were at least as honest as the average voter. But the average voter does not want someone who is only as honest as himself. He wants a man who is able to resist the temptations which he knows in his heart that he himself would not be able to resist. And in a sense he is right. After all, the average voter at least has the honesty not to put himself forward as an object of trust. . . .

Again and again the professionals will tell you, as they put the arm over the shoulders and lean close for the friendly word of advice, "Politics is a dirty game, John," or, in justifying some cute-but-slightly-soiled maneuver, simply, "That's politics." Often the man who tells you this is one whom, on over-all points, you would have to put down as a man of honor. He may have suffered for his integrity in the face of severe temptations. And his own career may have been fairly convincing evidence that moral carelessness is not essential to the profession. But still he persists in believing that he himself is a kind of exception to the general rule that to succeed in the game one must be ready, always, to look the other way.

All this is pretty dogmatic moralizing for a man who didn't make it himself. I became the first man in history to ring every doorbell (about eight thousand) in Ward 22. This is a minor distinction I shall carry proudly to the grave, but it wasn't enough to overcome my weaknesses as a candidate. One of these was that I had lived less than eight years in the ward and had spent very little time in local organizations—this in a ward where "born and raised in the district" is generally considered one of the first requirements for public office.

The best I could do was runner-up, third, in a field of ten. Looking back, I have to admit that this was better than I had any right to expect. It is a characteristic of political amateurs who make some pretense to idealism that they expect the electorate to roll over and beg as soon as they present themselves for office. But the electorate is neither a dumb dog nor an easy woman who can be swept off her feet by a whirlwind courtship. Like any sensible, decent woman she wants you to hang around awhile so she can get to know you, really know you, not just the party manners, but the real you.

There is no virtue in the political amateur that can exempt him from the discipline of politics: the laborious getting around and mingling, the hundred and one nights at the K. of C. meetings, the

American Legion meeting, the choir practice, the variety show rehearsals, the wakes, the weddings, the dinners. If you like people enough to enjoy it, fine, but if you don't, brother, resign yourself. There is no other way.

And are you needed, you political amateurs with the pretense of idealism? You certainly are, if the idealism is anything more than a pretense. The people cry out for you. Even the politicians are waiting and hoping that you will appear, convinced that you cannot succeed, hoping that you will, hoping that the Bible maxims are right after all, that honesty is the best policy, that Mr. Deeds *can* go to town and Mr. Smith to Washington. I believe that the woods are full of politicians who would like to be honest *all* the time, if only someone could convince them that it works.

Now consider carefully the following hypothetical situation as a case study in the problem of political campaigning, from the point of view of one of the candidates.

The Third Congressional District in the State of Sunshine has a population of approximately 400,000, and covers nine counties. Quentin, the largest city, has a population of about 105,000. Fifteen lesser cities, ranging in size from 5,000 to 10,000, have a combined population of 110,000. Some 90,000 people live in small towns or other rural nonfarm areas. About 20,000 farms of various sizes account for the remaining 95,000 of the population, some 8,000 of these being farm laborers. The latter are mostly Mexican-Americans, concentrated on a few relatively very large farms.

Three dams that provide sources of cheap hydroelectric power have recently been constructed in the area as part of a federal government development program. Mills and factories, attracted by the supply of cheap electricity, have been established in many of the small towns and cities during the past few years. Industry now accounts for about one-fifth of the employment in the District outside of Quentin, and for about half of the employment in Quentin. The new industries have brought with them a significant boom in building construction in which many local contractors and their employees have benefited.

Until the recent growth of industry the region had been over-whelmingly agricultural. The farming is diversified, with wheat, corn, and cotton accounting for 59 percent of the agricultural income. Most of the farms in the area are family farms and most of the farmers own their land. Of the 20,000 farms in the District about half yield annual net incomes of $5,000–$10,000, with a few exceeding $10,000. The new dams have resulted in inundating some valuable farm land, and forced some farm families to give up their homes. Some have established themselves on other farms; some have gone to Quentin or to smaller towns and taken jobs in industry. On the other hand the new industry and the new population it has brought with it has resulted in some enlargement of the local market for farm products, particularly for cotton to supply new textile mills and for poultry, vegetables, dairy products, and eggs sold for local consumption. Few farmers in the area belong to farm organizations, though some units of the American Farm Bureau Federation and the National Farmers Union exist.

There has been talk of using the water reserves building up behind the federal dams for irrigation purposes. The *New Era,* the leading newspaper in Quentin, has suggested a federally financed irrigation system to bring water to dry-land areas and to increase farm productivity in the region, but nothing has been done toward irrigation development. Some farmers are wary of irrigation proposals as a threat to their old way of life, while others, generally the more successful, favor an irrigation project as a step toward progress. Substantial dry-land areas do exist in the District, many of which could be brought under cultivation by irrigation.

The federal dams, the cheap electricity they provide, and the growth of industry have begun a basic transformation in the lives of most of the people in the District, particularly in the smaller cities and towns. A typical case is that of Fremont, where two paper mills have been established, each employing about 500 workers. The town's population increased sharply in a short time and is now nearly 8,500. The new mills were built by companies whose headquarters are in New York and the mill executives and supervisors were sent to Fremont from other plants owned by the companies. There has been a real estate boom as a result of the population increase and many new houses are now under construction. Bonds have been levied for a new school building to relieve the crowded classrooms. There is full employment in Fremont and the people are more prosperous than they have ever been before. The first chain supermarket, and A & P store, was established two months ago. Rumor is circulating that a Sears, Roebuck store will soon be built on the vacant lot across the street from the courthouse. Many merchants who welcomed the increase in trade are now beginning to fear that the arrival of chain stores will destroy their businesses.

Another result of the coming of industry has been the growth of labor unions in an area which had been traditionally "open shop," and often actively opposed to unions. Much of the new management in the area has been ready to sign union contracts in order to guarantee stable labor conditions, so important to getting the new plants into production. Employers longer established in the District, however, have resisted labor organization, often bitterly. Shortly after the new mills were built in Fremont, a newly organized AFL-CIO union in one of the older-established shops voted overwhelmingly to strike for wages comparable to those being paid in the new mills. The company fought the strike; after four months the workers went back to their jobs without their pay raise, and with their union virtually destroyed. Many of the "Old Timers" in Fremont agreed with the local newspaper, the Fremont *Courier*, that the strike was caused by "the grasping tendencies of the labor leaders, who won't let the men be satisfied when they're well off." The AFL-CIO unions in the area, faced as they are with the problems of getting organized and negotiating with management, have not so far undertaken any significant degree of political action.

The pattern of social and political leadership in Fremont is changing. People who have moved to Fremont to manage the new plants have begun to emerge as leaders in the city's social life, and two men who did not live in the area two years ago have been elected to the city council.

The picture in Fremont is similar to that in most of the small towns in the District. The economy has changed greatly in a short time. Established patterns of living and thinking are being challenged. The status and prestige of old community leaders is being threatened. On the other hand most people have derived financial advantage from the industries, and the Chambers of Commerce in many of the towns are working actively to attract more industry. There is no open hostility between the old and the new, but there is much latent dissatisfaction. This is voiced from time to time by "Old Timers" who see their way of life threatened.

The Congressional seat for the Third District will be vacant next term, as a result of the retirement of the incumbent Congressman. He has announced that he will take no part in the election to choose his successor. The Republicans always carry the District and the Republican primary is thus the effective election. Because of this one-party dominance party organization as such is weak, and candidates find it necessary to an unusual degree to conduct their own campaigns and build their own organization and following. A hard-fought Congressional primary is likely to bring out a total vote of 80,000 to 90,000.

One candidate has already filed for the congressional nomination in the Republican primary. He is Larry Copperwood, a fifty-nine-year-old druggist from Fremont and a bachelor. He has lived all his life there, is energetic, has many friends, and has been an important figure in his city and in the District for many years. He has served as mayor of Fremont and as state senator and is well known for his leadership of an effort in the state legislature of Sunshine to get better highways for the area. Copperwood is basing his campaign on a conservative appeal to local, independent businessmen, to old-established residents in the towns, and to farmers. He attacks the new industrial concerns and their officials from outstate as "foreigners" and "carpetbaggers" and denounces the "monstrous expansion of federal government power," particularly as represented by the federally built dams and hydroelectric generators in the District and by the proposals made by the Quentin *New Era* for federal aid to public schools in the region and broadening social security to include medicare for the aged. At the same time Copperwood calls for more federal aid to farmers as well as for laws to "restrict unfair competition from chain stores," and for new federal labor legislation to "curb the union bosses." He reminds his audiences of the uncomplicated "good old days" before the dams were built and new industry and labor disputes came into the area. He says that he will work in Congress "to keep old-fashioned sunshine in the hearts of the people of the Sunshine state." The Fremont *Courier* is supporting Copperwood vigorously by running news stories and editorials reflecting his campaign themes, and by picturing him as an ideal person to represent the District.

Only one other person, Glendon Jackson of Quentin, has announced for the Republican nomination. A youthful thirty-four, he is vigorous, has an attractive personality, possesses a wide circle of friends in Quentin and in Quentin County, and has often spoken on public affairs, particularly international affairs, at church and lodge meetings and over Quentin's TV station and local radio stations. He has an attractive, intelligent, red-haired wife, and three small children. A life-long resident of Quentin, he is not nearly as well known in small-town and rural areas as Copperwood is. He is a lawyer who has been active in Republican politics in Quentin and has served as prosecuting attorney of Quentin County. In the past his chief support has come from a group of businessmen in Quentin who have not been affected by the recent changes as much as the people in the smaller communities have been. While he has always been a businessman's lawyer, Jackson has never taken a position on the questions that are currently agitating many people in the Third Congressional District such as the federal dams, irrigation proposals, the influx of new industries, farm price supports, union activity and labor legislation, federal aid to education, medicare, and the like. Most people in the District have no clear picture of him in terms of his personality or of his stand on issues.

Though he knows he faces a tough fight Jackson thinks he can win, if he can devise a campaign that will appeal effectively to people or groups in the District who might be brought, for various reasons, to support him or to oppose Copperwood, his older and more experienced opponent. In short, Jackson sees himself as the underdog.

Review in your text and in your class notes materials relating to the role of interest groups, public opinion, candidates, and propaganda in election campaigns, and review any supplementary material you can find.

Assume that you work in Quentin as a member of a public relations firm. Candidate Jackson has come to you for advice on the substance and methods of publicity that would be most effective, given all the circumstances, in his campaign for the nomination. As a public relations specialist you know that one of the most important jobs in a winning campaign would be to build up, in the minds of as many voters as possible, a favorable "picture" or "image" of Glendon Jackson as a *personality* and as a *candidate*. You know that there are many ways in which such a picture or image can be built up: for example, by carefully painting Jackson's public personality in a certain way; or perhaps by contrasting his general background, character, and outlook with that of Larry Copperwood; or by trying to connect or identify him in the minds of the voters with certain groups or leaders in the District; or by developing and stressing positions he may take on certain important issues; or perhaps merely by identifying him in the minds of the voters with some general slogan or slogans. You also know that a favorable picture or image of Jackson may be built up by a careful *combination* of various possible approaches, including those listed above or others.

At the outset of his consultation with you Jackson lists seven possible alternative ways to focus his campaign that have been suggested to him, and asks for your criticism of these seven ways. They are:

1. Appeal for the support of the new industries and their employees and the new-industry leadership in the Third Congressional District, by denouncing Copperwood's "carpetbagger" charges and painting the new business leaders in the area as the advance agents of progress and prosperity. Paint yourself as a "forward-looking" man who can work with these new leaders. Stress the prosperity and payrolls more new industry can bring to Quentin and other areas.

2. Pitch the campaign toward the union members in the District, urging amendment of federal labor legislation so as to prohibit states from passing "anti-union" or "right-to-work" laws. Exploit Copperwood's opposition to unions, paint yourself as a "friend of labor," and try to get the solid backing of labor, which, it is argued, can give you organized and therefore effective support. In addition, go after the vote of the Mexican-American farm laborers, whose poor working conditions have been virtually ignored by other political leaders. Attack anti-union, low-wage employers and the factory-farm owners as "exploiters," who violate the "American way" and oppress the Mexican-American minority.

3. Wage a generally liberal and anti-Copperwood campaign. Frequently assert that Copperwood is reactionary, a petty man who lives in the past, an "Old Fogey," a "spokesman for the party of memory," a person who is not abreast of modern developments. Accuse him of being a tool of "vested interests" in the small towns, and paint yourself as a "progressive" leader.

4. Conduct a high-level campaign and rationally discuss the issues. Do not allow yourself to engage in mud-slinging, even if Copperwood does. Point out to the people the fallacies in Copperwood's arguments in regard to industry and to unions. Agree with him on the farm issue, disagree on the education and medicare issues. "Talk sense" to the people, taking specific positions on issues of concern to people in the District.

5. Concentrate on important issues facing the nation, rather than on issues of local interest. Take a stand on foreign affairs. Mention local issues, but subordinate them to "the national interest." Appeal, as a broad-gauge "statesman," to the better nature of the people to elect a Congressman who has the vision and the courage to make the nation as a whole his chief concern.

6. Run on your ingratiating personality in a personal-contact campaign, displaying your attractive wife and children as much as possible and flooding the District with pictures of yourself as the center of a happy family group. Imply but do not state directly that Copperwood is a crusty bachelor, an old curmudgeon, while you represent youth, the family, and vigor.

7. Conduct a highly general campaign around the slogan "Progress or Decay? The people must choose!" Support "progress," and identify yourself with "progress" in general terms.

As a public relations expert, give Candidate Jackson:

A. Your ESTIMATE of the probable success or failure of *each* of the *seven* possible strategies described above, 1 through 7.

B. Your own RECOMMENDATIONS as to the most effective publicity strategy for his campaign, which might be an elaboration of one of the seven strategies already suggested to him; or some combination of two or more of these; or a new strategy line, which might or might not incorporate within it one or more of the seven ideas already suggested.

Be as clear and specific as you can.

In both Questions A and B, above, *develop as fully as you can your* REASONS *for your estimates or suggestions*. Base your analysis and argument throughout on (1) your knowledge of factors that apparently influence the outcome of elections in general or the "rules of successful campaigning," and on (2) the situation in the Third Congressional District as it has been described.

Remember, your objective is to plan a winning strategy, or at least the best possible strategy to help Jackson get the nomination.

PART VI

The Legislative Power

PROBLEM 19

The Legislator's Choice

A variety of factors may affect a Congressman's decision to vote one way or another on the bills that come before him. As a representative in a democracy he is expected somehow to give heed to "the voice of the people," and not simply to vote as he pleases. Yet on many occasions he may find it hard to locate that voice at all, and on others he may feel that it contradicts itself or stutters. Even so, as a politician who depends on support and votes in his state or district, he usually tries to please as many people in his constituency as he can and offend as few as possible; and he is the target of innumerable interest-group pressures at home and in the capitol lobbies. As a Democrat or a Republican who is usually dependent to some degree on his party for election and for advancement in Congress he is generally inclined to go along with the party when he can and particularly if the president in office is of his own party the Congressman is likely to be subject to presidential leadership and influence. When an important roll call comes the Congressman may also consult another voice, the voice of his own values, judgment, or conscience. From the Congressman's point of view the legislative decision on important questions is seldom a mechanical one but is instead a choice, and a kind of choice that he must make day after day, month after month, bill after bill. He knows he is in some sense accountable to the political forces that play around and on him, but the voice that will in the end say aye or no is his.

Now read and ponder the following statements about the factors that may affect the legislator's choice.

The first statement is by the political scientist V. O. Key, Jr., from a summary of research in public opinion up to 1960 as it touched on Congressional voting behavior.[1]

In the long stream of rationalization and debate on the role of the representative, a continuous concern has been manifest about the proper relation between the representative and his constituency. The bald issue appears in the contrast between the representative bound by instructions from his constituents and the representative bound by conscience to exercise his best judgment in the interest of the nation. Burke, in his famed exposition of the second viewpoint, contended: "Parliament is not a congress of ambassadors from different and hostile interests, which interests each must maintain, as an agent and advocate, against other agents and advocates; but Parliament is a deliberative assembly of one nation, with one interest, that of the whole—where not local purposes, not local prejudices, ought to guide, but the general good, resulting from the general reason of the whole."

The practice of constituency instructions to representatives has long since ceased, in part because the broadening of the suffrage and the direct election of representatives left no organ competent, either legally or practically, to issue instructions. Nevertheless, the discussion of representation has continued in large measure in the terms set in Burke's time. Excessive devotion by the representative to his constituency has been thought to insure a sacrifice of national interest to local and parochial concerns. . . .

A concern about how representatives ought to respond to the

[1] V. O. Key, Jr., *Public Opinion and American Democracy* (New York: Alfred A. Knopf, 1961), 481–83, 487.

opinion of their constituents is a worthy preoccupation, but it is likely to be futile unless illuminated by some knowledge about how representatives respond. That legislators have an abiding interest in the nature of opinion in their constituencies there can be no doubt. How their estimates of that opinion bear on their work in the assembly is not nearly so clear. At times they bow down before constituency opinion, and at times they ignore it. On many questions there may be no discernible constituency opinion, but on a few issues constituency opinion may be imperious in its demands On all these matters, however, our information is limited. The objective in this [summary] is to assemble information that is available.

Most of the time the elegant prose spilled over the question of whether a legislator should be a man and vote his mature convictions in the national interest or be a mouse and bow abjectly to the parochial demands of his constituents is irrelevant to the realities. Few of his constituents have even the slightest awareness of most of the questions on which the legislator must stand up and be counted. On those few issues about which awareness is widespread among his constituents, he usually has no trustworthy estimate of the distribution of opinions of his constituents. In some districts on some issues the legislator may know well enough what opinion is. A southern congressman from a predominantly Negro district may have no doubt that his supporters—that is, the whites—oppose federal intervention in race relations. Such instances of clarity of opinion, however, are relatively few among all the questions a legislator must consider. On the same issue, the congressman from a northern, white constituency may vote in the opposite way from his southern colleague, though usually he has no reliable information on the attitudes of his constituency. Generally, a legislator may hear from a few people on a few issues. He must always, as he votes, assume the risk of antagonizing some constituents, but he is rarely faced by the difficult choice of rejecting or accepting the mandate of his constituency, for he does not know what it is. And, indeed, there may be none.

The sketchiness of knowledge about constituency opinion creates its embarrassments for any discussion of the relation between the voting of legislators and the attitudes of the people of their districts. Sampling the opinions of a congressional district—so strange are the properties of survey methods—amounts to almost as great a task as sampling the people of the nation. Hence, given the data now available, any treatment of how any representative links opinion in his constituency to the governing process must be less than exact. Political analysts approach the problem chiefly by indirection. They ascertain demographic characteristics of legislative districts. They reason that people of specified characteristics—industrial workers, for example—ought to have a specified outlook toward a given legislative issue. Therefore, it is concluded, a representative reflects the opinion of his district if he takes a position in harmony with the opinion imputed to a majority of his constituents.

[However], constituency influences upon a legislator are numerous and often mutually contradictory. The diversity of demands upon him, as well as the varying probability that these demands will affect the outcome on election day, leaves a range of freedom of choice for most legislators on many questions. That discretion is exercised in a manner to suggest a relationship between legislative voting and constituency characteristic, but at times the relationship is slight. Nevertheless, such correlations contribute to the description of the role of the legislator in the linkage of opinion to government. A summary of the chief findings on the matter may be useful.

Apparently party affiliation must be ranked as the factor most influential in the determination of a legislator's vote. Whether this phenomenon should be classified as an influence of constituency is not always clear. Party influence—that is, the influence of the party leadership—is usually reinforced by constituency; thus, the two types of influence may be indistinguishable. One type of constituency tends toward the Democratic party, and another toward the Republican. At the extremes there are working-class districts and silk-stocking constituencies. On those issues relevant to these constituency differentials, a legislator's perception of constituency opinion strengthens his inclination to vote with his party. On this type of issue the party effect also may strengthen the inclination of a Representative to vote with the sentiment of his constituency.

Yet the chances are that the party factor should be regarded as consisting, at least in part, of elements other than pure constituency influence—that is, something in addition to the legislator's concern about the views of the people who elect him. When he follows the party line, the legislator may be responding to the mandate of a constituency larger than his district. On occasion, this process even brings him to reject the dominant opinions of his own district. More often, party provides guides for position on measures about which the people of his own constituency have no real concern or about which the opinions of his constituency are divided or ambiguous. Although we have no district-by-district opinion data, our earlier occupational analyses of opinion support the assumption that in a considerable number of districts opinion and information on many issues must be low indeed.

The second statement is by the political scientist Lewis A. Froman, Jr., from a more recent study of constituency influences on the way members of Congress vote.[2]

Members of Congress, like people in other decision-making roles, operate in a more or less uncertain world. Congressmen are confronted almost daily with the necessity of making choices on a wide range of issues and problems. Besides their activities for constituents and their own personal affairs, members of Congress are faced with an enormous number of alternative choices in the performance of their legislative function. As many as three to four thousand different bills and resolutions are introduced in Congress every session, and of these, fifteen hundred may reach the floor for debate and a vote. These bills and resolutions vary from specific, local matters (such as relief for individual persons) to matters of great national and international importance (such as an education bill or foreign aid). There are also amendments to be considered to many of these bills and votes to be taken on the amendments . . .

Given the range, number, and complexity of choices to be made, how does a congressman make up his mind how to vote? What kinds of factors are influential in determining his vote? We can go a long way in answering these questions if we inspect just exactly what it is that Congress as an institution does and the kind of pressures which are likely to be placed on each congressman.

First . . . the decisions made by Congress (when signed into law by the President) make legal and legitimate the distribution of certain advantages and disadvantages. That is, laws have certain kinds of consequences for people. For some people the consequences will be favorable, for others, unfavorable. Civil Rights legislation

[2] Lewis A. Froman, Jr., *Congressmen and Their Constituencies* (Chicago: Rand McNally and Co., 1963), 3–7, 9–11.

which attempts to benefit Negroes suffering discrimination might serve as an example. Though certain groups of people would be aided, there are others who feel that they would be hurt, economically, socially, and/or psychically by such legislation. Hence, laws usually affect different people differently, depending upon their geographic and social location in society, their occupations, their skin color, religion, etc.

This leads us to . . . the pressures on congressmen. These pressures come in from multiple directions. Given the fact that the consequences of a law are likely to be different for different people, we would expect, on any given bill before Congress, that some people will be opposed to it, some will favor it, some will feel it does not go far enough, others will feel it goes too far, still others will want qualifying amendments, etc. On many pieces of legislation we would also expect party leaders, both in and out of Congress, to have preferences on the issue. Since party leaders have certain rewards and punishments at their disposal, they are in a position to influence the decisions of others. The President, too, is likely to be involved, as are executive agencies who must administer the program. A congressman's colleagues, especially friends, those from the same state delegation, and influential members of the committee handling the bill are also interested in the outcome of the legislation and are likely to make their preferences known. Last, but not necessarily least, a congressman himself is likely to have certain preferences about many pieces of legislation coming before Congress.

Although it may sometimes appear (especially to congressmen) that these plural pressures come from an infinite number of directions, they may be conveniently summarized in terms of five types: constituency, party, institutional, executive, and personal. Constituency pressures include written and personal contacts from the congressman's district. They also include communications from spokesmen for interest groups that are based or have affiliates within the congressman's district. . . . By party pressures are meant stands on issues which have been taken, either nationally or locally, by members of the congressman's party. Many of these positions are ambiguous and give the party members great leeway (for example, national party platforms), but nevertheless on many issues, such as social welfare programs, the parties do take stands which may serve as constraints on congressmen's behavior.

Institutional pressures include those from a congressman's colleagues, his friends, party leaders, committee chairmen, and others who may attempt, in various ways, to help the congressman make up his mind on a particular legislative matter. These pressures can range all the way from friendly discussion to promises of help or veiled threats of withdrawing favors. Executive pressures involve a great number of factors including service by executive agencies to the congressman's constituents, provision of information to the congressman, promises of aid, cooperation, etc. Personal factors involve a congressman's own values, convictions, preferences, attitudes, and beliefs.

Many of these pressures are quite closely interwoven. For example, members of the same party are more likely to be in contact with one another than members of opposite parties. In this case, institutional factors serve to reinforce party differences. Executive pressure is likely to be put more strongly on members of Congress of the President's party than on other members. Constituency pressures and party pressures are very often likely to be congruent . . . This interweaving of pressures makes it especially difficult to make a judgment, generally, as to the relative importance of each of these factors. However, two general comments are in order.

First, the importance of each factor is likely to vary from issue to issue. Some bills are more "important" than others in that they affect large numbers of people, are part of the President's program, involve large sums of money, or in other ways gain widespread attention. On these bills, all of the factors are likely to be operating at once, and not necessarily all in the same direction. It is on these bills that pressures from all five sources are the strongest and congressmen are often put in the most difficult conflict situations. On other issues, especially on bills and resolutions of a local nature, the congressman's own preferences, constituency pressures, and party pressures may become less important and institutional and executive factors, more important. It is on such bills that "logrolling" is most likely to take place.

Julius Turner provides evidence that these factors do vary considerably from issue to issue. Different issues had quite different consequences for *party cohesion* in the Congresses studied by Turner, indicating that different kinds of pressures were operating, depending upon the nature of the issue.

The results of this study of party voting in Congress [in 1921, 1931, 1937, and 1944] on various kinds of issues can be summarized in the following table, which indicates the relative degree of party cleavage on each kind of issue, and whether the parties took relatively consistent stands on the issue through the four sessions. . . .

1. Sharp cleavage, consistent. . . .	Tariff
	Government action
	Social and Labor
	Farm
2. Moderate cleavage, consistent .	Government regulation
	Negro
	Immigration
3. Sharp cleavage, inconsistent* . .	Patronage
	Control of House
	Bureaucracy
	Public Works, specific
4. Moderate cleavage, inconsistent*	States' Rights
	Executive and Congress
	Public Works, general
	Armament
	Foreign Affairs
	Business Claims
5. Little apparent cleavage	Veterans and Claims
	Women's Rights
	District of Columbia
	Civil Service
	Prohibition

*The designation "inconsistent" means that each party did not continue to support the same point of view on each roll call regardless of other circumstances. Usually such inconsistency was caused by changes in party rule, i.e., Republicans supported armament when in power, opposed it when out of office.

As this . . . table indicate[s], party pressures (or at least the success of party pressures) varied from issue to issue. Other factors than party were apparently influencing the votes of congressmen on many of the issues.

Second, in the long run, perhaps the most important pressures on congressmen are constituency pressures. Merely to assert this as a generalization, however, is much easier than to prove its validity . . .

Most congressmen like their jobs and wish to remain in office. The spectre of the next election is constantly before them, and most congressmen operate on the assumption that it is dangerous (and costly) to alienate constituents back home. Hence, congressmen are likely to pay relatively close attention to constituency opinion. Much of the time, constituency pressures are probably congruent with other pressures (for example, party positions), but when there is a conflict of pressures, we can expect the conflict to be solved in favor of a congressman's constituency. The cost of ignoring such constituency pressure (defeat at the polls) is much more severe than the cost of ignoring party, executive, institutional, or even personal pressures, at least for most congressmen in most situations. Even when constituency pressures are relatively ambiguous, the cost of not paying them at least some heed may mean trouble in the next election.

Constituency pressures on congressmen are of two kinds. First, most congressmen, in their campaigns and visits to their districts, have invited individuals and groups to contact them when the need arises. Congressmen, after all, seek votes, and one of the ways in which they do so is to be available to their constituents. The quid pro quo for such availability, in the congressman's mind, is the expectation of electoral support (such as votes, campaign contributions). Hence, congressmen are likely to receive pressure of a direct nature from constituents, including letters, telegrams, phone calls, and visits from individuals as well as interest group leaders.

Second, most congressmen are also quite well aware of the general nature of their constituency. That is, they have certain perceptions about the kinds of people who live within their districts. They would know, for example, with relative accuracy, the number of Jews, Catholics, Irish, Negroes, rich, poor, labor union members, business groups, etc. This knowledge comes with long familiarity with the people in the district, and a congressman develops a certain "feel" for what he believes his constituents want and how he, as a congressman, should vote on various issues. Hence, many congressmen probably feel that they know what is good for their constituency even in the absence of direct overt pressure. . . .

If what we have been saying is true, then we would expect the behavior of congressmen to vary depending upon the kind of constituencies from which they come, especially on legislation which has national importance.

Finally, read the following statement by John F. Kennedy, written before he became President but after he had served in the House of Representatives and the Senate for several years.[3]

Senators, we hear, must be politicians—and politicians must be concerned only with winning votes, not with statesmanship. . . .

Walter Lippmann, after nearly half a century of careful observation, rendered in his recent book a harsh judgment both on the politician and the electorate:

"With exceptions so rare they are regarded as miracles of nature, successful democratic politicians are insecure and intimidated men. They advance politically only as they placate, appease, bribe, seduce, bamboozle, or otherwise manage to manipulate the demanding threatening elements in their constituencies. The decisive consideration is not whether the proposition is good but whether it is popular—not whether it will work well and prove itself, but whether the active-talking constituents like it immediately."

I am not so sure, after nearly ten years of living and working in the midst of "successful democratic politicians," that they are all "insecure and intimidated men." I am convinced that the complication of public business and the competition for the public's attention have obscured innumerable acts of political courage—large and small—performed almost daily in the Senate Chamber. I am convinced that the decline—if there has been a decline—has been less in the Senate than in the public's appreciation of the art of politics, of the nature and necessity for compromise and balance, of the nature of the Senate as a legislative chamber. And, finally, I am convinced that we have criticized those who have followed the crowd—and at the same time criticized those who have defied it—because we have not fully understood the responsibility of a Senator to his constituents or recognized the difficulty facing a poli-

[3] John F. Kennedy, *Profiles in Courage* (New York: Harper and Brothers, 1955), 3–10.

tician conscientiously desiring, in Webster's words, "to push [his] skiff from the shore alone" into a hostile and turbulent sea. Perhaps if the American people more fully comprehended the terrible pressures which discourage acts of political courage, which drive a Senator to abandon or subdue his conscience, then they might be less critical of those who take the easier road—and more appreciative of those still able to follow the path of courage.

The *first* pressure to be mentioned is a form of pressure rarely recognized by the general public. Americans want to be liked—and Senators are no exception. They are by nature—and of necessity—social animals. We enjoy the comradeship and approval of our friends and colleagues. We prefer praise to abuse, popularity to contempt. Realizing that the path of the conscientious insurgent must frequently be a lonely one, we are anxious to get along with our fellow legislators, our fellow members of the club, to abide by the clubhouse rule and patterns, not to pursue a unique and independent course which would embarrass or irritate the other members. We realize, moreover, that our influence in the club—and the extent to which we can accomplish our objectives and those of our constituents—are dependent in some measure on the esteem with which we are regarded by other Senators. "The way to get along," I was told when I entered Congress, "is to go along."

Going along means more than just good fellowship—it includes the use of compromise, the sense of things possible. We should not be too hasty in condemning all compromise as bad morals. For politics and legislation are not matters for inflexible principles or unattainable ideals. Politics, as John Morley has acutely observed, "is a field where action is one long second best, and where the choice constantly lies between two blunders"; and legislation, under the democratic way of life and the Federal system of Government, requires compromise between the desires of each individual and group and those around them. . . .

The question is how we will compromise and with whom. For it is easy to seize upon unnecessary concessions, not as means of legitimately resolving conflicts but as methods of "going along.". . .

All of us in the Congress are made fully aware of the importance of party unity (what sins have been committed in that name!) and the adverse effect upon our party's chances in the next election which any rebellious conduct might bring. Moreover, in these days of Civil Service, the loaves and fishes of patronage available to the legislator—for distribution to those earnest campaigners whose efforts were inspired by something more than mere conviction—are comparatively few; and he who breaks the party's ranks may find that there are suddenly none at all. Even the success of legislation in which he is interested depends in part on the extent to which his support of his party's programs has won him the assistance of his party's leaders. Finally, the Senator who follows the independent course of conscience is likely to discover that he has earned the disdain not only of his colleagues in the Senate and his associates in his party but also that of the all-important contributors to his campaign fund.

It is thinking of that next campaign—the desire to be reelected —that provides the *second* pressure on the conscientious Senator. It should not automatically be assumed that this is a wholly selfish motive—although it is not unnatural that those who have chosen politics as their profession should seek to continue their careers— for Senators who go down to defeat in a vain defense of a single principle will not be on hand to fight for that or any other principle in the future.

Defeat, moreover, is not only a setback for the Senator himself— he is also obligated to consider the effect upon the party he supports, upon the friends and supporters who have "gone out on a limb" for him or invested their savings in his career, and even upon the wife and children whose happiness and security—often depending at least in part upon his success in office—may mean more to him than anything else. . .

The *third* and most significant source of pressures which discourage political courage in the conscientious Senator or Congressman —and practically all of the problems described in this chapter apply equally to members of both Houses—is the pressure of his constituency, the interest groups, the organized letter writers, the economic blocs and even the average voter. To cope with such pressures, to defy them or even to satisfy them, is a formidable task. All of us occasionally have the urge to follow the example of Congressman John Steven McGroarty of California, who wrote a constituent in 1934:

"One of the countless drawbacks of being in Congress is that I am compelled to receive impertinent letters from a jackass like you in which you say I promised to have the Sierra Madre mountains reforested and I have been in Congress two months and haven't done it. Will you please take two running jumps and go to hell."

Fortunately or unfortunately, few follow that urge—but the provocation is there—not only from unreasonable letters and impossible requests, but also from hopelessly inconsistent demands and endlessly unsatisfied grievances. . . .

Review in your text and class notes materials relating to Congress, members of Congress, and pressures on Congressmen.

Assume that the President sends a special message to Congress, urging the passage of a bill to authorize the granting of large sums to the states for education. He proposes a condition that no state will be eligible for such aid if any public schools in the state are segregated on the basis of color. The message further recommends that money be given only to *public* schools with no aid going to parochial or private institutions. In his message the President calls improvements in education a matter of national concern; he also stresses that his program would still vest administrative responsibility and educational policy making in the local school districts of the country. He emphasizes that the proposal is fully in accordance with the letter and the spirit of the Constitution, as interpreted by the Supreme Court. The next night, speaking at a party banquet, the President returns to the same subject. He points out that the recent party platform pledged "giant steps to make American education, already the finest in the world, still better," that it called for respect for the Supreme Court, and that it said, "this party stands firmly for that great American principle, equality of opportunity." As the administration's legislative liaison agents on school matters, spokesmen for the Department of Health, Education, and Welfare are also putting pressure on members of Congress to support school aid.

As a written exercise or for class discussion: Place yourself as a member of Congress in each of the following situations.

Assume throughout that the President's party has a majority in both houses of Congress:

A. You used to be a professor of international relations; now you are beginning your fourth term as U. S. Senator from a Southern state. In your state most schools are still segregated, but the schools of the state's largest city have been voluntarily and peaceably desegregated. On this issue you have long urged patience and moderation, without being specific about what steps, if any, should be taken. In the recent primary you narrowly defeated an aspirant who preached separation of the races and said that the Supreme Court justices should be impeached. Your chief interest is in foreign affairs. You are of the President's party, and for the last few years have been an eloquent senatorial supporter of his foreign policy.

Right now you know that there will soon be a close battle in the Senate over ratification of a treaty that the President has made with Ruritania. You feel that the ratification of this treaty is of vital importance to the country; you know, too, that ratification is ardently desired by the tobacco growers in your state, who expect to profit by renewed trade with Ruritania. The outcome may well depend on the votes of a dozen other Southern senators, ten of whom have regularly sought your advice and followed your lead in voting on foreign policy questions, but have thus far remained silent about the treaty.

B. You are a twenty-nine-year-old lawyer and Representative from a predominantly Catholic district in a Northern metropolis, serving your first term in the House. Last fall you were elected as the nominee of the President's party, receiving 80,020 votes to 77,153 for your opponent. About 10,000 voters in your district are Negroes; the ward where most of them live gave you a three-to-one advantage. The chief financial contributors to your campaign (including your uncle) were leaders in the local Chamber of Commerce, which has just adopted a resolution calling for lower taxes and condemning additional federal expenditures. Many of your most fervent campaigners were members of the Knights of Columbus in which you have been active, recently serving as president of the local branch in your city. In the House, you have been assigned to the Committee on the District of Columbia. This bores you; you are anxious to be assigned to the Committee on the Judiciary, where an early vacancy is likely. Committee assignments are made by a group of fourteen senior congressmen of your party, seven of whom are southerners. You are not very happy in Congress, partly because your wife and small children did not accompany you to Washington. Your secret ambition is to become a federal judge.

C. You are of the same party as the President; but when you were fighting successfully to be renominated last year for your second term in the Senate the President openly endorsed your primary opponent, a former member of his cabinet. You come from a small Western state which is rich in natural resources, and its people are justifiably proud of their public schools. Many wealthy men live in the state. By profession, you are a journalist. Some years ago you wrote several syndicated articles alleging inadequacies of parochial schools and urging that schools be upgraded somehow, although you did not specify how. Since that year most of your articles have centered on the question of whether federal dams should be built on western rivers. You favor such dams; the President opposes them. On the Senate floor you have criticized the President very sharply for his stand against the dams. He has taken offense and neglected "accidentally" to invite you to a recent White House reception for Western Senators.

D. You are one of the senior Representatives in the minority party. Your predominantly rural district is in a rather poor border state, where schools used to be segregated but have been voluntarily and peacefully desegregated. You have won re-election by smaller and smaller margins, the last time by only 2,000 votes. Conservative business interests regularly support you, because you agree with them on tariff and labor questions. Organized labor, mainly members of the United Mine Workers of America, is strong in your district and its leaders have long opposed you; they now favor the President's education proposal. So does a small branch of the National Association for the Advancement of Colored People. In past years you have strongly and sincerely opposed federal aid to education on the ground that financial aid would soon be followed by federal control of the schools' programs. You made a special point of your fear that money would go to parochial schools which you feel would be very undesirable. Among your closest friends and supporters are the owners of a television station who are seeking Federal Communications Commission approval of their application for a new channel. There is a vacancy on the bipartisan FCC, which by law, must be filled by the presidential appointment of a member of your party. You have been urging the appointment to this post of your able nephew for whom you have great affection and admiration. A presidential assistant has told you that your nephew seems well qualified and "appears to be in the lead for that job."

Now for *each case*, A through D, separately, as the member of Congress described:

1. Analyze the situation carefully. How would you vote?

2. Select and evaluate, in terms of their importance in the situation as you see it, the specific factors that would lead you to take a particular position with reference to the President's proposal.

PROBLEM 20

Strategic Pressure Points in the Legislative Process

THERE are many ways of approaching the process by which Congress makes laws. Some may wish to evaluate the congressional process in terms of the extent to which it meets the needs of the contemporary international situation; some in terms of the extent to which Congress conforms to a model of democratic government; and others in terms of the extent to which Congress satisfies particular political or economic interests. Prior to any such evaluation, however, there must be a thorough understanding of how Congress operates to achieve its results; of the procedures it follows; of the relationships between the presidency and Congress; of the impact of party leadership; and of the relationships between Congressmen and their constituents. To further this understanding, the student is here thrust into the role of a leader of an interest group with an important stake in the fate of a bill in Congress. In this role he is asked to calculate as thoroughly and as fully as possible all the possible steps he might take in order to influence the course of the legislation.

There are five general techniques one might use in order to influence legislation. First and most obvious is *direct lobbying*, in which the interest-group representative personally contacts legislators and tries to persuade them of the virtue of his case. Second, *indirect lobbying* may also be useful as the group tries to stimulate public opinion through a propaganda campaign in the hope that the opinion so generated will be fed back from constituents to the Congressmen and affect their thinking. Third, many interest groups have spokesmen for their point of view who are members of Congress; these *spokesmen in Congress* need no particular convincing on an issue, but only data and arguments from the interest group in order to enable them to make the best possible case within Congress. Fourth, an interest group may try to use its *voting strength* to reward its political friends and punish its enemies. Finally, a group may try to work through *party leaders* both inside and outside Congress, men with whom they have sympathetic associations, in order to get such leaders to exert whatever influence they may possess on other Congressmen. On any particular major issue it is likely that an experienced interest group will use all these techniques in one way or another to develop a maximum of influence.

For background material on pressure-group techniques, see the discussion by Henry A. Turner in Problem 13, "Interest Groups in the Political Process," above. See also the brief statements concerning the AFL-CIO and the NAM in Problem 15, "Toward More Responsible Political Parties?" above.

Another point to remember is that to the legislative agent of an interest group there are a number of strategic agencies in Congress. These include the standing committees, committee chairmen and other particularly influential or strategically located members, and strategic points on the legislative track itself, where a bill may be halted or run off the rails. It is of particular importance for these points of decision and these persons to be influenced. Thus the lobbyist will not try indiscriminately to persuade any and all Congressmen, all of the time, but will concentrate his attention on those who can be of the most service at a critical point.

Now assume the following situation:

In the second session of the Ninety-third Congress (1974) a bill has been introduced which seems to have substantial support in

Congress and which the leaders of union labor interpret as a very serious threat to the health of the labor movement. This bill has been introduced following a long and widely publicized Congressional investigation of several labor unions. This investigation revealed that corruption and racketeering were rife in some unions, though by no means all; and the many headlines produced by the investigation have helped create an unfavorable image of labor generally in the minds of much of the public. The American Federation of Labor-Congress of Industrial Organizations has itself taken disciplinary action against the unions demonstrated to be corrupt, but the public image of labor—insofar as this image is reflected in the nation's press—has not been much affected by these measures.

The bill itself provides that labor unions will be fully subject to the antitrust laws, thus repealing the substantial exemption from such laws that has been in the statutes since 1914. Before then liability of unions to prosecution under the antitrust laws effectively prevented unions from improving the economic position of labor through action designed to compel collective bargaining. Whether this liability would be reimposed by the proposed legislation is not clear, since the bill does not repeal other federal statutes that guarantee collective-bargaining rights to unions. Although the effects of the proposal are unclear, the bill's proponents have made effective use of the symbol of "labor monopoly," arguing that they propose only to restore antimonopoly controls over labor unions just as they apply to business corporations. In particular the National Association of Manufacturers and other business pressure groups have played up this theme.

The Democrats have majorities in both houses of Congress. In the Senate, largely because of the persuasive skills of Majority Leader Walt Whitson, the Democrats have exhibited substantial party unity. Whitson and a few other Democratic leaders have been able to mobilize about 75 percent of their party members in the Senate to support almost any position on which they take a strong stand; and when Democratic leaders outside Congress (for example, former presidential candidates) also agree, nearly

90 percent of the Democrats vote together. On the bill in question many Democratic leaders outside Congress have voiced strong opposition to the bill, but so far neither Whitson nor the other prominent Democratic Senators have publicly taken a position.

In the House, Democratic party leaders are not nearly as influential. Although Speaker Avery Blackburn is usually able to command the support of twenty or thirty Democratic Representatives, and other Congressmen are influential with small groups, no strong man or group of men can "deliver" the House Democrats.

In both houses of Congress the Republicans have shown little unity. Again, as with the House Democrats, particular leaders have a few followers, but except when the Republican President takes a strong stand, most Republicans in the Ninety-third Congress have tended to make up their minds on an individual basis rather than look to their party leaders. So far the President has adhered to the position he took in a press conference a year ago when he said that he had no particular opinion on the question and would bring no pressure on Congress, one way or another. Some but not all of the Republican leaders in Congress have announced their support of the bill, but none of the most influential Democrats in the Senate or House has taken a stand.

In the House there are 235 Democrats and 200 Republicans. Speaker Blackburn presides; he is a faithful party wheelhorse whenever the interests of the party, as he sees them, are involved in legislation. Perhaps 120 Democrats in the House regularly support the interests of organized labor, while about forty Republicans usually can be counted on for such support. The AFL-CIO classifies about 140 Republicans and fifty Democrats as "usually antilabor." The rest of the members are publicly uncommitted on the bill, and their voting tendencies on labor questions are uncertain.

The thirty members of the House Committee on Education and Labor include seventeen Democrats and thirteen Republicans. Eight of the Democrats are opposed to the bill and three are for it, and nine Republicans on the committee support the bill and two oppose it. The remaining eight members are uncommitted. The six uncommitted Democrats include the chairman, Kew Garden, who is regarded by labor and everyone else as "unpredictable." He professes to make up his mind on most questions of public policy in terms of whether the proposed policy squares with his religious convictions. The other five uncommitted Democrats normally follow the lead of Garden, who rules his committee with a firm hand; and policies that Garden opposes have small chance of reaching the floor of the House. His district contains no significant organized labor groups, and his political support back home is such that he has been unopposed in either primary and general election for the past four elections.

The House Rules Committee is chaired by Representative Jonah Hale (Democrat, Missouri), who usually goes along with the President but who is highly unpredictable when the President takes no stand. Two of the other nine Democrats on the committee and four of the five Republicans favor the bill, and two Democrats are uncertain.

In the Senate there are fifty-one Democrats and forty-nine Republicans. Thirty-two of the Democrats can probably be counted on to oppose the bill, and eight have indicated that they were sympathetic to its purposes, leaving eleven uncommitted. The best estimate of Republican sentiment places thirty-four for the bill and eight against, with the remaining seven neutral. Senator John Sanders is one of the Republican "neutrals," and his opinion on labor matters is valued by many other Republicans including some of those who have indicated sympathy for the bill. Sanders is from a state that until recently had little industry or labor, but since World War II automobile factories have been built in his state and a rapidly growing organized labor movement is becoming a political force that Sanders must reckon with.

The Senate committee that will consider the bill is composed of seven Democrats and six Republicans. The chairman is one of the bill's sponsors and one other Democrat has announced his support of the proposal, while three Democrats oppose the bill. Three Republicans on the Committee have spoken in favor of the bill while the others, including the ranking Republican, Sanders, are uncommitted.

Review material in your text and lecture notes relating to Congress and the legislative process, and to the techniques of interest groups.

For class discussion, or as a written exercise, place yourself in the two following situations:

A. Assume that you are a registered lobbyist for the AFL-CIO and are responsible for planning and carrying out the actions necessary to win acceptance for the AFL-CIO positions on legislation of interest to labor. You have a large though not unlimited budget, and you can call upon the nationally known leaders of labor and on the labor press whenever it seems necessary. Prepare a full plan of strategy to defeat the proposed bill. Do not concern yourself with the substance of the proposal unless you intend to use this in some way in your campaign.

In preparing your plan, carefully undertake each of the following:

1. List the strategic points in the Congressional process where you might attempt to have the bill killed. Include not only the strategic agencies and strategically located Congressmen, but also the major rules of procedure in each house which might be used to your advantage.

2. Evaluate your chances, considering carefully the resources or pressures you have available, of successfully killing the bill at each strategic point. Explain the reasons for your evaluation in each case.

3. Show specifically how you would use particular techniques of influence or pressure at the particular strategic points that seem most promising to you, so as to give you the best chance of defeating the bill.

NOTES: Regardless of whether you think you can kill the bill at any one point or use successfully any particular technique of influence, consider explicitly all the available alternatives.

B. Assume that you are a registered lobbyist for the NAM, and that your organization has officially endorsed the proposed bill and instructed you to do everything you can to get it passed. You too have a large but finite budget and can call upon prominent members of your organization whenever you need to. Prepare a full plan of strategy to secure the passage and presidential approval of the proposed bill. Repeat each of the steps indicated in Part A, but this time aiming at the passage of the bill.

PROBLEM 21

Seniority and Power in Legislation

FOR years controversy has raged concerning the seniority system or seniority rule in Congress. The fact that length of service is the highroad to crucial committee chairmanships, committee assignments, and other perquisites in the Senate and House, critics have argued, gives undue power or influence to older men and to men who represent "safe" states or districts which are little affected by changing currents of national opinion. Defenders of the seniority system have maintained that it brings men of depth of knowledge and mature wisdom to top places in the legislative process, and that it is difficult to envisage another procedure for staffing committees of Congress that would not generate serious tensions or conflict. On the one hand the cry has often been for "democracy" against "oligarchy"; on the other, for the value of "experience" and "order."

In a strong statement on the subject, Senator Joseph Clark (Democrat, Pennsylvania) has criticized what he called the "Senate Establishment." Read carefully the following selection from an address by Senator Clark in February 1963, paying particular attention to the force of precedent and the role of seniority in perpetuating what he calls the "establishment" and its power.[1]

MR. CLARK: Mr. President, I desire to address the Senate on the subject of the Senate establishment and how it operates. . . .

I believe that the concept of an establishment in America is something which all of us who try to understand the sometimes almost

[1] *Congressional Record*, February 19–21, 1963, 2413–14, 2705–07.

inexplicable ways in which we in this country act would do well to contemplate. Just as Great Britain has its establishment and the United States of America perhaps has its establishment, so . . . the U.S. Senate has its establishment. I wish to discuss today what that establishment is, how it operates, and why in my opinion the present establishment is not operating in the interests of the future of the United States, or the future of the U.S. Senate, and certainly is not operating to the benefit of the future of the Democratic Party.

The Senate establishment, as I see it, after a relatively brief sojourn here—I am now in my seventh year—is almost the antithesis of democracy. It is not selected by any democratic process. It appears to be quite unresponsive to the caucuses of the two parties, be they Republican or Democratic. It is what might be called a self-perpetuating oligarchy with mild, but only mild, overtones of plutocracy. The way it operates is something like this:

There are a number of States, most of them Democratic, but one or two of them Republican, which inevitably and always return to the U.S. Senate members of one party, and under a custom which has grown up over the years of following the rule of seniority in making committee assignments, and in connection with the distribution of other perquisites of Senate tenure, the result has been that those who have been here longest have become chairmen of committees, and as such chairmen, have exercised virtual control over the distribution of favors, including committee assignments and other perquisites of office in the Senate, and largely—although not always, and not entirely, because there are exceptions—determine who shall be selected to posts of leadership in this body.

As I see it, the Senate establishment pretty well controls the assignment of members to committees. How is that done? I think it is interesting to note that it is not only the present Senate establishment which does that. From time to time, going back at least to the early days of the present century, the same system prevailed. There have always been those who fought against the establishment, who thought that the Democratic caucus and the Republican caucus should determine who would select the members of committees and the other perquisites of office. One of the most eloquent men to speak in that vein was, at the time he spoke, a Republican. It was that very much revered and able Senator from Wisconsin, the elder Robert La Follette.

We now stand at the beginning of the third session of what might be called a Kennedy Congress, but actually it is not a Kennedy Congress, and it seems to me that it is not going to be a Kennedy Congress. The principal reason why it is not going to be a Kennedy Congress, so far as the Senate is concerned, is, in my opinion, that we are operating under archaic, obsolete rules, customs, manners, procedures, and traditions—and because the operation under those obsolete and archaic setups is controlled by this oligarchical Senate establishment, a majority of the members of which, by and large, are opposed to the program of the President.

I do not wish to overstate the case. There are able and effective members of the establishment who will support the program of the President in many areas. There are a few members of the establishment who will support the program of the President in some areas. But, by and large, the two-thirds majority of the Democratic Senators who are Kennedy men, and therefore liberals, and therefore want to get the country moving again, and therefore believe in the inevitability of change, are represented sparsely, if at all, in the Senate establishment.

Mr. President, why all this fuss? Why should I have taken the time of the Senate . . . to raise these matters? The first reason is that procedure is the heart of justice. Without just procedure, whether it be due process of law, enshrined in the 5th and 14th amendments to the Constitution, or whether it be the rules, customs, manners, and traditions which are unjust, unfair, and undemocratic.

So while I sympathize with the majority leader when he suggests that we should get to the Senate business, I say there is no more important Senate business than assuring, at the beginning of a session, that the procedures of the Senate are just. . . .

So I close, as I began, with the plea to my colleagues to make a beginning in the modernization of the Senate and its procedures; to make a beginning in the elimination of control by a small group of bipartisan Senators, fine persons, I say at the end, as I said when I began—friends of mine they have been in the past, friends of mine I hope they will continue to be in the future—who are committed to the status quo, who seem to be committed to sectional rule; who, with all due deference, I suggest—and I do defer to those fine and honorable Senators—have an unawareness of the modern world and

of the dangers confronting us from a resourceful antagonist over-
seas, whose government is able to act in a crisis because the Senate
of the United States has rendered itself, by its ancient, archaic,
and obsolete rules unable to act when its majority is ready for action.

In the end, the Republic is in jeopardy. Perhaps not today, perhaps not tomorrow, but who knows when? It is later than we think.
The Senate should bring itself up to the needs and the challenges
of the seventh decade of the twentieth century.

Mr. President, I yield the floor.

Now read carefully the following statement taken from an
article by Representative Emanuel Celler (Democrat, New York),
for many years Chairman of the Judiciary Committee of the
House, bearing in mind that Representative Celler's views of what
constitutes desirable public policy would be very nearly the same
as those of Senator Clark.[2]

It is a rare session of Congress that does not produce its share of
proposals to abolish that perennial red herring—the so-called
"seniority rule." This long-standing congressional tradition, under
which the House and the Senate organize their working committees,
has become as popular a target as sin itself. It is intermittently
bombarded by Democrats and by Republicans, by liberals and by
conservatives, depending largely upon whose ox is being gored.

I do not entirely understand why this should be so. True, it is
sometimes expedient to explain the defeat of a locally popular
measure in terms of the tyranny of a committee chairman. Also, able
and energetic young men and women who come to Congress and
find the best seats occupied will understandably chafe at the tardi-
ness with which their talents are recognized and rewarded by assignments to coveted posts. Thus, a distinguished United States
Senator, after two years of service, called the seniority rule a "strait-
jacket," described it as "rigid, inflexible, and unyielding," and urged
its discontinuance as "the sole determinant of Congressional sovereignty and influence" in committee chairmanships and assignments.
An example of the intermittent assaults upon congressional seniority
is the joint resolution, H.J. Res. 253, of the 86th Congress, which

[2] Emanuel Celler, "The Seniority Rule in Congress," *Western Political
Quarterly,* 14 (March 1961), 160–67.

would have rendered senators and representatives who have served twelve years ineligible for re-election for a two-year period.

But the tendency to attack the seniority principle has not been confined to members of Congress, nor, indeed, to politicians. Students of political science regularly excoriate the rule for theoretical imperfections which no method of selection designed by human beings could conceivably eliminate. Even members of the working press—practical men and women who know their way around Capitol Hill—fall in with this approach. The seniority bugaboo is always good for a couple of sticks on a dull Monday, or for a feature in the Sunday Supplement, predicting what the Hill "leadership" will or will not "permit," with the clear implication that the congressional power is too narrowly held and dictatorially exercised.

From the tone of some of its critics, one would suppose that the seniority principle is firmly entrenched and sanctified by law, and that little short of a constitutional amendment could dislodge it. Properly speaking, however, it is not a rule at all, but is rather a custom or convention. Although operative in both the Senate and the House for many years, it is embodied in no formal rule of either chamber. And, far from being sacrosanct, seniority has been overridden by both parties, when circumstances appear to require. Instances of this include the ouster of Stephen A. Douglas from the chairmanship of the Senate Committee on Territories in 1859, and the removal of Charles Sumner from the chairmanship of the Committee on Foreign Relations in 1871. It was a Democratic caucus that ousted Douglas, a Republican caucus that removed Sumner. Moreover, the rigor of the seniority rule has been modified in the current practice of Senate Democrats to allow no senator a second committee choice until each freshman shall have received at least one major committee assignment.

Recurrent criticisms also create the impression that the seniority criterion has wrested control of legislation from the members of Congress and concentrated it in the hands of autocratic committee chairmen, for the gratification of their personal whims. Yet despite these repeated assertions, no steps are even taken to change the basic operation of the system. Like the weather, much is said, but nothing done about it.

Just what role does seniority actually play in the operation of

Congress, and why, if it is as unsatisfactory as its critics assert, has it not long been abandoned?

My thirty-eight years of continuous service in the House of Representatives, spent first in acquiring the experience and understanding of legislative work which are implicit in "seniority" and more recently in the exercise of the responsibilities that go with a committee chairmanship, have given me a better than average opportunity to observe the working of the system. I believe that the seniority principle, though far from perfect, performs an indispensable function in the organization of the Congress, and that the alternatives that have been offered as a cure for its deficiencies would aggravate, rather than relieve them. . . .

Neither house of Congress could conceivably give detailed attention to all the facets of its legislative program in regular session. Preliminary consideration of legislative proposals is therefore delegated to standing committees, which, with the aid of specialized subcommittees, study the bills, conduct investigations, hear and attempt to reconcile divergent needs and views, and finally report a measure to the full body. Thereafter the committee members perform their individual responsibilities in the ensuing debate. In addition, each committee has the task of keeping itself informed as to the effectiveness with which existing laws within its jurisdiction are being enforced.

What is more, legislation destined for ultimate enactment frequently fails of passage in the Congress in which it is initially introduced. Indeed, it is not unusual for legislative history of a measure to extend over more than two biennia. In such cases, although new bills must be introduced in each new Congress, the committee has a virtually continuing responsibility for managing, or processing, the legislative issue.

Against this background, the rationale of the seniority principle becomes evident. Over the years, manifestly, the effectiveness of a committee will bear a direct relationship to the stability of its personnel. If the legislative committees were to be reshuffled after each election—beyond what is necessitated by the retirement of members and the arrival of new ones—all issues pending unresolved in the House, and to a lesser degree those pending in the Senate would require consideration de novo. The time and effort necessarily expended by committee members in familiarizing themselves with the nature of the committee's work, the intricacies of its problems, and the identity and character of interested parties would indeed be lost. What has been said of the members applies with peculiar force to the committee's chairman. Upon the chairman rests the administrative responsibility for the committee's program and for the functioning of the subcommittees. He supervises the professional staff. Continued availability of the chairman's accumulated expertness, experience, and prestige is a central factor in a committee's effectiveness. Interruption of his tenure, other than is necessitated when the control of the Chamber passes from one political party to the other, would needlessly impair the efficiency of the committee's operations.

Fundamentally, the seniority system avoids the waste implicit in instability of committee composition and management. It invokes the presumption that, other things being equal, the man or woman with the greatest experience in a particular job is best fitted to participate and to lead in its performance. To quote Luce, in his work on legislative procedure, "Whatever the activity, we all know that experience counts for more than anything else, and promotion by seniority is nothing but the recognition of this." Since a senior congressman is more experienced than his junior, and since all congressmen aspire to posts of influence, choice of committee assignments may safely be left to seniority. Within a committee, similarly, since effectiveness is presumptively related to length of uninterrupted service, the seniority ladder properly defines the succession to the chairmanship.

The seniority criterion for selecting committee chairmen has the added virtue of being objective. It automatically eliminates the intrigues, deals, and compromises that characterize election campaigns. By the same token, committees are able to get down to work immediately, without having first to bind the wounds of disappointed aspirants to leadership.

To counter these salient advantages, opponents of the system offer two principal criticisms. The first is addressed to its alleged effect upon the functioning of the committees. Here it is contended that the capacity to achieve re-election has no necessary relation to the qualities ideally embodied in a chairman; that under a seniority

rule the potential contribution of an exceptionally able young legislator is sacrificed to the entrenchment of an aging incumbent whose
energies may be waning; and that the relative inviolability of the
custom operates to immunize chairmen against retribution, no matter how arbitrary and dictatorial their conduct of office.

Each of these claims has surface plausibility—and each has been
overstated. Although seniority, alone, does not guarantee superior
ability, success in effectively serving the state or district remains an
indispensable attribute of the perennially successful candidate for
election. The most backward electorate will not indefinitely return
a congressman who wholly fails to serve its needs. Such a man is
retired, if not in election, then in a primary contest. By and large,
the so-called "safe" state or district is one that has been getting the
kind of representation it wants. And inevitably, the affirmative
qualities that keep a man in office do contribute to his effectiveness
as a committee chairman.

Each of us must some day lay down his burdens, but nature has
not uniformly decreed when this must be. Some men remain
vigorous and effective in their eighties; others may fail at fifty. As
stated by Gross in *The Legislative Struggle,*

> The seniority system has often been mistakenly attacked on the
> ground that it puts too much power in the hands of old men. This
> argument misses the real implications of the seniority system. Age
> alone does not cause diminution of mental vigor, alertness, and
> leadership ability. Nor does it mean that a man becomes more con-
> servative. Some of the outstanding liberals in Congress have been
> old men who have fought valiantly despite the other handicaps of
> age. . . .

Public servants with long tenure should be able to retire with a
measure of security, and recent amendments of the retirement
system make this increasingly possible for members of Congress.
But most men know when they have had enough, and I fear that by
imposing compulsory retirement of committee chairmen upon the
attainment of any particular age we would as often lose as gain in
terms of the vigor and capacity of the successor. With respect, also,
to the criticism that able young legislators with special skills must
today go too long without appropriate outlet for their talents, it is

noteworthy that increasing use of subcommittees, as well as select committees, are enabling greater utilization of such members in chairmanships.

By far the most serious of this group of criticisms is that which implies arbitrary, one-man rule of committees. It is true that the prerogative of calling meetings and the control of agendas gives some chairmen wide powers, sometimes amounting to the practical equivalent of a veto. But it would be a mistake to attribute this to the seniority system. Seniority does no more than designate the chairman; it does not write the committee's rules of procedure, nor does it prescribe despotism in the conduct of the committee's affairs. Recent years have seen an increasing incidence of well-developed rules of procedure for the governance of committee business. It is always possible for the members of a committee to out-vote its chairman. That this happens from time to time is whole-some. That it does not happen more often is as reasonably at-tributable to the respect and confidence with which the members regard their chairman as to any sinister implication of dictatorship. I believe that the charge of dictatorship is often an attempt to saddle the chairman with sole responsibility for the committee majority's unwillingness to act.

As Luce puts it: "Somebody must lead. If it is not the strong, it will be the weak. If it is not the experienced, it will be the inex-perienced. Otherwise chaos." Under any method of selection, the chairman will remain the committee's most powerful member. The cure for despotism, where it may still exist, is not to deprive the committee of the services of its most seasoned member, but to insist on democratic procedures. In this way, the committee itself can guarantee that the chairman will act as a guide and leader, responsive to the will of the majority, and not as a dictator.

The other major objection that has been leveled at the seniority system is that it concentrates the power implicit in chairmanships in congressmen from so-called one-party states and districts, at the expense of areas whose political complexion is mixed. It is further asserted that the prestige and influence of a high-seniority congress-man becomes a political asset in warding off assaults upon his tenure, thus further entrenching him in office. Here, again, some truth and some exaggeration are encountered.

In a Democratic Congress, like the present one, the argument is usually illustrated by pointing to the preponderance of southerners, traditionally more conservative than northern and western Democrats, at the helms of the committees. It is true that of 36 standing committees in the House and the Senate, 21 are headed by men from the South. On the other hand, many important chairmanships are in the hands of northerners and westerners. Indeed, the dean at this writing among Senate Democrats, in his eighties, is the exceptionally able Senator Carl Hayden, chairman of the Committee on Appropriations, who speaks for Arizona. So, too, the states of Nevada, Washington, New Mexico, and Missouri, none of them classed as southern, are represented among Senate committee chairmanships.

In the House, likewise, the important Committees on Appropriations, Banking and Currency, Education and Labor, Foreign Affairs, Government Operations, Interior and Insular Affairs, Judiciary, Public Works, and Un-American Activities, are chaired by men from non-southern states, including New York, Illinois, Pennsylvania, Missouri, Kentucky, and Colorado. And four of the six House committee chairmen having the greatest length of uninterrupted service are from non-southern states. Numerous northerners are also chairmen of powerful subcommittees.

Withal, it cannot be denied that the seniority system produces some disproportion in the distribution of committee chairmanships. Whether this justifies abandonment of the rule raises the question whether the one-party districts can properly be penalized, simply for being able to make up their minds, by being deprived of the fruits that normally accrue from the acquisition of experience and expertness by their representatives. Such considerations tend to become academic, however, unless some satisfactory substitute for the existing rule can be found.

It is my conviction that the reason why the seniority principle has not long been abandoned lies not only in its demonstrable advantages but also in the difficulties that beset alternative proposals. I know of no substitute for the present system whose disadvantages would not outweigh its benefits. Proposals to require chairmen to step down at a specified age, or after a specified period of service, and to rotate chairmanships among committee members having a specified period of service would destroy continuity without necessarily producing more capable leadership. Proposals to elect chairmen in party caucuses would additionally give rise to campaigning with its attendant evils—again without any real assurance of the election of the best fitted candidate. Resort to secret ballot would slightly, but not wholly obviate this objection. The practice of foreign parliaments in which chairmen are predominantly elected by committee members may be appropriate in situations in which the members are themselves selected by lot. Such a system, however, makes knowledge or interest on the part of the committee members improbable. In systems like our own in which a premium has always been placed on continuity, election by committee members would be subject to all the infirmities of election by caucus. Appointment by the Speaker would generate inordinate pressures upon him from within and without Congress and would inordinately enlarge his power over legislation. I doubt whether the present Speaker would want such power. None of these alternatives would go to the real heart of the problem—the evolution of committee procedures that will guarantee democratic functioning.

I suspect that we shall continue to follow the custom of respecting seniority in the selection of congressional committee chairmen, not because it is perfect, but because it is better than any other method that has yet been proposed. And we could do much worse, for, to paraphrase Speaker Rayburn, the rules of both Houses of Congress are such that a determined majority can always work its will.

Some of the arguments for and against the seniority principle have been summarized by George Goodwin,[3] and his statements should be carefully compared with the views of Senator Clark and Representative Celler, as given above.

It is well to remember at the outset that very few human institutions ignore seniority entirely. Champ Clark, in his autobiography, noted that it is observed in all the affairs of life:

No sane man would for one moment think of making a graduate from West Point a full general, or one from Annapolis an admiral, or one from any university or college chief of a great newspaper, magazine or business house. A priest or a preacher who has just taken

---

[3] George Goodwin, Jr., "The Seniority System in Congress," *American Political Science Review*, LIII (June 1959), 412, 418–20.

orders is not immediately made a bishop, archbishop or cardinal. In every walk of life "men must tarry at Jericho till their beards are grown."

Yet, as George Galloway states, "in no other place, perhaps, does seniority or length of service carry so much weight as it does in the Congress of the United States." It is more than a means of choosing committee chairmen; it is a means of assigning members to committees, of choosing subcommittee chairmen and conference committee members. It affects the deference shown legislators on the floor, the assignment of office space, even invitations to dinners. In short, "it is a spirit pervading the total behavior of Congress." Its significance for constituencies was expressed by Senator Byrd, who, when he was persuaded to run again for his seat, explained that "seniority of service and committee rank have importance over and above the capabilities of the members." . . .

The debate over the seniority system generally centers on the choice of committee chairmen. The favorable arguments stress the harmony which results from the system, the emphasis which it places on experience, and the lack of any more suitable alternative. The unfavorable arguments stress the effect of the system on party responsibility and Presidential leadership, the lack of any dependable relation between seniority and qualified leadership, and the fact that the committee leaders in Congress are by no means representative of many of the dominant interests either in the party or in the nation.

The most telling argument of the proponents of seniority is that the system promotes legislative harmony. It prevents hurt feelings on the part of those passed over in the struggle for appointment, and incidentally, it keeps pressure groups out of this struggle. As a result, it helps to create a more cooperative atmosphere, both in the legislative body as a whole, and on the various committees. Committees can act as more of a unit, and in a more nonpartisan manner. . . .

Another argument of the proponents is that the system produces experienced chairmen—experienced both in the subject matter of the committee on which they have served so long, and in legislative procedure. They may also be better acquainted with the officials at working levels in the executive branch with whom they have to deal than the more transient department heads, who come and go with changes of Presidents. . . .

People on both sides of the fence tend to agree that when and if Americans turn toward party responsibility, "seniority will be an early casualty." The proponents of seniority, as one might expect, emphasize the harmonizing, rather than the issue-defining role of political parties, while the most outspoken critics of seniority favor responsible parties. They emphasize the diffusion of leadership among the 36 standing committees of Congress, and the fact that there is no adequate way of integrating their various programs. In fact, they hold, the people most likely to become chairmen, the people from one-party constituencies, are the ones most likely to be out of tune with the party's program:

A chairman, after all, is the position of a quarterback on a football team. It should not be given to someone who refuses to be part of the team or who might even carry the ball across the wrong goal line.

The system, the critics argue, is no guarantee that chairmen will be well qualified. A hardy constitution and the ability to get re-elected in the home district do not necessarily fit a man to preside over committee meetings or to defend committee reports on the floor. If the system puts so much emphasis on experience, why, they ask, is a man who leaves to take an administrative post, but who returns later to Congress, given little or no credit for his previous experience? There have been examples, also, of chairmen who were too senile to be effective. When Senator Capper became chairman of the Agriculture Committee he could neither make himself understood, nor understand others. "The seniority principle is followed mainly because the seniors are pleased with themselves and see no sufficient reason for consigning their powers to others."

Finally, the critics suggest that the system produces a large number of chairmen who are representative of only one element of the party, and that, generally, a minority element. They represent "stagnant" districts made safe by restrictions on voting, by a one-party monopoly, by the ascendency of a major interest group, or by an effective rural or urban political machine. Thus, the leaders of

Congress, produced by the seniority system, are almost guaranteed to oppose the President, regardless of party, and a new non-constitutional dimension is added to our constitutional system of separation of powers.

Review carefully materials in your text and class notes relating to the operations of Congress in general and the seniority rule or seniority system in particular.

Now read and ponder the following alternative formulations of rules which might be used to govern the selection of committee chairmen in either branch of Congress, whether the Senate or the House:

1. The member of the majority party with the longest continuous service on a standing committee shall be designated chairman of that committee.

2. The chairman of each standing committee shall be selected by lot from among the committee members at the beginning of each session of Congress.

3. The question of the selection of a chairman and all other questions which come before a standing committee of Congress shall be determined by a majority vote of the members of the committee.

4. The designation of committee chairmen shall be made by the elected leaders of the majority party: the Speaker, the Majority Leader, and the Assistant Majority Leader in the House, or the Majority Leader and the Assistant Majority Leader in the Senate.

5. The designation of committee chairmen shall be made by majority vote of the whole membership of the House, or, of the Senate.

As a written exercise or for class discussion:

A. On the basis of your understanding of the dynamics of the congressional process, forecast the probable main consequences of each of the alternative rules given above if the rule were adopted and put into practice. Emphasize the impact of the rule on the power or influence of specific groups with an interest in national politics.

B. Assume that you are the chairman of the Committee for a More Democratic Congress. Draft and justify a "model" or "ideal" rule to govern the selection of committee chairmen in Congress. Your stated goal is to maximize three objectives: "fairness in representation," "effectiveness in the legislative process," and "the public interest."

PART VII

The Executive Power

PROBLEM 22

The President and Domestic Policy: Innovator or Routineer?

IN the crisis-ridden years since the Great Depression of 1929 the United States has witnessed a significant expansion of presidential power and influence, particularly in the realm of legislation. Most occupants of the White House since Franklin D. Roosevelt took office in 1933 have sought to be "strong" presidents who labored to carry out new policies and new programs. In so doing they were working more or less consciously in the tradition of Thomas Jefferson or Andrew Jackson, Abraham Lincoln or Theodore Roosevelt, all of whom undertook the role of *innovators* in policy making and in presidential politics. In the crisis decades Dwight D. Eisenhower was at least a partial exception; he hoped to make his presidency a period of consolidation and calm. Nonetheless, the notion of the presidency as a source of domestic policy innovation and legislative influence has become familiar in the twentieth century and has been continued by Lyndon B. Johnson in our own time.

Yet there is another tradition of the presidency, whose adherents often cite the presumed original intention of the framers of the Constitution as authority. This is the tradition of the president as an executive and administrator who leaves the problem of legislation and the broader areas of domestic policy making to Congress, and thereby holds to a more limited or passive view of the proper role of presidential power. Men in this tradition include presidents like James Madison or James Monroe, William McKinley or Calvin Coolidge, who have by and large acted as *routineers* in office. Generally, though not invariably, times of crisis have been associated with innovators in office, while times of relative calm have tended to coincide with routineers in the presidency. Generally also innovators have sooner or later come to points of sharp conflict with Congress, not only on the substance of legislative policy but over the prerogatives and pride of the legislative branch. Routineers have less often precipitated such conflict, but the price has been a relative minimum of presidential influence over legislation as national policy making.

It is useful to think of innovator and routineer as ideal-typical poles at either end of a continuum. Most presidents would not in fact fall at either end of the continuum, but at various intermediate points along the line.

Now consider the following hypothetical situation and the possible courses of action open to the president:

In 1976 the United States had enjoyed for some time a period of genuine peace, prosperity, and tranquillity. A reasonably harmonious coexistence between this nation and the Soviet bloc had been worked out and the two great national powers were engaged in a peaceful, not unfriendly, competition in which each nation expected its way of life to prove most successful in promoting the happiness of its people. International control of nuclear weapons, ballistic missiles, earth satellites, and space platforms had at last been achieved; and American and Russian space men often rocketed to visit with one another on either nation's space platforms. Domestically the economic uncertainties and maladjustments that had troubled the United States in the late 1950's and 1960's had been brought into a relatively stable balance, and observers remarked that even the "poverty problem" appeared to have been "solved." Conflicts over issues of racial equality had been largely resolved also, and the nation was enjoying substantial internal tranquillity.

The Republican candidate for president in 1976 was Josiah Cabot, who was described by a history-minded journalist as "a modern, more capable Cal Coolidge with a great record as an effective administrator." During the campaign the Republican and Democratic parties found few issues on which to disagree, save one. The incumbent President, a Democrat, had followed a pattern of strong, insistent leadership in his relations with Congress reminiscent of Franklin D. Roosevelt, Harry S. Truman, and Lyndon B. Johnson, and had repeatedly played the role of "Chief Legislator" as well as of "Chief Executive." Cabot, in his campaign, commented on the "international peace" and "domestic tranquillity" of the times, and said that he thought a president ought to avoid any action that might "rock the boat." In a major address at the Second Century Jubilee of the Declaration of Independence in Philadelphia he had declared, "I do not conceive of the president as properly the legislative leader or general policy maker of this nation. In our system of separation of powers and responsibilities, the people elect the *Congress* to make the laws of this fair land; they elect the *President* to assure the able administration of those laws." The Republican party platform for 1976 reiterated these views and committed the party to a conception of the president as an administrator who should leave the matter of legislation entirely in the hands of Congress. In addition the party's congressional leadership itself was strongly committed to this view. As the Republican leader in the House, Carl Halpin, put it, "The executive department of a government like ours should be subordinate to the legislative branch; in short, the president should enforce the laws, leaving to the people the task of correcting any errors or omissions Congress may commit; this, and only this, is our conception of the proper role of the presidency in relation to Congress." The stand taken by Cabot, the Republican party platform, and the party's congressional leaders seemed sound doctrine about the proper source of national policy to most voters at the time. It was a major factor in Josiah Cabot's election by a majority of 52 percent of the popular vote to 48 percent for his opponent, and in the election of Republican majorities in both houses of Congress.

There was, however, one flaw in the national tranquillity. The tempo and pressures of an increasingly complicated and perplexing life generated tensions that took toll of the nation's health. The rate of heart ailments had risen sharply through the 1960's and early 1970's. In May 1977, four months after President Cabot had taken office, announcement was made of a new cortisone derivative, C2D, which when processed proved to be a positive preventive and cure for heart disease. The General Pharmaceutical Corporation had developed the new drug as an application of basic research activities that had been going on for some time in the nation's medical schools and other centers of biological, biochemical, and chemical research. Before it announced the development of C2D, General Pharmaceutical had, through patents on its processes, obtained sole rights to its manufacture and distribution. The supply that General Pharmaceutical was able to provide was limited and, taking into account the limited supply and the probability of a great demand, General Pharmaceutical fixed a very high price for C2D.

Following the announcement concerning the development and marketing of C2D, members of Congress were virtually flooded with mail. This mail reflected a widespread popular opinion that the federal government should take action to ensure manufacture of C2D in quantity, fair and impartial distribution, and a lower price. Important newspapers echoed these demands, as did a number of nationally organized interest groups including the Council for the Nation's Health, the American Federation of Labor-Congress of Industrial Organizations, and the powerful National Association for the Welfare of the Aged. Spokesmen for these groups compared the development of C2D to the development of the atomic bomb in the early 1940's, arguing that the General Pharmaceutical Corporation had only made "a lucky breakthrough" in the application of basic research carried on by thousands of scientists and physicians over the years, and that C2D like the atomic bomb was really "a national discovery." Thus, they argued, the drug should be used "for the benefit of all, fairly and impartially, regardless of ability to pay," and they declared that federal government action was the only effective way to assure that this would be done. On the other hand, other newspapers opposed federal government action, and such groups as the National Physicians' Association, the American Pharmacists' Institute, and the Committee for States' Rights denounced national governmental intervention as "an abuse of the federal government's proper powers."

In June 1977, Senator Daniel Deer Benton (Republican, Winnemac) introduced a bill to "ensure fair standards for the manufacture, distribution, and pricing" of C2D. It would have provided for a special commission of physicians and government officials to operate the program. The bill was referred to the Committee on Labor and Public Welfare and thence to a subcommittee headed by Senator Thomas Meadows Linn (Republican, Sunshine), which had jurisdiction over such legislation. It soon became apparent that Senator Linn, a former druggist, who acted frequently as a Congressional spokesman for the National Physicians' Association and the American Pharmacists' Institute, intended to smother the bill in committee if he could; and furthermore that he was exerting all his considerable influence in the Senate and in the House to prevent any action on the C2D issue. In the House confusion developed when party and committee spokesmen disagreed on the kind of legislative action that was in order. Most influential House leaders supported a proposal contained in a bill introduced by Carl Halpin, the Republican Majority Leader, which would have required General Pharmaceutical to license other drug firms to manufacture and sell C2D. On the other hand, many House members opposed any legislation. In addition, observers predicted that, if legislation was passed in the Senate or in the House, the Senate on the one hand and the House on the other would each insist on its own plan—that is, a federal commission in the Senate, or compulsory licensing in the House.

In short, it seemed highly probable that a deadlock would develop in Congress. In this situation President Cabot was informed by friends in Congress that Senator Linn's influence, the confused situation in the House, and the chances of a Senate-House deadlock might prevent *any* action on the issue, *unless* the President himself entered the controversy and took leadership in the fight for a national policy. He was also advised by his Attorney General that existing statutes did not provide an adequate basis for purely executive or administrative action with reference to the manufacture, distribution, or pricing of C2D. As a man at once humane and astute, President Cabot was sensitive to the welfare aspects of the problem and also to its political potentialities.

The problem was summed up in an editorial that appeared in the Washington *Intelligencer* in mid-June 1977:

The President has up to now not indicated whether he will or will not take a position on this question, and although his active support is not absolutely essential for some sort of action, the general opinion is that without it there is a good chance of stalemate within Congress. The discovery itself is of unquestionable benefit to mankind, but the issue before the nation is whether in the light of its importance it should or should not be made a public trust.

The President, if he decides to act, can recommend and support a bill for the creation of a federal government commission to manufacture and distribute the drug C2D. Or, instead, he may decide that the real issue is not one of governmental control, but rather one of the monopoly on the drug obtained by one company. If this is the case, he may urge legislation to provide compulsory licensing of other firms to produce, distribute, and sell C2D. Thus, if the President is wary of governmental management through a special commission, even with representation from physicians and the public, he can push for solution of the problem in terms of licensing to bring about "old-fashioned" competition. In either case, however, new legislation will be required.

This, of course, is the big question, the real problem—whether President Cabot, in view of his and his party's past position on the proper role of the president, will elect to do anything at all. He may choose to do nothing and leave the problem squarely up to Congress. In any case the public will watch with deep interest for his decision, and his justification for acting or not acting.

Review in your text and in your class notes materials relating to the presidency, the role of the president and presidential leadership in legislation, different conceptions of the proper role of the presidency, and presidential-Congressional relations.

Next, read the following statements from men who were well placed to articulate conceptions about the role of the president. The Ohio Republican who served as President from 1909 to 1913, William Howard Taft, had this to say: [1]

> The true view of the Executive functions is, as I conceive it, that the President can exercise no power which cannot be fairly and reasonably traced to some specific grant of power or justly implied and included within such express grant as proper and necessary to its exercise. Such specific grant must be either in the Federal Constitution or in an act of Congress passed in pursuance thereof. There is no undefined residuum of power which he can exercise because it seems to him to be in the public interest. . . . There have not been wanting, however, eminent men in high public office holding a different view and who have insisted upon the necessity for an undefined residuum of Executive power in the public interest. They have not been confined to the present generation. We may learn this from the complaint of a Virginia statesman, Abel P. Upshur, a strict constructionist of the old school, who succeeded Daniel Webster as Secretary of State under President Tyler. He was aroused by Story's commentaries on the Constitution to write a monograph answering and criticizing them, and in the course of this he comments as follows on the Executive power under the Constitution:

> The most defective part of the Constitution beyond all question is that which related to the Executive Department. It is impossible

[1] William Howard Taft, *Our Chief Magistrate and His Powers* (New York: Columbia University Press, 1916), 139–41.

to read that instrument, without being struck with the loose and un-guarded terms in which the powers and duties of the President are pointed out. So far as the legislature is concerned the limitations of the Constitution, are, perhaps, as precise and strict as they could safely have been made; but in regard to the Executive, the Convention appears to have studiously selected such loose and general expressions, as would enable the President, by implication and construction either to neglect his duties or to enlarge his powers. *We have heard it gravely asserted in Congress that whatever power is neither legislative nor judiciary, is of course executive, and, as such, belongs to the President under the Constitution.* How far a majority of that body would have sustained a doctrine so monstrous, and so utterly at war with the whole genius of our government, it is impossible to say, but this, at least, we know, that it met with no rebuke from those who supported the particular act of Executive power, in defense of which it was urged. Be this as it may, it is a reproach to the Constitution that the Executive trust is so ill-defined, as to leave any plausible pretense even to the insane zeal of party devotion, for attributing to the President of the United States the powers of a despot; powers which are wholly unknown in any limited monarchy in the world.

The view that he takes as a result of the loose language defining the Executive powers seems exaggerated. But one must agree with him in his condemnation of the view of the Executive power which he says was advanced in Congress. In recent years there has been put forward a similar view by executive officials and to some extent acted on. Men who are not such strict constructionists of the Constitution as Mr. Upshur may well feel real concern if such views are to receive the general acquiescence.

The man who preceded Taft in the presidency and then tried to regain the office after Taft's tenure, Theodore Roosevelt, took a quite different stand on what responsibilities the man in the White House should assume.[2]

The most important factor in getting the right spirit in my Administration, next to the insistence upon courage, honesty, and a genuine democracy of desire to serve the plain people, was my

[2] *Theodore Roosevelt: An Autobiography* (New York: Charles Scribner's Sons, 1914), p. 357.

insistence upon the theory that the executive power was limited only by specific restrictions and prohibitions appearing in the Constitution or imposed by the Congress under its Constitutional powers. My view was that every executive officer, and above all every executive officer in high position, was a steward of the people bound actively and affirmatively to do all he could for the people, and not to content himself with the negative merit of keeping his talents undamaged in a napkin. I declined to adopt the view that what was imperatively necessary for the Nation could not be done by the President unless he could find some specific authorization to do it. My belief was that it was not only his right but his duty to do anything that the needs of the Nation demanded unless such action was forbidden by the Constitution or by the laws. Under this interpretation of executive power I did and caused to be done many things not previously done by the President and the heads of the departments. I did not usurp power, but I did greatly broaden the use of executive power. In other words, I acted for the public welfare. I acted for the common well-being of all our people, whenever, and in whatever manner was necessary, unless prevented by a direct constitutional or legislative prohibition. I did not care a rap for the mere form and show of power; I cared immensely for the use that could be made of the substance.

Finally, John F. Kennedy, a President firmly in the Rooseveltian tradition, summed up his thoughts about the role of the presidency at the beginning of the year of his election.[3]

The history of this Nation—its brightest and its bleakest pages—has been written largely in terms of the different views our Presidents have had of the Presidency itself. This history ought to tell us that the American people in 1960 have an imperative right to know what any man bidding for the Presidency thinks about the place he is bidding for, whether he is aware of and willing to use the powerful resources of that office; whether his model will be Taft or Roosevelt, Wilson or Harding. . . .

During the past 8 years, we have seen one concept of the Presidency at work. Our needs and hopes have been eloquently stated—but the initiative and follow-through have too often been left to

[3] *Congressional Record*, January 18, 1960, A353–54.

others. And too often his own objectives have been lost by [President Eisenhower's] failure to override objections from within his own party, in the Congress or even in his Cabinet.

The American people in 1952 and 1956 may have preferred this detached, limited concept of the Presidency after 20 years of fast-moving, creative Presidential rule. Perhaps historians will regard this as necessarily one of those frequent periods of consolidation, a time to draw breath, to recoup our national energy. . . .

But the question is what do the times—and the people—demand for the next 4 years in the White House?

They demand a vigorous proponent of the national interest—not a passive broker for conflicting private interests. . . . They demand that he be the head of a responsible party, not rise so far above politics as to be invisible—a man who will formulate and fight for legislative policies, not be a casual bystander to the legislative process.

Today a restricted concept of the Presidency is not enough. For beneath today's surface gloss of peace and prosperity are increasingly dangerous, unsolved, long-postponed problems. . . .

Ulysses Grant considered the President "a purely administrative officer." If he administered the Government departments efficiently, delegated his functions smoothly, and performed his ceremonies of state with decorum and grace, no more was to be expected of him. But that is not the place the Presidency was meant to have in American life. . . .

We will need instead what the Constitution envisioned: a chief Executive who is the vital center of action in our whole scheme of Government.

This includes the legislative process as well. The President cannot afford—for the sake of the office as well as the Nation—to be another Warren G. Harding, described by one backer as a man who "would, when elected, sign whatever bill the Senate sent him —and not send bills for the Senate to pass."

Assume now that you are one of President Josiah Cabot's trusted special assistants. He says that he has been urged by some to intervene actively in the C2D policy conflict and lead a fight for effective legislation of some sort; and that he has been urged by others to abide by the conception of the president's role he, his party platform, and Republican leaders in Congress have expressed, and let Congress alone determine what action, if any, to take. He says that he does not object to either the federal commission or the licensing proposals as such; that his decision will not be determined by such catch phrases as "socialized medicine" or "sacredness of patent rights," which may be misleading and immaterial in the present situation. He says that he looks upon both Senator Benton and Majority Leader Halpin as vigorous, effective Congressional leaders, but he is not sure whether they can overcome the obstacles to getting legislation passed. He is undecided as to whether he, President Cabot, should try to be a legislative leader or leave the policy issue entirely to Congress. He knows that whatever decision he makes, he will have to justify it to the nation.

As his assistant, you are asked by President Cabot to prepare for him three different, well-informed, carefully thought-out documents:

Document 1. A draft of part of a message which he could send to Congress, *if* he decides to assume legislative leadership on the C2D issue; this part should justify President Cabot's undertaking such policy leadership in view of the differing conceptions of the president's role with reference to legislation, pro and con, as given above.

NOTE: Another assistant will prepare those parts of the draft message that will deal with the details of the legislative proposals the President may finally decide to recommend.

Document 2. A work paper, as detailed as possible, setting forth the most successful *strategy* and *tactics* you think President Cabot could employ in order to secure legislation, *if* he decides to take legislative leadership.

NOTE: This paper would have to deal with presidential-Congressional relationships on legislation and the ways in which the president could marshal support for his proposals, directly with Congressmen, through his potential role as party leader, through appeals to public opinion as these might affect Congressional action, and through any other means at his disposal.

Document 3. A draft of a press release which President Cabot could issue, *if* he decides to leave the C2D policy question entirely up to Congress; this release should justify as fully as possible, on general grounds, his refusal to assume legislative leadership on the issue, without being based on disapproval of either Benton's or Halpin's bill.

As a written assignment, or for class discussion, work out in a careful, orderly fashion, and a minimum of mere rhetoric, the contents of the three documents indicated above. Cite as many precedents as you can for your argument in each document.

PROBLEM 23

The Institutionalization of the Presidency

YOU are an Englishman and a Fellow in Government at Oxbridge University. You have recently finished the manuscript of a book on American government in which you emphasized the following point:

The leadership of a series of strong presidents has made the man in the White House the most important man in the land. The president of the United States makes the biggest decisions on public policy all by himself and no one effectively can challenge him. Congress cannot, for he dominates Congress; the courts cannot, for they have largely withdrawn from the hope of checking the president in major policy areas. The job of president, therefore, is one bearing fearsome responsibility and demanding enormous capacity, first to absorb the relevant data on the host of major problems confronting the country, and then to decide the issues of war and peace, prosperity and poverty, equality and rewards, not only for the United States but for much of the rest of the world as well. Such concentration of power in the hands of one man might present as serious a threat to the health of democracy as it does to the health of the president were it not for one continuing fact: the president of the United States must each four years present himself and his decisions to the people for their approval. The judgment rendered by the electorate ensures that the president's power will not be abused.

Shortly after submitting your manuscript to the publishers you are having dinner in Washington with two American governmental officials: Roger Cash, who is Assistant to the Director of the Bureau of the Budget under a vigorous chief, Arthur Savage;

and James Mars, who is Executive Secretary to the National Security Council. Over coffee, Cash and Mars begin to talk shop.

CASH: Well, the agencies have submitted their budget requests to us. Now we have to pare them down to the over-all figure the White House gave us. There will be plenty of howls when we begin to slice some of those programs.

MARS: Who will be hit hardest?

CASH: There is some sentiment to cut the farm programs, but most of them are set by legislation and there isn't much we can do to cut them. Military spending can't be cut much in these times, not since the reductions that were put in at the time of the "big shave," anyway. Veterans' programs are also required at about the present levels by existing legislation and there is no chance of repealing or modifying it. I guess public works and foreign aid will get most of the blow. Especially since the run-in between Savage and those western senators, there will be little money for new dam construction when we get through preparing the budget.

MARS: I thought Congress had already authorized those dams to be built.

CASH: They did, but they haven't appropriated much money for them yet; and in order for them to do it this year, they will either have to cut the military program or run into deficit spending. Savage thinks that they will settle for much talk and little money this year.

YOU, THE OXBRIDGE DON: I thought the President had promised to build those dams. How can Savage cut them out of the budget?

CASH: I doubt if the President is really enthusiastic about the dams. Anyway, Defense says they must have so much, State says the same thing, and the political advisors say that a balanced budget is an absolute necessity. So the White House sends down an over-all figure and Savage and the rest of us decide how to break it down among the various agencies. The President doesn't interfere with the details.

MARS: Don't you have any idea what the White House wants?

CASH: Not any very definite idea, except that we can't cut military spending much, and of course the programs required by legislation have to be kept up unless things like grants-in-aid for old-age assistance and highways are repealed, and nobody is seriously suggesting that they should be. The President said in his press conference that we would have to make sacrifices in order to stay ahead in the space race into the 1970's, if we can manage it; but when Savage asked Herman Williams, the President's chief assistant, just what this meant he didn't give us much help. Usually Williams is more on top of budget details than anybody else around the White House, but he can't say much beyond the broad outline until the President gives him a lead.

MARS: Who set the over-all spending limit?

CASH: Savage himself and Treasury provided the figures on requests and anticipated tax revenues, and Williams insisted on two things: money for an overhauled antipoverty program and adequate funds for the "man-in-the-moon" program. The cities are where the party people hope to make their real gains in the next election. Add this to Savage's disapproval of federal power projects as a matter of principle and it spells little money for dam construction.

MARS: What is the scuttlebutt on foreign aid? I understand that the President wanted a big increase and was talked out of it.

CASH: Didn't you settle that in the National Security Council?

MARS: Not really. We talked about it, but the Treasury people weren't at the meeting, so the question was postponed. I heard it was taken up at a Cabinet meeting.

CASH: My information is that the Congressional leaders told the President an increase was impossible and that ended it. The State Department wouldn't settle for less than last year's figure so that fixed the size of the request.

MARS: We did decide the size of the defense budget in the NSC.

CASH: That was done while the President was away at the NATO meeting, wasn't it?

MARS: Yes. He was in on the earlier discussions, but the main problem was getting some kind of compromise worked out between the various branches of the armed forces that would come within the over-all limits insisted on by the Treasury people and the Budget Bureau people. The President wanted to knock some heads together to get the research programs under one unified control, but nobody could agree on *who* should control, so the matter was left pretty much as it had been. The Secretary of Defense may get some additional authority over the services but—

CASH: I doubt that. That request from Defense needs legislation from Congress, and until the State Department is convinced that Defense is on the right track we can't clear the request.

YOU: What do you mean?

CASH: All requests for legislation emanating from executive agencies come to us in the Bureau of the Budget before they are submitted to Congress and we clear them—get the views of other agencies, see how they square with the President's legislative program, and so on. Until they are cleared and the major agencies involved agree, they can't be submitted.

YOU: Wait a minute. You mean if the President wants to ask Congress for legislation, he can't just go ahead and do it?

CASH: Of course he *can*, but he won't as a rule. The agencies that have to carry out the program, or whose interests are affected by the program, must support the recommendations, or there would be an awful hassle. The President wouldn't risk that even if he wanted to, which he doesn't because he doesn't really know enough of the details to have an opinion. So clearance is our job.

MARS: Your man Savage and the Treasury boys are not so dominant in the National Security Council as they were. Defense and State and the Joint Chiefs of Staff have been calling the shots for the last few weeks. I hear that Defense and State dominate the Cabinet too.

CASH: They're bound to with the international picture dominating everything the way it has lately. By the way, what do you think of Alsmann's column that the Cabinet is being revived as the truly deliberative body it was supposed to be?

MARS: I don't think it is, not yet anyway. *We* make the decisions on defense and a whole lot of other foreign policy, which in turn means two-thirds of the budget. You people are the key agency for the rest of the budget and for the legislative program. The influential members of the Cabinet also attend NSC meetings and exert their influence there, but several of the Cabinet people are hardly involved. Between Budget and NSC the important questions are taken care of. What is there left for the Cabinet to do as an institution? Ultimately it might become the agency that coordinates you with us and brings in the viewpoint of, say, Health, Education, and Welfare, but not now.

CASH: I agree. And since patronage is handled by the party National Committee and Williams there isn't any party work for them to do. The Council of Economic Advisers has been getting increasingly secure jurisdiction over economic policy questions. You know, I don't think that many people really understand what is involved in the way executive agencies are piling up and handling the planning and coordination of the policy-making side of things. Even the newspaper boys write very little about it, and precious few of the academics even suspect what is happening.

YOU: Look here, I'm an academic and an outsider as well. I've heard a little about the kind of thing you've been discussing, but I didn't think this sort of thing was a permanent part of the presidency.

CASH: Much of this machinery was established under Roosevelt and Truman, then under Eisenhower the process was extended, and a lot of it stayed on under Kennedy and Johnson too. We both had our present jobs under previous administrations. The developments have been a little more dramatic recently, but I think this machinery will survive and continue to function with increasing authority.

YOU: Well, where is the President? What is his role?

CASH: Well, of course he is around. He is the one exposed to the public spotlight and he performs a lot of ceremonial duties. He doesn't play much part in making policy, though. That is our job: Mars, me, and a lot of others like us.

Having listened carefully to this conversation, you the Oxbridge Fellow, go out and check as thoroughly as you can the validity of what Cash and Mars have said. You find that their specific statements of fact are accurate, and that these facts are a fair sample of what normally goes on within the executive branch. However, there are many who disagree, some rather violently, with Cash's final evaluation of the President's role. They insist that the President still must make, personally, the broad policy decisions and that the responsibility is still his in the last analysis.

Next, you reread with fresh interest three summaries by American political scientists of certain aspects of recent developments in the presidency. The first, by Edward S. Corwin, stresses what he sees as the progressive institutionalization and routinization of the presidential office and its powers.[1]

The "Institutionalized Presidency" pivots, so to speak, on two hinges. The first is the Executive Office of the President, the product chiefly of legislation; the second is the White House Office, which has taken on unprecedented importance under President Eisenhower.

Dealing with the former, a recent writer remarks:

We have routinized the President's responsibility to take the policy lead. And at the same time, we have institutionalized, in marked degree, the exercise of that responsibility. President and presidency are synonymous no longer; the office now comprises an officialdom twelve-hundred strong. For almost every phase of policy development there is now institutional machinery engaged in preparations on the President's behalf; for the financial and administrative workplan of the government, the Budget Bureau; for the Administration's legislative program, the White House counsel and the Budget's clearance organization; for programming in economic and social spheres, the Council of Economic Advisers (and to some degree the Cabinet, Eisenhower-style); in foreign and military fields, the National Security Council; in spheres of domestic preparedness, the Office of Defense Mobilization; these pieces of machinery among others, each built around a program-making task, all lumped

[1] Edward S. Corwin, *The President: Office and Powers*, 4th ed. (New York: New York University Press, 1957), 300–304.

together, formally, under the rubric "The Executive Office of the President," an institutional conception and a statutory entity less than two decades old.

These are significant developments, this routinizing, institutionalizing, of the initiative. They give the presidency nowadays a different look than it has worn before, an aspect permanantly "positive." But the reality behind that look was not just conjured up by statutes or by staffing. These, rather, are *responses* to the impacts of external circumstance upon our form of government; not causes but effects.

Presidents have, of course, always had some kind of help in the discharge of their duties, but . . . it is in the Eisenhower regime that tendencies toward bureaucratization, exhibited during the incumbencies of Truman and F.D.R., have become controlling, thanks in part to Mr. Eisenhower's military experience with the Chief of Staff work concept, in part to his settled preference for consensus and security as against debate and adventuring, and in part to intervals of bad health. In consequence of all these factors combined, the institutionalizing process has been carried beyond the Truman model in four respects: (1) in the employment of Sherman Adams as Chief of Staff; (2) in use of the Cabinet for collective consultation; (3) in more effective use of the Vice-President; and (4) in regular, planned consultation with congressional leaders on legislative policies.

Sherman Adams is, in fact if not in name, the "Chief of Staff" called for by the First Hoover Commission. Today he is accorded the title and enjoys a power in the White House second only to that of the President himself. Indeed, in the light of what is now known about the matter it would seem that Mr. Adams was for all practical purposes President during the early stages of Mr. Eisenhower's illness. . . .

Eisenhower has also made conspicuous use of the Vice-President, not only inviting him to Cabinet meetings, but assigning him to preside over meetings of the Cabinet and the National Security Council when the President does not attend, and giving him a succession of extracongressional duties. . . .

Another marked characteristic of the Eisenhower administration is the frequent detachment of the President from the conduct of his subordinates. On several occasions he appears to have accomplished what President Truman and many commentators have said was impossible, "passing the buck" to the Secretary of Agriculture, the Secretary of State, the Secretary of the Army, the Attorney General. Each of these gentlemen, according to the President is an independent officeholder with his own views of appropriate policy, with which the President has no warrant to interfere. . . .

Just how durable is President Eisenhower's impact on the presidency apt to be? Certainly the time is long past when the conception of the President as a sort of "boss of the works" had convincing connection with reality.

Rather, I suggest, there is a long-term trend at work in the world that consolidates power in the executive departments of all governments, first in the person of one individual, then in an "administration." The era of Roosevelt, Churchill, Stalin, Hitler, Mussolini—each a cornerstone of the national "cult of personality"—has been followed by collegial rule, collective responsibility, and *ad hoc* policies flowing out of completed staff work.

The second statement you review is by Richard E. Neustadt, who discusses various ways in which two occupants of the White House sought to assert presidential leadership and power in order to avoid becoming altogether the prisoner of the institutionalization of the office.[2]

It has been a quarter century since the President's Committee on Administration Management, chaired by Louis Brownlow, blessed by Franklin D. Roosevelt, heralded a major innovation in our constitutional arrangements: substantial staffing for the Presidency distinct from other parts of the executive establishment—in Edward Corwin's phrase an "Institutionalized Presidency." The Executive Office, which throughout our prior history has been essentially a "private office" in the English sense, was to become a "President's Department." . . .

So far as I can find, Roosevelt did not theorize about the principles which underlay his operating style in later years. But he

[2] Richard E. Neustadt, "Approaches to Staffing the Presidency: Notes on FDR and JFK," *American Political Science Review*, LVII (1963), 855–58, 861–62.

evidently had some principles, or at least premises, or touchstones, or instinct, for his practice was remarkably consistent in essentials.

The first of these "principles," I suggest, was a concern for his position as *the* man in the White House. If he began the institutionalized presidency, he did not for a moment mean that it should make an institution out of *him*. The White House was *his* House, his home as well as office. No one was to work there who was not essential for the conduct of his own work, day by day. "This is the White House calling" was to mean *him*, or somebody acting intimately and immediately for him. The things he personally did not need firsthand, were to be staffed outside the White House. The aides he did not have to see from day to day were to be housed in other offices than his. This is the origin of the distinction which developed in his time between "personal" and "institutional" staff. The Executive Office was conceived to be the place for "institutional" staff; the place, in other words, for everybody else.

Not only did he generally try to keep second-string personnel out of his house, he also shied away from second-string activities which smacked of the routine (except where *he* chose otherwise for the time being). This seems to be one of the reasons—not the only one —why he never had "legislative liaison" assistants continuously working at the White House. Reportedly, he foresaw what came to be the case in Eisenhower's time, that if the White House were routinely in the "liaisoning" business, Congressmen and agencies alike would turn to *his* assistants for all sorts of routine services and help. "It is all your trouble, not mine," he once informed his Cabinet officers, with reference to the bills that *they* were sponsoring. This was his attitude toward departmental operations generally, always excepting those things that he wanted for his own, or felt he had to seize because of personalities or circumstances. . . .

The second "principle" I would note is FDR's strong feeling for a cardinal fact in government: that presidents don't act on policies, programs, or personnel in the abstract; they act in the concrete as they meet deadlines set by due dates—or the urgency—of documents awaiting signature, vacant posts awaiting appointees, officials seeking interviews, newsmen seeking answers, audiences waiting for a speech, intelligence reports requiring a response, etc. He also had a strong sense of another fact in government; that persons close to presidents are under constant pressure—and temptation—to go into business for themselves, the more so as the word gets out that they deal regularly with some portion of his business.

Accordingly, he gave a minimum of fixed assignments to the members of his personal staff. Those he did give out were usually in terms of helping him to handle some specific and recurrent stream of action-forcing deadlines he himself could not escape. . . .

The third thing I would emphasize is Roosevelt's sense of need for mobile manpower and multiple antennae. In addition to his aides with fixed assignments, FDR took full advantage of the Brownlow *Report's* proposal for a number of "Administrative Assistants" on his personal staff, each with a "passion for anonymity." After 1939 and on into the war years, he had several men so titled—and so enjoined —about him, all of them conceived as "generalists," whom he could use, *ad hoc,* as chore-boys, trouble shooters, checker-uppers, intelligence operatives, and as magnets for ideas, gripes, gossip in the Administration, on the Hill, and with groups outside government. These men were also used, as need arose, to backstop and assist the aides who did have fixed assignments.

FDR intended his Administrative Assistants to be eyes and ears and manpower for *him,* with no fixed contacts, clients, or involvements of their own to interfere when he had need to redeploy them. . . .

Put these three operating "principles" together and they add up to a *fourth:* in Roosevelt's staffing there was no place for a Sherman Adams. Roosevelt made and shifted the assignments; *he* was the recipient of staff work; *he* presided at informal morning staff meetings; *he* audited the service he was getting; *he* coordinated A's report with B's (or if he did not, they went uncoordinated and he sometimes paid a price for that). Before the war, reportedly, he planned to keep one of his Administrative Assistants on tap "in the office," to "mind the shop" and be a sort of checker-upper on the others. But he never seems to have put this intention into practice. . . .

But suppose a President whose operating instincts were not unlike FDR's faced complications of the sort I have ascribed to wartime Washington without the wartime benefits . . . ? There is no need to be supposititious. This, roughly speaking, is John F. Kennedy's plight.

There are some obvious affinities between the operating "principles" in Kennedy's own mind and those I earlier ascribed to FDR. His staffing demonstrates this rather plainly. He evidently shares Roosevelt's concern for the distinction between "personal" and "institutional" staff. From Administration to Administration, White House staff has grown inexorably; "this is the White House calling" has less meaning every decade. But Kennedy quite consciously has tried to slow the trend; he cut back Eisenhower's growth and started small.

Kennedy, moreover, has run his personal staff with a feeling as keen as Roosevelt's (or was it Brownlow's?) for organizing around action-forcing processes. Like FDR, this President has operated with a small core of senior aides on relatively fixed assignments . . . each handles a distinctive aspect of the work-flow which the President must get through, day-by-day. Like their Rooseveltian counterparts these men also do other things, *ad hoc*. And as in Roosevelt's day their general-purpose services are supplemented by the services of others who do not have comparable fixed assignments. . . .

The differences grow greater as one moves beyond the personal staff toward the realms of institutional staff and departmental relations. Roosevelt was lucky; he wrote on a clean slate and then he got a second slate "war government." Roosevelt innovated, Kennedy inherited.

From Truman he inherited an Executive Office larger and much more diffuse than Roosevelt's Budget Bureau, encompassing by statutory mandate NSC [National Security Council] staff, CEA [Council of Economic Advisers], and what we now call OEP [Office of Emergency Planning]. From Eisenhower he inherited a complex "staff system" and cabinet-committee structure, as well as a variety of specialized staff units. From both his predecessors he inherited classic and unresolved dilemmas of relationship between a President and certain key departments, notably Defense, State, Justice, Treasury. Kennedy's approach to staffing has been shaped in major part by his attempts to cope with this inheritance. The outcome naturally resembles Roosevelt's pattern less than does the White House staff, *per se*.

Commotion over Kennedy's deliberate dismantling of his predecessor's staff and cabinet system has obscured the fact that he retained and has elaborated on four features of the Eisenhower era.

For one thing, Kennedy disposes of his time with much the freedom Eisenhower painfully acquired from a heart attack. . . .

But Eisenhower's cut-back on the set-appointments list is not the only way in which his practice has been carried forward. Kennedy has also kept, indeed enlarged upon, the White House staff for legislative liaison, a notable departure from Rooseveltian practice, which Eisenhower was the first to introduce in a serious way. Similarly, Kennedy has followed and indeed elaborated Eisenhower's staff for science and technology. . . . Further, the Special Projects Fund which Eisenhower added to White House resources has been used by his successor, very much as he had done, to bring assorted special staffs with special purposes—including status-recognition for an interest-group or program—into the presidential orbit as need be from time to time. This evidently has become an indispensable adjunct of presidential life as it will be lived from now on.

Finally you consider the following conclusions from an article by Harlan Cleveland on the federal bureaucracy and the presidential office, in which he agrees that the presidency has become institutionalized but is unwilling to accept this as meaning that the individual who holds the office is necessarily lacking in responsibility or power.[3]

Whether, under our system, the government ultimately serves the public interest, or merely obliges the private and sectional Trojan horses encamped inside the walls of the Federal bureaucracy, depends on the President to an extraordinary and alarming degree. He is the chief mediator among the veto groups, the one political executive whose whole job is to consider the situation as a whole. He is the one remaining safety man available to stop a specialized interest which breaks through the normal line of checks and balances and threatens to gain too much yardage at the expense of other groups.

In a revealing passage of his autobiography, Mr. Truman regarded it as quite natural that nobody should consider the public interest but the President, "I was always aware," he wrote, "of the

[3] Harlan Cleveland, "Survival in the Bureaucratic Jungle," *The Reporter,* April 5, 1956, 30–32.

fact that not all my advisers looked at the . . . problem in the same manner I did. This was nothing unusual, of course. It is the job of the military planners to consider all matters first and always in the light of military considerations. The diplomat's approach is—or in any case should be—determined by considerations of our relations to other nations. The Secretary of the Treasury thinks in terms of budget and taxes. Except for the members of his personal staff, each Presidential adviser had and should have a departmental outlook."

Though we sometimes make gods or supermen of our Presidents, they have not generally been more moral than most of us. The difference is that in the White House they are compelled to stand a little higher on the mountain than anybody else, and they consequently see farther at the horizon. It is this unique and lonely vantage point that lends grandeur to the American Presidency.

Yet the President's high rank does not necessarily mean that he makes more "decisions" than other political executives below. Indeed it is arguable that in our government, the higher one's rank the fewer decisions one makes. The man who buys paper clips makes a number of unreviewed decisions without consultation—what size and shape of paper clip, from whom to buy, at what price. As you go up the ladder of authority each official is beset with more committees, more horizontal clearances, more veto groups and political personalities whose views must be reconciled or discounted before the "final decision" is reached. . . .

The saving grace of our Executive bureaucracy, [however], is that nearly everybody in it works for the President. To be sure, each political executive is also responsible horizontally to four or five Congressional committees; he has to deal with several outside interest groups whose leaders feel the executive is answerable to them; and within the Executive Branch he is constantly evading his own responsibility by burying it in collective decisions by interdepartmental committees. But when the chips are down on any one issue, all political executives are accountable to the President—which is another way of saying that if they get into a tight spot, they can generally pass the buck to him. . . .

Government is politics, but the Executive Branch has to be run by executives. And in government, as in other hierarchies, the buck can travel in one direction only—up.

Bear in mind that all of the above analyses were written before the death of President Kennedy, and that other presidents might bring still other approaches to the problem of the presidential office and staff.

Review materials in your text and lecture notes relating to the presidency, and, more specifically, to the operations of the Bureau of the Budget, the National Security Council, and other major agencies in the Executive Office of the President.

On the basis of the new material, but also bearing in mind the data on which your original analysis was based, prepare a written exercise or for class discussion answers to the following in your role as the Oxbridge Fellow in government:

1. To what extent, if any, does your original summary statement concerning the job of president of the United States need to be revised? ~~Great~~

2. What particular changes would you make in your manuscript? *Many decisions are made by others (Bureaucrats)*

3. Is your conclusion concerning the democratic control of the president's action still valid? If not, explain why not and suggest the changes that might re-establish democratic control without upsetting the performance of functions by the executive branch. If you believe that your conclusion on this point is still valid, be sure to justify it in terms of the newly acquired data.

4. What factors have contributed to the process that has been called the institutionalization of the presidency? Be as specific as possible.

5. Would Mars and Cash agree with the statement that the president "stands higher and sees farther" than anyone else; that he is the one man who can reflect the interests of the nation as a whole? If not, why not? *he depends on them*

PROBLEM 24

The President and Foreign Policy: Democracy in Action?

IN the 1830's a perceptive Frenchman, Alexis de Tocqueville, visited the United States. One of his observations about American society and democracy has as much relevance in the 1960's as it did a century and a quarter ago. Tocqueville believed that "Foreign politics demand scarcely any of those qualities which are peculiar to a democracy; they require, on the contrary, the perfect use of almost all those in which it is deficient . . . [A] democracy can only with great difficulty regulate the details of an important undertaking, persevere in a fixed design, and work out its execution in spite of serious obstacles. It cannot combine its measures with secrecy or await their consequences with patience." Students since the time of Tocqueville have echoed his sentiments. In particular the question of democratic control over foreign policy has captured interest.

Read the following statements about the process of making foreign policy with careful attention to two questions: first, what is the relationship between public opinion and executive decisions about foreign policy? and second, what is the responsibility of the executive branch in the making of foreign policy?

Statement I [1]

[There are] . . . four hard challenges to the basic workings of our democratic system.

For one thing, if ever the line between domestic and foreign affairs could be drawn, it is now wholly erased. Whether we realize it or not, we can no longer assure ourselves that what we do in one place is unrelated to what we do in a second place; that if we slip domestically, the effect will not be felt abroad—or the other way around. The strength of the American economy, for example, enters directly as a factor in our power to build a versatile military establishment, or to export capital in ways that will contribute to the orderly growth of newly independent peoples. In a reverse view, if those people and their resources along with those of our European allies should ever be drawn into the Communist orbit, it is difficult to see how we could for long maintain our present economy or, indeed, anything resembling our present way of life.

Secondly, because America's paramount strength has vested in us the role of leadership for a coalition diplomacy, our Executive and Legislative organs of government must bear two constituencies in mind. One is the voting constituency from which the chief officers of American government draw their title of office. The second constituency begins at the three-mile limit. It is formed by many hundreds of millions of people around the globe who, though they don't cast a single vote in any American election, are vitally affected by the decisions of American lawmakers.

Out of this there arises a recurrent dilemma. In the event of a conflict of interest between the two constituencies, which one should have a prior claim on the support of the American lawmaker? If the prior claim is that of his nonvoting constituency, then he risks a repudiation by American voters. If the prior claim is that of his voting constituency, then he risks the loss of trust by the nonvoting constituency—whose support he must have if he is to attain what both constituencies want above all other things, namely, the conditions for a just peace.

[1] Senator J. W. Fulbright, "What Makes United States Foreign Policy?" *The Reporter*, May 14, 1959.

Thirdly, the very process of coalition diplomacy tends to exercise a gravitational pull that centers the business in the hands of the Executive, and downgrades the role of the Congress and the electorate as direct parties to the affair. For the Congress is simply not structurally equipped to deal simultaneously with all the day-to-day problems of coalition diplomacy. And the people, for their part, are even less well equipped to follow the intricate twists and turns of any contemporary diplomatic transaction.

The fourth difference between the past and present represents so great an intensification of the old problem of amateur-expert relations in government as to constitute an almost new problem. What I have in mind here is the fact that many of our leading questions of foreign affairs nowadays are entwined with infinitely complicated scientific and technological questions. For example, should we or should we not stop the testing of the hydrogen bomb? Should we put more or less effort into missile-launching submarines or into the support of foreign allied armies? You can search all the great treatises on the American polity from the *Federalist* papers on forward and they will not give you a single clue to the right answer. Even that second great source of popular doctrine, *Poor Richard's Almanac,* which is so much evoked today, also fails in this respect.

Public ignorance of these new-style political-scientific-military questions is widespread, to put it mildly, and reaches into high places, including the United States Senate. It is matched by the respect and awe we hold for the expert practitioners of these new arts—a respect which we do not accord experts in other fields. The economists of this country rarely, if ever, agree on precisely the monetary policy to be followed by the Federal Reserve Board. But this does not in the least inhibit people who don't know the difference between Adam Smith and John Maynard Keynes from expressing the most profound judgments on the matter. Yet these same people are quite willing to leave vastly more important questions to a handful of scientists and military strategists who sharply disagree among themselves.

One reason for this paradox, I suggest, is that whereas the economists carry on their disputes in public, what the military scientists have to say is funneled almost exclusively to the Executive, where the cutoff stamp of Top Secret comes into play. But what is cut off simultaneously is any real power by the people or the

Congress to judge whether the agents of the Executive acted wisely or not on the basis of the word they alone were privileged to hear. . . .

Statement II [2]

A joint responsibility of the Congress and the Executive that deserves special emphasis is that of maintaining effective relations with the public which ultimately sets the limits of maneuver within which those who shape and execute policy must operate. The climate of opinion that emerges from the public is the product of many interacting factors—the impact of mass media, the activity of hundreds of interest groups, the initiatives of public leaders, the influence of foreign opinion, and the weighing of issues and individuals through the channels of party politics.

The anticipated course of future world developments promises to impose greater burdens than ever on the public in relation to foreign policy. At the same time, the obstacles to public understanding threaten to become even more severe. These include the secrecy that often shrouds official deliberations, the bewildering pace of change, and the intricacy of the issues. While this report cannot accommodate a detailed treatment of the role of public opinion, it is pertinent to consider briefly a few alternative approaches to thinking about the relationship between the Government, particularly the Congress, and the general public with respect to foreign policy.

One point of view would place minimal emphasis on governmental efforts to cultivate contacts with the public through informational activities. This attitude stems largely from the feeling that such efforts run the risk of putting the Government in the position of "selling" programs to the people, of manipulating them. There is also the concern that the general public cannot be expected to be well informed or active in relation to the daily flow of international affairs.

Another view is that the Congress and the executive branch should support a stronger foreign policy information program for

[2] "The Formulation and Administration of United States Foreign Policy," A Study Prepared by the Brookings Institution for the Committee on Foreign Relations, U.S. Senate, 86th Congress, 2nd Session, 1960, 822–23.

the general public. The lives of all Americans are touched by the Nation's international policies; it is their survival which is at stake. The public's attitudes toward crucial foreign policies may be seriously distorted by the tendencies of some media toward sensationalism and superficiality.

A third view holds that a more systematic and energetic effort should be made to bring leaders of public opinion into closer touch with the officials and processes that shape U.S. foreign policy. These leaders are extremely important in informing and mobilizing the public and are most likely to make the best use of such an opportunity.

Many devices could be used to implement this third alternative. More high-level briefings might be conducted by the executive departments for selected groups. . . . More opportunities might be given to leading individuals to take part in the policy process as consultants, temporary staff members, delegates, or visitors abroad. Arrangements to provide information and other services for groups conducting programs in world affairs could be strengthened. The Congress could contribute by reinforcing its relations with special groups and the media that reach those groups. Hearings could be held in various parts of the country, and Members of the Congress might more frequently form bipartisan teams to explain aspects of foreign policy and to sample attitudes. A few Members have already performed valuable services in this regard and have developed effective means of discussing the essence of policy with community audiences.

Of these three broad alternatives, the second and third are the most promising. If the Government is to move in the direction of bringing the public into closer touch with governmental policy, it will be necessary to have more adequate continuing collaboration between the two branches regarding both substantive and procedural aspects of the effort. The Congress should provide broad directives for this purpose and the necessary authority and funds to give life to the directives.

The factor of secrecy is of vital importance here. Some secrecy is necessary, but it can be used as a shield against legitimate criticism. As more governments impose restrictions on the flow of information the public becomes increasingly dependent upon governmental releases. This can lead to serious distortion of public attitudes. Because there will always be justification for some measure of secrecy, especially in relation to matters close to the heart of national security, the solution must be one of degree. The direction should generally be toward a more permissive balance between concealment and disclosure that will provide the public with the basic information it needs to fulfill its responsibilities with regard to fundamental issues. . . .

Review in your text and lecture notes material relevant to the presidency, the executive branch, public opinion, and foreign policy. Then consider the following hypothetical situation:

In a public meeting in Bonn, West Germany, a rising star in West German politics named Hans Burger, a man with a considerable following throughout Western Europe, launches an attack on the United States. His chief argument is that the United States has lost any claim that it might have had to the support of Western Europeans in the struggle against totalitarian aggression because the United States has itself become undemocratic. Burger argues that since the United States is no longer a democracy, West Germany and other free nations must turn elsewhere for leadership in the effort to defend the standards of freedom. In support of his arguments Burger introduces seven statements taken from American publications. All of these statements are correctly quoted and come from responsible sources, and Burger asserts that they prove his contention that the United States is no longer a democracy.

1. It is not too much to say that since it was organized in 1947 the National Security Council has made the most basic decisions in the field of international affairs. In fact, the decisions of the Council very probably will fix the course of the whole world for peace or war.—*Prominent Journalist*

2. The decisions of the National Security Council are not fit subjects for public discussion.—*Member of the NSC*

3. I will never reveal what goes on in the meetings of the NSC. —*President of the United States*

4. Politics must stop at the water's edge. American foreign policy cannot be allowed to fall prey to the devious ins and outs of machine bosses and the unscrupulous efforts of men who seek political office without regard for the welfare of the nation. Issues of foreign policy should be decided without regard for the fortunes of a political party, and, once decided, they should receive the united support of all Americans.—*Member of the Senate Foreign Relations Committee*

5. Too much information concerning the defense potential of the United States has been revealed to the public. Such information may well give aid and comfort to the enemy.—*Secretary of Defense*

6. Surveys consistently show that 20 percent to 25 percent of the American public is not interested in even the most pressing problems of foreign affairs. Three years after the establishment of the United Nations, one-fourth of the American public was not aware of its existence. A substantial percentage of the public cannot answer such questions as "Where is Viet Nam?" and "Who is Fidel Castro?" A similar proportion is totally unaware of current international problems. Only 15 percent can identify the Alliance for Progress; and whereas 92 percent were keenly interested in cost-of-living news, only 54 percent were vitally concerned with United States relations with the Soviet Union.—*Public Opinion Analyst*

7. The military establishment of the United States has grown tremendously in size and in influence in the making of foreign policy. Even though civilians occupy the top positions in the Defense Department they speak for military values and objectives, and their voices are heard with great respect in the highest councils in the land. Military expenditures comprise two-thirds of the national budget and are beyond any really effective control by Congress.—*American Political Scientist*

Apparently there is considerable support for Burger's view in the audience, an audience which many newspaper correspondents believe accurately reflects the thinking of many Western Europeans. A substantial number of people in the audience, however, are confused and uncertain. They are unsure of the advantages to be obtained from following the lead of the United States in world affairs and are therefore willing to be convinced by Burger that they should seek other leadership. They do not understand, however, the connection between the statements Burger has read and the conclusion he has reached—namely, that the United States is undemocratic. Neither are they sure what difference it makes if the United States *is* undemocratic.

After Burger has spoken a young German named Karl Klaus rises to challenge Burger's argument. Klaus has recently returned from the United States where he spent a year as an exchange student in music composition. He is not an expert in American politics and he does not have quotations from American publications to support his argument. Nevertheless, he says that during his stay in the United States he saw many examples of what he considered to be vigorous democracy with respect to foreign policy. He cites the many lively arguments he heard among students over foreign policy questions. He tells of the strong criticisms leveled against the Democrats for their policy in the Far East or Cuba, and against the Republicans for alleged failures in missile research and development. Klaus points out that members of Congress were constantly advocating changes in policy and threatening to withhold foreign aid appropriations unless the president shifted his stand on one policy or another. Foreign policy issues were frequently debated at length during election campaigns, and Klaus remembers a study which showed that most Americans continued to receive much of their information and opinion about foreign policy issues from the leaders of the political party they normally supported. Various organizations devoted to the study and discussion of foreign policy problems could be found all over the country; and most interest groups, even though their primary concerns were domestic, had something to say about foreign policy. Klaus said that the American press was filled with information about all sorts of matters related to foreign affairs, from guided missile research to the latest gossip about the Soviet ambassador.

You are an American political scientist engaged in research on West German politics. During your researches you have become acquainted with several responsible and thoughtful West Germans who are widely respected in their country for their opinions about foreign affairs. These people are genuinely puzzled. They have been impressed by the warm regard which Klaus holds for the United States, and his argument has softened the force of Burger's charges considerably. Yet they are afraid that Klaus's rather fragmentary impressions do not give an accurate picture of the United States, and that, even if they do, the United States is still not really democratic in the way in which it makes foreign policy decisions. Your friends turn to you, with your expert knowledge in this field, and ask where the truth lies.

For a written exercise or for class discussion:

1. Explain to your friends as carefully and clearly as you can the way in which each statement quoted by Burger is related to his charge that the United States is undemocratic.

2. Explain to your friends the extent to which Klaus's impressions support the conclusion that the United States remains vigorously democratic.

3. Explain to your friends the other facts and arguments that you, on the basis of your broad knowledge and understanding of the American political system, believe should be included in arriving at a balanced judgment on this question.

Remember, your job is not to defend the United States uncritically, nor should you uncritically condemn foreign policy-making procedures. Rather you should provide a candid, balanced, and full statement of the significant facts and problems involved.

PROBLEM 25

Factors in Presidential Decision Making

DECISIONS and policies affecting the entire society or its relations with other societies are the ultimate products of political systems. Whether a given decision is to take action in a situation or not to take action and let the situation remain or develop as it will, a choice is involved. As a student of administrative behavior has put it: [1]

All behavior involves conscious or unconscious selection of particular actions out of all those which are physically possible to the actor and to those persons over whom he exercises influence and authority. The term "selection" . . . refers simply to the fact that, if the individual follows one particular course of action, there are other courses of action he thereby forgoes. In many cases the selection process consists simply in an established reflex action. . . . In other cases the selection is itself the product of a complex chain of activities called "planning" or "design" activities . . . At any moment there are a multitude of alternative . . . possible actions, any one of which a given individual may undertake; by some process these numerous alternatives are narrowed down to that one which is in fact acted out.

Men in all walks of life make decisions with an eye to attaining their goals. By the nature of their jobs, politicians are men whose waking hours are filled with the problems and questions which accompany what we may call public policy decision making. Some decisions, for example, Supreme Court judgments, are made after extensive study and weighing of all the relevant factors.

[1] Herbert A. Simon, *Administrative Behavior* (New York: The Macmillan Co., 1961), 3–4.

Other decisions must be made in response to a crisis situation or unanticipated event; for example, a military decision made in response to an aggressive action. In one way or another most of the problems in this book have been concerned with premises of policy making, that is, with the question of what factors are taken into account as the policy maker chooses from among the available alternatives. An implicit assumption has been that politicians, like the rest of us, collect *information* which is pertinent to the situation calling for action or the problem demanding a solution. This question is discussed in a general way in Problem 1, "Facts and Values in Political Analysis," and has been touched on in other problems. Information is essential if decision making is to be rational.

Because of the complexity of the changing world and the necessity for rapid decisions, there has been an increasing reliance on political staffs and professional information gatherers for information. This is true at all levels of government and in every type of political institution. The city council may have its city manager, the Congressman has his office staff, Supreme Court judges have their clerks, and so on. In particular the role of the adviser, the information expert, the consultant, or the professional staff has become apparent in the executive branch of the federal government. Some of the reasons for this development are set forth in Problem 23, "The Institutionalization of the Presidency," above. The collecting of relevant information and the garnering of expert advice is a process with its own kind of political consequences. The following two selections provide some insights into the relationship between the adviser and the advised, and between information and the political decision.

Statement I [2]

Delegation to experts has become an indispensable aid to rational calculation in modern life. In business, government, education, mili-

[2] Robert A. Dahl and Charles E. Lindblom, *Politics, Economics, and Welfare* (New York: Harper & Brothers, 1953), 73–75.

tary affairs, communications—indeed, in almost all organizations—leaders and non-leaders decrease the number of variables they must deal with by delegating some choices to individuals who have "special skill or knowledge in a subject." The choices delegated to experts range from determining what set of facts is correct to choosing the goals to be maximized. How to delegate to experts choice of factual assumptions without granting them an unwanted choice among the very goals to be maximized is, however, a staggering problem. In this sense, delegation to experts is both an indispensable aid and an unremitting threat to rational calculation.

If prescribed superiors are to make rational calculations, the relationship between them and experts must be such that the superiors can specify goals and the experts will indicate the relative costs and gains of the various alternative means for maximizing the achievement of these preferences. For example, the House Committee on Irrigation and Reclamation might have employed some engineers, accountants, and economists to sort out the various alternatives for pricing electric power at reclamation dams and to estimate what each alternative would probably involve in costs to taxpayers, indirect subsidies to power and water consumers, effects on agricultural growth and production, population, and the like. Applying their own schedule of preferences, committee members could then choose among these alternatives.

But committee members could be led into irrational decisions in two ways: if for the preferences of his superior the expert surreptitiously substituted a different set to be maximized; or, alternatively if on a question in which the committee member was less competent he substituted his judgment for the expert analysis of the relative costs and gains of alternative techniques. Yet to keep these types of judgment separate is difficult. The superior may not be able to articulate his preferences to the expert, and will find it even more difficult to articulate the points at which one preference should give way to another. In government advisory commissions, for example, top leaders usually specify goals so vaguely that the experts can and must load the policy proposals with their own private preferences.

Experts have their own axes to grind, and it is easy for them to rationalize (e.g., as being in "the public interest") the substitution of their own goals for those of their superiors. One suspects, for example, that the House Committee on Irrigation and Reclamation could have obtained little help from the Department of the Interior in examining alternative power prices. For the Reclamation Bureau and Solicitor's Office would have been strongly tempted to load the data to suit their own policy preferences. But even experts employed directly by the committee might have done the same; no technical field is more marked by moral fervor than reclamation and conservation. Then, too, whether or not the lay superior is more competent than the alleged expert to decide a particular factual question is itself frequently unclear in the real world. In 1944 some western governors and the Bureau of Reclamation in the upper Missouri Valley disagreed vociferously and publicly with army engineers over the question of whether a deepening of the Missouri River channel from six to nine feet from Sioux City to St. Louis would or would not significantly reduce the water available to upstream farmers.

Sometimes these differences simply indicate a stubborn unwillingness on the part of the layman to recognize his own limits. Sometimes they reflect a well-grounded suspicion of self-appointed "experts." But there is a more profound source of difficulty: there is no satisfactory and easily accessible body of knowledge for determining the kinds of questions on which a lay judgment is likely to be superior to an expert judgment in a particular case. Almost everyone who is not an expert in a field quickly sees the proverbial limitations of the expert: that his superior knowledge of certain specialized kinds of repetitive events does not usually fit well with the conditions of real life. For in real-life decisions many different kinds of events are relevant to a rational judgment; yet each kind of event may be the bailiwick of a different specialty—or none at all. Successful administrators—tested by their capacity for maximizing the goals of the organization—know that the judgment of experts must be overruled at many points, not because the experts' body of factual propositions is wrong, but because it does not apply closely enough to real life. "In an emergency the able but unimaginative expert is a public danger," said Lloyd George, who had no hesitancy in overruling the experts in the War Office. "On the one hand their thorough knowledge of the details of the business, and their high reputation, give them an authority which it is difficult for the amateur to set aside. While in a situation for which there is no precedent experience often entangles the expert."

Statement II [3]

A President is helped by what he gets into *his* mind. His first essential need is *information*. No doubt he needs the data that advisers can provide. He also needs to know the little things they fail to mention. To illustrate, it is reliably reported that by mid-December 1956 the Secretary of the Treasury was declining to take phone calls from the Director of the Budget. In effect, [George M.] Humphrey had broken off diplomatic relations with Brundage. This is a little thing and an affair of "personalities"; a thing of just the sort that Eisenhower seemingly disliked to hear and his associates disliked to tell him. But what could be more useful for a President to know while those two personalities conversed at Cabinet table? If nothing else aroused his sense of danger to himself, this knowledge might have done it. In January 1957, immediately after Humphrey's press explosion, Brundage was prepared to argue strongly for the rightness of the Eisenhower budget as it stood, and for the practical necessity of rallying to its defense in public. Brundage went so far as to prepare a White House press release for issuance that very afternoon. But he got no encouragement from White House staff officials, and he did not feel he could appeal over their heads. Within a week he had lost heart and changed his tune. Eisenhower, it appears, was spared the knowledge that his Budget Director once had thought it right as well as politic for him to disassociate himself from Humphrey's stand. Yet few things could have helped as much as this to give the President a sense that *he* was playing in a hard game for high stakes. No matter what he might have done with Brundage's advice, the very force of Brundage's reaction was a warning sign.

It is not information of a general sort that helps a President see personal stakes; not summaries, not surveys, not the bland amalgams. Rather, as these illustrations will suggest, it is the odds and ends of tangible detail that pieced together in his mind illuminate the

[3] Richard E. Neustadt, *Presidential Power* (New York: John Wiley & Sons, 1960), 153–155.

underside of issues put before him. To help himself he must reach out as widely as he can for every scrap of fact, opinion, gossip, bearing on his interests and relationships as President. He must become his own director of his own central intelligence. For that directorship two rules of conduct can be drawn. . . . On the one hand, he never can assume that anyone or any system will supply the bits and pieces he needs most; on the other hand, he must assume that much of what he needs will not be volunteered by his official advisers.

To fill one's mind with odds and ends is only the beginning. What helps is not the information, merely, but its meaning. Not only need a President know tangible details, he also needs to have a frame of reference. The information that a Brundage wanted White House disavowal of a Humphrey might mean no more than "parochialism" to a President unless he grasped the workings of the budget process well enough to sense that every agency and scores of congressmen were treasuring commitments which they took to be from *him*. Yet sensitivity to processes, to who does what and how, is hard to gain except by joining in the doing. The same thing can be said of sensitivity to substance; one gains by joining in the argument. Presidents are always being told that they should leave details to others. It is dubious advice. Exposure to details of operation and of policy provides the frame of reference for details of information. To be effective as his own director of intelligence, a President need be his own executive assistant. He need be both, that is to say, *if he would help himself*.

This is the help that starts a man along the road to power. Information in his mind and rightly understood alerts him to his personal stakes when choices come before him. By taking his own stakes into account he does what he can do to make a choice contribute to his influence. By choosing he builds power in the only way he can. If power is his object, to inform himself is help indeed. By the same token, though, it is not help enough.

A President in search of power cannot rest content to be informed. Along with data in his mind he needs the choices in his hands. But power-laden choices may not reach him; others may pre-empt them or foreclose them. Or they may reach him so late that personal perspective has no bearing on his options. Situations of both sorts will be familiar to the readers of case studies in this book. In theory, any President, informed enough and sensitive enough to what he knew, could make such situations go away, at will, by reaching out and down for just the choices that he wanted. In practice, though, he rarely has the time. However much he knows, however sharp his senses, his time remains the prisoner of first-things-first. And almost always something else comes first.

Problems of information and advice are particularly difficult when the decision maker is working against a deadline. Foreign and military policies, for example, must frequently be made without time for thorough examination of pertinent data and leisurely evaluation of the alternatives. In the foreign policy field the president is often involved in the "putting out fires," in the manner suggested in the following selection.[4]

A President's own use of time, his allocation of his personal attention, is governed by the things he *has* to do from day to day: the speech he has agreed to make, the fixed appointment he cannot put off, the paper no one else can sign, the rest and exercise his doctors order. These doings may be far removed from academic images of White House concentration on high policy, grand strategy. There is no help for that. A President's priorities are set not by the relative importance of a task, but by the relative necessity for him to do it. He deals first with the things that are required of *him* next. Deadlines rule his personal agenda. In most days of his working week, most seasons of his year, he meets deadlines enough to drain his energy and crowd his time regardless of all else. The net result may be a far cry from the order of priorities that would appeal to scholars or to columnists—or to the President himself.

What makes a deadline? The answer, very simply, is a date or an event or both combined. The date set by MacArthur for a landing at Inchon, or the date set by statute for submission of the budget, or the date set by the White House for a press conference, these and others like them force decisions on a President, pre-empt his time. And statements by MacArthur, or a Humphrey press explosion, or a House appropriations cut, or sputniks overhead, may generate such pressure inside government or out as to affect him in precisely the same way. Dates make deadlines in proportion to their certainty; events make deadlines in proportion to their heat. Singly or com-

4 *Ibid.*, 155–56.

bined, approaching dates and rising heat start fires burning underneath the White House. Trying to stop fires is what Presidents do first. It takes most of their time.

Review thoroughly in your text and class notes materials concerning decision making in general, foreign policy making in particular, and the executive branch.

Now assume that on one Saturday afternoon in late November, the following events occur:

A. A small band, led by a Mexican general who is in revolt against his government, invades El Paso, Texas, shoots up the town, captures twenty leading citizens and, holding them as hostages, goes back across the border into the mountains of northern Mexico.

B. The press services report that vacationing United States Senator Roy Ladu, powerful and popular chairman of the Senate Foreign Relations Committee, rose at a bibulous banquet in Paris and, apparently with tongue in cheek, urged that France extend its east border to the Rhine, saying: "Don't worry, *mes amis,* you can do it. We are with you. The Yanks are coming. Lafayette, we are here!" A cable from the United States Ambassador to West Germany states that the West German government is demanding a formal retraction and apology from the United States. The West German Ambassador to the United States happens to be home in Bonn, on vacation. A newly signed treaty of mutual assistance with West Germany will be referred to the Senate Foreign Relations Committee when Congress reconvenes in January.

C. An earthquake in India destroys two new dams and power plants, floods thousands of miles of farm lands, renders millions of people homeless, and smashes the chief water main and water purification plants of a large city. A telephone call comes from the Indian embassy reporting that the Prime Minister of India momentarily expects to receive an offer of emergency aid from Red China.

D. An armed clash occurs between the troops of Pakistan and

Afghanistan, on the border between the two countries. Each country denounces the other as the aggressor. One hour before the battle, Moscow radio announces that Afghanistan has been invaded and that the USSR is committed by treaty to defend Afghanistan.

You are Assistant to the President, who, that afternoon, is attending the Army-Navy football game at Philadelphia. Congress is not in session. You reach the President by telephone, between the halves, and tell him the news. He says he will return to Washington at once; and, with respect to these four matters, he gives you the following instructions:

1. You are to arrange a conference or series of conferences, to be held that evening in the White House.

2. You are to invite conferees on the basis of who has access to relevant information and on the basis of what political issues or bargaining will be involved in the decisions taken in response to *each* of the four situations.

3. You are to prepare for each conference an agenda—a carefully organized and detailed outline of topics to be discussed, issues to be raised, alternative choices to be explored.

For class discussion or as a written exercise:

Prepare a paper which states who you would invite to attend such conference(s), in what order you would place matters on the agenda(s), and what topics you feel should be discussed as having a bearing on the four situations. This paper should be one which, long after you cease being Assistant to the President, you can proudly show your grandchildren as an example of how a responsible public official acted promptly, wisely, and efficiently, within the narrow limits of his authority, at a time of crisis—and how, by his selection of issues and his knowledge of governmental organization, he contributed to important policy decisions. Remember that a crucial question throughout would be the kind(s) of information necessary, and the available sources of information within the government.

PART VIII

The Judicial Power

PROBLEM 26

The Task of the Judge

THERE are many conceptions and misconceptions of the task a judge performs in deciding cases. The mechanical theory of jurisprudence suggests that the judge merely takes the facts presented to him and applies the law in question to those facts, and that his decision is the result of this process. It presumes that the judge is influenced by no extralegal factors and that he decides only on the basis of what the law requires. The mechanical theory is illustrated by the following statement: [1]

> It is sometimes said that the court assumes a power to overrule or control the action of the people's representatives. This is a misconception. The Constitution is the supreme law of the land ordained and established by the people. All legislation must conform to the principles it lays down. When an act of Congress is appropriately challenged in the courts as not conforming to the constitutional mandate the judicial branch of the Government has only one duty—to lay the article of the Constitution which is invoked beside the statute which is challenged and to decide whether the latter squares with the former. All the court does, or can do, is to announce its

[1] Justice Roberts in *U.S.* v. *Butler,* 297 U.S. 1, 62–3 (1936).

considered judgment upon the question. The only power it has, if such it may be called, is the power of judgment. This court neither approves nor condemns any legislative policy. Its delicate and difficult office is to ascertain and declare whether the legislation is in accordance with, or in contravention of, the provisions of the Constitution; and, having done that, its duty ends.

In Justice Roberts' view, determining facts, applying the law, and putting the two together to reach a decision is a straightforward, unambiguous task which, to the trained judge, presents no serious problems or possibilities of error. We know, however, that judges take quite different positions in deciding the same issues; that many decisions in appellate courts are divided; that appellate courts reverse lower court decisions; and even that an appellate court overrules previous decisions made by itself. The application of the law is obviously not automatic and simple.

A second theory of jurisprudence recognizes that *extralegal* influences affect judicial decisions. An extreme version of this point of view suggests that the trappings of law and facts are mostly decoration; that the decisions are based on "what the judge ate for breakfast," or on whether the defendant reminds the judge of his father. Most statements of the "theory of free legal decisions" are not so bizarre. Instead it is recognized that judges must often exercise discretion in the choice of legal rules. Advocates of free legal decision are doing more than stating a necessity; they are often arguing that "better" law is the result. Deciding cases is a creative task demanding of the judge more than knowledge of law; he must also ask himself how ought the law be applied in particular situations. It has been maintained that "the judge who would think and act rightly in his function of rendering judgment must be able, as far as inelastic provisions of the statute do not prevent him, to discover the law and make effective that which he himself, if placed in the situation of the parties, would feel to be right and just." In other words it can be argued that the act of judging may involve a considerable range of discretion.

Neither of these interpretations completely describes the intellectual processes through which judges arrive at a decision, the things they think about, the questions they ask themselves, the sources they consult for advice and information. Judging cases in a court of law, like reaching judgments that will affect the lives of others in any walk of life, is a terribly difficult and responsible task, and one which must therefore be undertaken with full deliberation and use of all the resources available to the judge. This is especially true when the judge is called upon to decide great issues of public policy. It is difficult to see how he can escape his social and economic environment and his personal values as they have been shaped by experiences in that environment. President Theodore Roosevelt recognized this fact when, in a message to Congress in December 1908, he observed: "The chief law-makers in our country may be, and often are, the judges, because they are the final seat of authority. Every time they interpret contract, property, vested rights, due process of law, liberty, they necessarily enact into law parts of a system of social philosophy; and since such interpretation is fundamental, they give direction to all law-making. The decisions of the courts on economic and social questions depend upon their economic and social philosophy."

Yet no judge acts alone. He is the heir to centuries of judicial tradition and he makes his decision surrounded by the learning and opinion of countless others.

From another perspective the judge may be said to be playing a particular role in a political process, as the following statement maintains.[2]

> A judge is in the political process and his activity is interest activity not as a matter of choice but of function. Judicial participation does not grow out of the judge's personality or philosophy but out of his position. A judge who defers to the legislature is engaging in interest activity just as much as the judge who avowedly writes his own preferences into his opinions. . . .

[2] J. W. Peltason, *Federal Courts in the Political Process* (New York: Random House, Inc., 1955), 3–5.

However . . . despite the washing of mechanical jurisprudence in the acid of critical observation, the notion persists that judges should not be studied in the same terms as other politicians.

James Madison long ago pointed out in *Federalist* No. 10 that the most important acts of legislation are "but so many judicial determinations . . . concerning the rights of large bodies of citizens," but students of politics willing to describe legislators in terms of group conflict still resist applying these categories to judges. They argue that legislators are concerned with political controversies which are resolved by group struggle, but judges are concerned with legal controversies which are resolved by applying the "law." Legislators choose among competing values; judges apply the law.

Of course, most political scientists and legal scholars do not believe that "the law" is an external objective phenomenon that controls judges. The traditional explanations of judicial behavior are no longer in good standing among sophisticates. Yet judges will not admit to judicial legislation and the official explanation of public men and practicing lawyers is that the law is independent of the judge and controls his behavior. This explanation is ideological, not theoretical, and although it affects conduct, it does not describe the behavior of public men, practicing lawyers, or deciding judges.

Many skeptics of the orthodox ideology, after admitting that judges sometimes do make value choices and that the law does not necessarily control judges, nevertheless explain that in most cases a properly trained judge can determine the proper rule and arrive at the correct decision by looking at statutes or at past judicial decisions. The policy-making activity of judges is thought to be an exception to the general course of judicial business and not to justify treatment of the judiciary as an integral part of the political system. Some scholars would hold that courts are political agencies when deciding constitutional questions, but should be described differently when deciding nonconstitutional matters.

It is of course true that judges make their decisions in terms of the law. The prevailing ideology requires that choices be so stated. And in many areas there is no conflict within the community about the interest to be supported. The law to be applied is clear. The judge's task is to apply rules about which there is little dispute. Judges who make decisions contrary to the widely accepted meaning of the law will discover that these decisions do not long survive. Where there is widespread agreement as to the rules which should be applied, the judge's task is relatively simple, his behavior predictable. However, whenever there is serious contention, he must choose, and he will find that he cannot turn to deductive logical machines for answers. The law becomes the judge's conclusion, not his starting point.

Compare, for example, the status of the separate-but-equal formula in 1910 with its status in the 1930s. In 1910 the formula was securely established, there was little agitation for change, the segregation interest was dominant, the law clear, the decisions predictable. By the 1930s the group struggle had unsettled the law. In 1910 there was substantial agreement on the interest to be supported, the rule or major premise was settled, and the conclusion was inevitable. By the 1930s there was conflict over the major premise, the particular interest the judge would support became less predictable. But whether the judge speaks for an interest supported by the entire community or for an interest supported by a small portion, it is necessary to describe his activities as participation in the group struggle.

More important, in order to justify an attempt to describe judges as participants in interest conflict, a discussion of whether judges discover or make law is somewhat beside the point. Whether judges make the choices or the law through the judges makes the choices, the choices are interest activity. It may be comforting to the group adversely affected to believe that the decision came not from men making value choices, but from scientific technicians. But this comfort-providing function of the official explanation of judicial behavior does not bear on or negate the importance of describing judicial choice-making in the same descriptive system used to describe other agencies of government.

To recognize that judges represent values and make choices is not to recognize that they are free to choose as they want. But then neither are legislators free. Both judges and legislators are required by the community to behave in certain ways. Both are required to explain their conduct and justify it in terms of some long-range considerations other than personal preference. A legislator explains his votes as being "required by the national interest" or "against the selfish special interests"—seldom as purely personal preferences. A judge is required to explain his decisions in terms of precedents, "intent of the framers," "intent of the legislators," "plain words of the statute." Failure to conform to the role imposed by the community can result in various kinds of sanctions.

Again, to recognize that judges participate in the political process as legislators do is not to assert that judges necessarily represent the same interests as legislators or that the consequences of judicial representation are the same as the consequences of legislative representation. Relations among judges and other decision-makers, public expectations about judicial behavior, functions allotted to judges, these and many other factors make the pattern of interest activity of judges different from that of legislators. Both judge and legislator are engaged in the group struggle, but the manner of participation varies.

Review in your text and lecture notes the material relating to judges and the judicial process.

Now consider the following case:

John Larsen is charged with using the mails with intent to defraud. He has been indicted by a federal grand jury and waived a jury trial. The facts of the case are developed as follows: Larsen inherited from his father a secret formula for making a "magic bag," somewhat similar to an asafoetida bag. This bag contained an extremely aromatic combination of rare herbs, and both Larsen and his father claimed that when worn around the neck the bag would ward off a large variety of diseases. Larsen himself always wore such a bag and insisted that his family do likewise. Larsen worked at a regular job and engaged in no large-scale effort to promote his secret. However, he did praise the bag's qualities to all the people he met. Over a period of time, a good many people persuaded Larsen to make bags for them. The ingredients were difficult to obtain, and Larsen had to engage in correspondence to secure the necessary items and on two occasions wrote letters to prospective buyers of the bags. Larsen charged $250 apiece for the bags, which price resulted in a profit to Larsen of $100 on each bag sold. With only two exceptions the purchasers of the bags were as enthusiastic about them as Larsen was himself. Expert witnesses testified, however, that the bags offered no medical benefits of any significance and certainly could not prevent the diseases claimed.

The law under which Larsen was indicted and under which conviction is sought is as follows: [3]

Whoever, having devised or intending to devise any scheme or artifice to defraud, or for obtaining money or property by means of false or fraudulent pretenses, representations, or promises, or to sell, dispose of, loan, exchange, alter, give away, distribute, supply, or furnish or procure for unlawful use any counterfeit or spurious coin, obligation, security, or other article, or anything represented to be or intimated or held out to be such counterfeit or spurious article, for the purpose of executing such scheme or artifice or attempting to do so, places in any post office or authorized depository for mail matter, any matter or thing whatever to be sent or delivered by the Post Office Department, or takes or receives therefrom, any such matter or thing, or knowingly causes to be delivered by mail according to the direction thereon, or at the place at which is directed to be delivered by the person to whom it is addressed, any such matter or thing, shall be fined not more than $1000.00 or imprisoned not more than five years, or both.

As a written exercise or for class discussion:

Assume that you are a federal district judge before whom this case is being tried. DO NOT concern yourself with arriving at a decision on Larsen's guilt or innocence. DO, carefully and thoughtfully, indicate *what considerations you would take into account, what procedures you would go through, what operations you would perform,* in order to answer the following questions:

1. Is the law valid?
2. Does it apply to the facts of this case?
3. Under this law is Larsen guilty?

Again, *do not try to answer the questions themselves.* Rather tell what you would do in order to find out the answers.

Now, *justify* each *procedure* you have suggested. What reasons

[3] Adapted from 18 *U.S. Code* 338.

have you for doing these things rather than something else? Do these procedures offer the best possibility of arriving at a *just* conclusion?

Finally, in what ways would you consider the procedures you went through to be a part of the *political* process?

PROBLEM 27

The Supreme Court, Democracy, and the American System

THE "independence of the judiciary," designed to assure the impartiality of judges and to enable them to stand fast against the gusts of political forces and public passion, is a value that has long been recognized as a constitutional principle by many Americans. Thinking of the federal judiciary and especially of the Supreme Court, they assume that the desired independence is achieved by the system of appointing judges for life instead of electing them for specified terms. Thus the judiciary is expected to be removed from the control of the voters, Congress, the presidency, or the states. This overlooks the fact that in the United States most of the judges of state and local courts are elected to office for a specific term, usually in a typical party contest. Yet the framers of the Constitution made much of the independent judiciary as a bulwark for a "government of laws and not of men," a safeguard against the shifting winds of public opinion, and a protection for individual and minority rights.

Nonetheless there have been recurring controversies over the role of the Supreme Court and the federal judiciary in the American political system. In the sea-change of the New Deal in the 1930's the Supreme Court held unconstitutional a number of federal and state statutes regulating various aspects of the economy, often by five-to-four majorities of the justices. As a result the high court was assailed by many critics as an obstacle to important regulatory or reform measures which, it was argued, had the support of a majority of the nation's voters. More recently the Supreme Court has come under attack on a variety of issues—its decisions outlawing segregation in public schools and other areas; its ruling that prayers in the public schools are a violation of First Amendment guarantees of the separation of church and state; its decisions requiring reapportionment of state legislative districts to meet the requirements of equal population in accord with the rule of one man, one vote. Criticism has been particularly vehement when decisions have impinged sharply on claims of states' rights or on local customs or mores, which may have majority support in a particular area even though they represent a minority position in the nation as a whole. Cases which have touched on such matters recently include those dealing with segregation and the reapportionment of state legislative districts.

In the 1920's and early 1930's, when the Supreme Court invalidated numerous federal and state laws regulating economic activity, the Court's majority interpreted the due-process clauses of the Fifth and Fourteenth Amendments as forbidding laws which prohibited child labor, for example, or established a minimum for wages. Most of these decisions were later overruled. In the 1950's and the 1960's the Court struck down state segregation statutes and laws establishing legislative electoral districts of widely varying size on the ground that these enactments conflict with the Fourteenth Amendment's provision that no state shall deny to any person the equal protection of the laws. As a result, criticism of the Supreme Court has come from different sides or points of view in the two periods, mostly from a liberal position in the 1930's and mostly from conservatives today. In both eras, however, there have also been strong defenders of the independence of the judiciary even though the action of the Supreme Court may seem too conservative for some at one moment, or too liberal for others at another.

After being angered by a number of negative decisions on important pieces of legislation in the mid-1930's, President Franklin D. Roosevelt proposed that Congress should increase the size of the Supreme Court—an action that would have given him an opportunity to appoint several new justices who would presumably have voted to uphold the validity of the challenged legislation. Appearing before the Committee on the Judiciary of the Senate in hearings on this proposal as an eloquent opposition witness, the columnist Dorothy Thompson argued in part: [1]

There are always hundred percenters for democracy, those who want pure democracy. They want to do away with every impediment and march at high speed toward what they call a real or modern democracy, or the democracy in harmony with the times. But precisely in such revolutionary times—and we live in one—it is most necessary to have a point of reference, a warrant, an instrument which confidently assures the legitimacy of what is being done. For without such a point of reference, there ceases to be a spontaneous social cohesion and what you then get as sure as fate is social cohesion by coercion. . . .

I think the disciplines of law are particularly needed in democracies and are especially needed at any moment when a powerful majority is in temporary control of the current political situation almost to the exclusion of minority representation. We have such a situation in this country now. The men who designed the structure of this Republic realized this. They did not believe that the cure for the evils of democracy was more democracy. They believed that the prevention against a democracy running away with itself, the prevention against a powerful majority riding roughshod over the temporary minority and selling short the whole future of the country, the prevention against today's majority mortgaging tomorrow's majority, lay in a written constitution and an independent Supreme Court to interpret that constitution.

There is a reason why Supreme Court judges are appointed for life, and removable only by impeachment. That reason is obvious. It was certain that successive executives and successive Senates would seek to put upon the Supreme Court Bench men responsive to their own ideas. Everybody is human, but it was arranged that the Supreme Court, only by the merest chance, by a very remote mathematical chance, would ever coincide with the majority of the

[1] Hearings Before the Committee on the Judiciary, United States Senate, 75th Congress, 1st Session on S. 1392 (Washington: Government Printing Office, 1937), 861–62.

moment. It was so arranged that the Court should represent, not the momentary dominant majority, but the continuity and tradition in American life. . . .

It is true that the Supreme Court is conservative. I think it is conservative by its very nature. And that, gentlemen, is its function —to conserve. It represents, the opponents say, the past. Yes; perhaps it does. It represents continuity; it demands that today's laws shall be checked against the whole body of law and the principles governing the state, and thus it insures that new laws shall be designed in some conformity with certain long-established customs and ways of life. And just because it represents continuity, because it exerts a constant reminder on the people that they have a past, a past to which they have a duty; just because it reminds them that when they act, however radically, however drastically, they must keep an eye on long-established patterns of law and behavior—just for that reason I think it safeguards the future. . . .

More is involved in the controversy, however. When the Supreme Court struck down laws for minimum wages as "arbitrary and unreasonable," for example, even though they were the product of long consideration and debate in legislative halls, critics said that the judicial branch of government was usurping the functions of the legislative branch elected by the people. If indeed judges appointed for life tenure engage in law making, is not the exercise of such power by men who are not subject to control by the voters a defiance of the fundamental principle of democracy? Read and analyze the following statement of democracy as a system of government ultimately responsible to a national majority of the voters, as set forth by the political scientist William H. Riker, bearing in mind that it was written before the school desegregation decision of 1954 set the Supreme Court on its recent course: [2]

Democracy is more than an ideal; it is also a method. . . . The method is government responsible to the people. Hence, the essential democratic institution is the ballot box and all that goes with it.

[2] William H. Riker, *Democracy in the United States* (New York: The Macmillan Co., 1953, 28, 32, 34, 110–112, 247–248, 279–284.

All [of the great advocates of democracy] place electoral responsibility at the very center of the democratic system. . . .

[Electoral responsibility] promotes self direction through participation in making public policy. The ballot and the system of political parties are the means and the assurance of that participation. They are the means because, however much the process of voting may be obscured, the basic decision on policy is always the choice of the policy-makers. They are the assurance because all the paraphernalia of participation (campaigning, petitioning, canvassing, propagandizing) is the one essential way to compel rulers to respond to pressure from the ruled. . . .

Democracy is a form of government in which the rulers are fully responsible to the ruled. . . .

If government is to be fully responsible, [elections and parties] ought to make [popular] majorities effective. If the rulers chosen by electoral majorities do not have the power to govern, then responsible government is as impossible as if there were no majority at all. The idea of [an electoral] sanction is simply praise and blame leading to rewards and punishments. Yet praise and blame cannot be rationally assigned unless rulers have in fact the power to carry out the majority will. If rulers have not the power to govern, how can they be fairly blamed for failure to enact electoral decisions? . . . Government truly responsible to the people . . . can thus be said to depend upon [popular] majorities. . . .

[According to Aristotle], "Another attribute of democracy is to dispense with all life offices—or at least to curtail the powers of any such offices, if they have been left surviving from some earlier epoch. . . ."

A latent obstructiveness lies deep in the [Supreme] Court's nature. Although most of the time it is rationally repressed, now and again it breaks loose and springs upward to direct judicial action. . . .

Of course, the danger would be insignificant were it not that the Court really has enough resources, even when besieged for a long time, to refuse to unite with the rest of government. Its granary is its irresponsibility, life tenure uncontrolled by popular sanction. Its armory is its share, small but crucial, of the power to govern. We do not need the goggle-eyed perceptiveness of a man from Mars to see the inconsistency in our constitutional myth. Dispassionate analysis, as well as the amazement of casual visitors from Europe and Asia, ought to point it out. We say that Sovereignty resides in elected officials, yet we regularly permit the Court, whose responsibility to the people is very indistinct, to exercise a sizable share of it. . . . Many people may prefer an only vaguely responsible Court to elected representatives; but they cannot possibly reconcile their preference with the democratic method. What is democracy, but government by public opinion determined in partisan elections? and what public opinion can there ever be but the public opinion of the most recent election or "hour"? If one does not wish to speak as bluntly as Hamilton of legislative oppression or popular incapacity, one can then . . . cast slurs on the democratic process itself, suggesting by the words "passionate party campaigns" or "mob passion" that Congressional legislation is first cousin to lynch law. The slander is insidious. It does not argue the case; it merely hints of some vague dire peril. Mob passion there may be in the United States, but judicial review has never been used against it. Rather the statutes the Court has nullified have been enacted after mature and lengthy deliberation. Consider the AAA, for example. During the late twenties, and early thirties, bills dealing with farm surpluses were, as Solicitor General Reed pointed out in his argument in the Butler case, reported out eight times by the House Committee on Agriculture, ten times by the Senate Committee. Of these the Senate passed five, the House four, and Presidents signed two. The slow and tortuous path of a bill through Congress . . . can hardly be called mob passion. And the proposal that finally matured as the AAA had been before Congress since 1923, so that it can hardly be called the product of a passionate party campaign. The mob passion, from which the proponents of judicial review say the Court saves us, was in this case a popular emotion stable and thoughtful enough to endure through five campaigns and a decade of argument. . . .

American democrats should not be misled by insinuations about mob passion or by the suggestion that life tenure works better in democracy than the electoral sanction can. They should understand the justification of life tenure for what it is: a distrust of democratic government and a preference for irresponsibility.

The Court is indispensable to the constitutional system. Without a highest court of appeal, differences in decision between equal courts would produce intolerable confusion. Even the basic outlines of law would be different in different jurisdictions. And without a supreme federal court, state courts could not be relied upon to enforce federal law. Hence democrats cannot simply abolish the Court. They might perhaps return to the medieval tradition, still partially continued in England, in which the legislature is the high court of appeal. So Senator La Follette suggested during his campaign for President in 1924: appeal to Congress when the Court has refused to enforce one of its acts. Theodore Roosevelt had earlier (during his 1912 campaign) suggested popular referendums on Court-nullified law. The disease, as Theodore Roosevelt rightly saw, is judicial pride.

[T]o expect that judges can always restrain themselves requires a faith in fallen human nature greater than democrats dare have. The propensity of pride pervades the black-robed judges no less than other men; and as democrats are well aware, neither humility nor responsibility endures unless enforced by formal sanctions. Should the Court again be about to thwart majority leadership, again about to harass us with the most unworkable of separated powers, we then ought to remember the advice of Jefferson:

"Before the canker is become inveterate, before its venom has reached so much of the body politic as to get beyond control, remedy should be applied. Let the future appointments of judges be for four or six years, and renewable by the President and Senate. This will bring their conduct, at regular periods, under revision and probation. . . . We have erred in this point, by copying England, where . . . it is a good thing to have the judges independent to the King. But we have omitted to copy their caution also, which makes a judge removeable on the address of both legislative Houses. That there should be public functionaries independent of the nation, whatever may be their demerit, is a solecism in a republic, of the first order of absurdity and inconsistency."

Now it appears that in "pure" democratic theory there is something highly anachronistic about allowing major decisions to be made by either an unrepresentative group, such as the Supreme Court, or a minority of a representative body, such as the United States Senate. Yet even in the Senate it is true that a minority can sometimes force the Senate to make a major decision, namely, the decision not to pass a bill. True, like the Court's nullification of a law, such a decision is a negative one; the Court strikes down a statute, and the Senate minority prevents a statute from being made. Yet the nullification of a law and the defeat of a bill are examples of important governmental decision making. They are decisions to put things back to where they were, or to leave them where they are.

The method by which a minority of senators can cause the Senate to make this kind of negative decision is the *filibuster*. A filibuster is a determined effort of a group of Senators to talk so long about a pending bill that the Senate, wishing or needing to get other business done, eventually agrees to withdraw the bill from consideration. The Senate rules make it possible to shut off a really determined filibuster, but only if at least two-thirds of the senators present vote in favor of a motion to terminate debate.

It is true that if two-thirds of the senators are sufficiently determined to see a bill passed, they stop a filibuster. Some senators, however, are reluctant to vote for any curtailment of unlimited debate; and many bills, of course, are supported by a majority of the Senate yet by fewer than 67 senators. Such bills can be killed by a persistent and long-winded minority. The right to filibuster in effect sometimes deprives the majority of its right to make laws. Nevertheless, the antimajoritarian principle of the filibuster has been earnestly defended by a number of people, including the columnist Walter Lippman in the following statement: [3]

> Although the question before the Senate is whether to amend the rules [to make it easier for the Senate to close debate] the issue is not one of parliamentary procedure. It is whether there shall be a profound and far-reaching constitutional change in the character of the American government. . . . If the amendment is carried, the existing power of a minority of the states to stop legislation will have been abolished.
>
> "Stripped of all mumbo-jumbo and flag waving," says *The New York Times*, the issue "is whether the country's highest legislative

[3] Walter Lippmann, *New York Herald-Tribune*, March 3, 1949; Copyright, 1949, New York Herald-Tribune, Inc. By permission.

body will permit important measures to be kept from a vote through the activities of a few leather-throated, iron-legged members who don't want democratic decision." This is an unduly scornful and superficial way to dispose of a great constitutional problem. For the real issue is whether any majority, even a two-thirds majority, shall now assume the power to override the opposition of a large minority of the states.

In the American system of government, the right of "democratic decision" has never been identified with majority rule as such. The genius of the American system, unique I believe among the democracies of the world, is that it limits all power—including the power of the majority. Absolute power, whether in a king, a president, a legislative majority, a popular majority, is alien to the American idea of democratic decision.

The American idea of a democratic decision has always been that important minorities must not be coerced. When there is strong opposition, it is neither wise nor practical to force a decision. It is necessary and it is better to postpone the decision—to respect the opposition and then to accept the burden of trying to persuade it.

For a decision which has to be enforced against the determined opposition of large communities and regions of the country will, as Americans have long realized, almost never produce the results it is supposed to produce. The opposition and the resistance, having been overridden, will not disappear. They will merely find some other way of avoiding, evading, obstructing or nullifying the decision.

For that reason it is a cardinal principle of the American democracy that great decisions on issues that men regard as vital shall not be taken by the vote of the majority until the consent of the minority has been obtained. Where the consent of the minority has been lacking, as for example in the case of the prohibition amendment, the "democratic decision" has produced hypocrisy and lawlessness.

This is the issue in the Senate. It is not whether there shall be unlimited debates. The right of unlimited debates is merely a device, rather an awkward and tiresome device, to prevent large and determined communities from being coerced.

The issue is whether the fundamental principle of American

democratic decision—that strong minorities must be persuaded and not coerced—shall be altered radically, not by constitutional amendment but by a subtle change in the rules of the Senate.

The issue has been raised in connection with the civil rights legislation. The question is whether the vindication of these civil rights requires the sacrifice of the American limitation on majority rule. The question is a painful one. But I believe the answer has to be that the rights of Negroes will in the end be made more secure, even if they are vindicated more slowly, if the cardinal principle—that minorities shall not be coerced by majorities—is conserved.

For if that principle is abandoned, then the great limitations on the absolutism and tyranny of transient majorities will be gone, and the path will be much more open than it now is to the demagogic dictator who, having aroused a mob, destroys the liberties of the people.

In recent years criticisms of the Supreme Court have played more and more on the argument that the judiciary has been engaged in a usurpation of power at the expense of the states. A powerful statement of this kind of argument is given by James Jackson Kilpatrick, a Virginia editor and student of constitutional problems in the Southern tradition: [4]

The decision in the school segregation cases [of 1954] was not the first major usurpation of power by the Supreme Court in the post-war period. It was merely the most flagrant. It is keenly important to understand that the trend put newly in motion under Vinson's court continues, at increasing speed, under Warren's administration. If States outside the South are to comprehend the peril before them, they would do well to look beyond the frontal fight of Brown vs. Board of Education to the flanking decisions in which State powers also are being steadily destroyed.

Half a dozen such mileposts will suffice to mark the way. They involve drillers for oil off California and the Gulf; a small trucker in Pennsylvania; a railwayman named Hanson; a Communist, Steve Nelson; a professor of German, Harry Slochower; a thief named Griffin. Their cases are all a part of the ending and beginning. . . .

[4] James Jackson Kilpatrick, *The Sovereign States* (Chicago: Henry Regnery Co., 1957), 286–87, 304–05.

These cases (and countless others could be cited) define a trend: the deification of the Federal government, and the steady stultification of the States. They point to a problem, a great and difficult constitutional problem. It certainly is not a new one. It existed in Jefferson's day, and in Calhoun's, and for that matter, in Teddy Roosevelt's also. It is to preserve unto the States, for good or ill, that which is rightfully the States', and to guard with equal jealousy the proper function of the Federal government. Yet to an ominous degree, the problem now is far more acute than it has ever been before. When Jefferson and Calhoun were protesting most furiously, enormous areas of public administration remained to the States; even at the turn of the century, States' rights still held some meaning. Now, month by passing month, the States steadily are being stripped of the last of their sovereign powers—not by their own wish, as expressed through constitutional amendment—but by judicial usurpation. Those who had conceived the Constitution itself to be the supreme law of the land are now told, imperiously, that today's opinions of the Court, however palpably in violation of the Constitution these mandates may be, are supreme above all things. We are told to bow and fawn before a judicial oligarchy which has asserted unto itself powers as arrogant as those of any tyrant: "This is compassionate," says the Court, "*therefore* it is constitutional." This, in the Court's view, is socially desirable; therefore the Court will make it the law. And to resist, as in Clinton, is to travel in handcuffs to Knoxville, there to face prosecution for contempt.

The end of this process is the corruption of a constitutional Union, by judicial fiat, into a consolidated government in which the States are mere political dependencies. The end is a centralization of all meaningful powers in the hands of Federal authority. And so long as the constructions placed by the Court upon the Constitution are agreeable to one-third of the House of Representatives, plus one, timely remedy cannot even be found in constitutional amendment.

The remedy lies—it must lie—in drastic resistance by the States, *as States,* to Federal encroachment. "If those who voluntarily created the system cannot be trusted to preserve it," asked Calhoun, "who can?" The checking and controlling influence of the people, exerted as of old, through their States, can indeed preserve the constitutional structure. The right to interpose the will of the sovereign people, in order that the evils of encroachment may be arrested, once more can be exerted toward the preservation of a Union and the dignity of States.

A long time ago, a great Virginian had this to say: "So far as our (Federal) government is concerned, I venture to predict that it will become absolute and irresponsible, precisely in proportion as the rights of the States shall cease to be respected and their authority to interpose for the correction of Federal abuses shall be denied and overthrown."

Abel Parker Upshur's prediction of 1840 has been grimly fulfilled. The American people have lost sight of the old concept that the States, as such, form the balance wheel—in Upshur's term, "The only effectual check upon Federal encroachments." We have lived to see the truth of his prophecy, that the danger to constitutional separation of powers is "not that the States will interpose too often, but that they will rather submit to Federal usurpations, than incur the risk of embarrassing the government, by any attempts to check and control it."

The States have submitted too long to Federal usurpations. At their grave peril, they can submit no longer. Through every device of interposition they can bring to bear—political, legislative, judicial—once more they must invoke their sovereign powers to insist that Federal encroachments be restrained.

Bearing in mind the points made in all four of the statements given above, assume the following situation:

The Supreme Court, after a long series of decisions which have given offense to various segments of the population, is being subjected to the glare of public scrutiny. For more than a decade sentiment has been growing to restrict the power of the Supreme Court and subordinate federal courts. Portions of the press, influential private citizens, and some leaders in both parties have condemned what they call "the Court's usurpation of power."

In this situation a resolution is introduced by Senator Abner Marksen to amend Article III of the Constitution. It would provide that while federal judges will be appointed as heretofore, they shall serve not for life but for a term of six years, after which they can be reappointed by the president with the concurrence of a two-thirds majority of the Senate. A large majority of senators have stated publicly that they will favor the amendment. While the resolution is still before the Senate Judiciary Committee, however, a group of twenty senators, calling themselves "The Defenders of the Faith," announce that they are prepared to filibuster "till hell freezes over," in order to prevent a vote ever being taken on the resolution. Thereupon Senator Marksen moves to amend the rules of the Senate, to provide that after every senator has had the opportunity to speak for one hour on any bill or resolution debate may be terminated by a simple majority vote. The first question before the Senate next week will be Senator Marksen's motion to amend the Senate rules. After that on the Senate's schedule will be the Marksen resolution to amend the Constitution.

You are a senator. You have always leaned heavily for advice and counsel on an ancient friend who taught you political science in college long ago. From this friend comes a letter which says:

"Joe, for Heaven's sake, go slow. Remember Madison! Remember the separation of powers! Read Walter Lippmann! But far be it from me to tell you how to vote. Whatever you do, though, try to be true to yourself. Be *consistent*, Joe. You're going to have to make two difficult decisions. My advice is, be sure of what you believe about government, clarify your principles in your own mind, and vote in accordance with those principles."

From your twenty-five-year-old son, a highly skilled technician in the airplane industry, comes another letter:

"It took us a long time to get together in an organization in our industry, and our Engineers and Technicians Union wouldn't last a week if we didn't all abide by the principle of majority rule. And our union president might ruin the whole organization if he had the job for life and didn't have to stand for re-election every two years. You brought me up, Dad, to revere Abraham Lincoln. Lincoln said: 'government of the people, for the people, by the people.' You'll remember that, won't you, when you vote next week? You'll remember the basic principles of the American system and majority rule, I'm sure, Dad, and vote accordingly."

From a friend of yours from law-school days who now lives in Mississippi, you receive still a third letter:

"You know, Joe, this independence of the judiciary is really just the judges taking over—schools, restaurants, hotelkeepers, the states—everybody's got to knuckle down. It doesn't have anything to do with majorities, either—most of us in our state have been against the orders of this Supreme Court even that school case in 1954. It has to do with whether the sovereign states are going to be allowed to protect the rights of their people to live the way they're used to. These are the things I think it's your duty as a Senator to protect, so go it, Joe, and don't let up!"

Think carefully about all of the reading assigned in this problem exercise. *Then, as a written exercise or for class discussion, prepare thoughtful replies to all three letters.* Indicate how you expect to vote on BOTH issues, and EXPLAIN your reasoning. In your replies, remember that you are to deal with the points raised by your friend the professor, your son, and your Mississippi correspondent. Make it clear to them that you have pondered their advice. Remember also that your replies should emphasize your REASONS for the votes you intend to cast on both the issues before the Senate.